PRAISE FROM THE CRITICS

"Interesting and fast-moving. This is a book for everyone who wants to know what being a cop is *really* like."
—Cornelius J. Behan, Baltimore County (Md.) Chief of Police.

"The sights, sounds and smells of urban policing. A masterful effort. . . It delivers on its promise and dispels many of the myths."
—Anthony V. Bouza, former Minneapolis Chief of Police, and author of *The Police Mystique*.

"Excellent reading material for anyone contemplating a career in law enforcement."
—Sgt. John Spiroff, Community Relations Division, Baltimore County (Md.) Police Department.

"An authentic and well-written in-depth look at the police culture by a reporter who, like *Dragnet's* Sergeant Friday, 'just wants the facts.' "
—Dr. Harold E. Russell, co-author of *Understanding Human Behavior for Effective Police Work*.

"Gellman's beautifully written portrayal of life as a cop guides us through every important facet of police work and explores the profound impact that policing has on the personal lives of officers."
—Sari Horwitz, Crime Reporter, *The Washington Post*.

"Accurate and realistic. I recommend this book to anyone who would like to know what is involved in the making of a cop."
—Edward J. Spurlock, Deputy Chief, Metropolitan Police Department, Washington D.C.

COPS: IN THEIR OWN WORDS

THE SUSPECTS

"Many of them can't wait to talk It seems the first thing they want is a cigarette. I tell the suspect, 'When we get to the station, I'll take the cuffs off and I'll get you a cigarette.' If he's just bullshitting me, what has it cost? Just someone else's cigarette."

Arresting a childhood friend: "He didn't know I had become a cop and I didn't know he had become a crook."

THE ADRENALINE EXPRESS

Rene Gomez to an assault suspect who outweighs him by nearly 100 pounds: "Jim, don't you ever walk away from me when I'm talking to you. You come here *now!*" Rene's partner is stunned: "All I'm thinking is I'm going to die. That man could have wasted us both with his bare hands."

"If it's going to be balls to the wall, I'm going to try to make sure that it's *their* balls."

After fatally shooting a woman who has shot two men and then pointed a gun at his partner: "I don't remember analyzing it, but I think there was a conscious decision on my part that I didn't want to go look at her. I didn't want to see what I had done."

A despondent woman has shot herself, and part of her face has been blown away. As Robert Garcia checks for a pulse "which I know she can't have, a voice whispers, 'Hi.' I got goosebumps up and down my arm. I thought I was going to die next to her."

THE PUBLIC

On traffic stops: "I'll listen to their problems or excuses and some-times let them off with a warning. Maybe it will help turn around their day. If they keep cursing at me and chewing me out, though, I just keep writing citations. They usually get the message after two or three of them."

"These are my people, even though I don't live in their neighbor-hood. The important part is to try."

"Some people will act like dipshits no matter how you approach them, but I like to give them a choice."

THE HUMOR

Anita Sueme, in uniform at an undercover drug bust: "I asked what I was supposed to do and was told, 'You're just here for your body. Keep your mouth shut and stay out of the way.'"

Greg Strom suggests that hospital nurses keep a violent, drunken man strapped down until the effects of the alcohol wear off. "I'm not taking them off, ever," a nurse responds.

THE DRUNKS

"They're people, too. They weren't just born on the street."

On female drunks: "They're the worst. One of them nearly broadsided me and then sped off. When I caught up to her, she pulled down her top, grabbed her boobs and said, 'Here, do you want some of these?' She blew a .31, and I arrested her."

THE DANGER

"I know that something could happen and I might never see (my family) again, but I don't dwell on it. We're trained to recognize danger and respond to it, but cops make mistakes, too."

Racing to a 'man with a gun' call: "You're scared shitless and all the time you're pushing down harder on the accelerator rushing to get there, you know you might just be rushing to get killed."

THE POWER

"That can be pretty heady stuff and you learn quickly that it must be held in check."

THE CHANGES WITHIN

"I always felt you could trust your neighbors. Now I know it's possible that my neighbor could be a pervert."

"I hear so many lies and half-truths that I'm initially skeptical of almost anything I'm told. I don't like that attitude, but it's there."

"I've gotten where I'm not so idealistic as to think I can make a major difference. It's sure not what you see on *T. J. Hooker*."

COPS

The Men and Women Behind the Badge

Published by Horizon Press
7272 Broadway Blvd., Suite 400, Tucson, Arizona 85710
Telephone (602) 749-1000
Fax (602) 722-0363

First Printing October 1990
Printed in the United States of America by Banta Company

Cover design by Holly Moga

Cataloging-in-Publication Data
Gellman, Stuart
COPS : The Men and Women Behind the Badge
1. Police — United States — Biography.
2. Police Patrol — Arizona — Tucson.
3. Police Training.

ISBN 0-9627628-4-9
363.2

$11.95

With best wishes,
Stuart Gellman

COPS

The Men
and Women
Behind
The Badge

Stuart Gellman

HORIZON PRESS

"COPS: The Men and Women Behind the Badge"

is dedicated to

Pat Batelli, Les Beach, Derek Campbell,
Robert Garcia, Rene Gomez, Bernie Harrigan,
Jeff Moore, Greg Strom and Anita Sueme.

Without them, this book would not exist.

ACKNOWLEDGMENTS

Researching and writing a book is almost never a one-person endeavor. In the case of "COPS: The Men and Women Behind the Badge," the list of helpers is lengthy.

The project couldn't have begun without the permission and encouragement of Tucson Police Chief Peter Ronstadt, and it could not have proceeded without the nine officers to whom the book is dedicated, and their willingness to 'go public' with their stories.

In many ways it was a family endeavor. Some of the best ideas and feedback came from my children, Alan, Bart and Sheri; my sister, Barbara Kates; and my ex-wife, Alex.

Several supportive and talented friends were also kind enough to review my manuscript. In addition to leaving notations and 'happy faces' in the margins to indicate what they liked, they took me at my word and also provided constructive — sometimes even harsh — criticism. This book is far better because of Phil Corrigan, Laurie DeCorte, Carol Freundlich, Kathy Heitzmann, Wanda Kerr, Judith Kidd, Mimi Kirk, Robert Powers, Leonard Rosenthal, Jennifer Schneider and Viki Sharp.

Others were also generous with their time and expertise, and many of their names appear within the text of the book. Among those whose names do not appear elsewhere are Steve Auslander, Leann Bonhorst, Maureen Bureson, Linda Burkett, Max Cannon, Joe Carillo, Lois Cross, Richard Diffenderfer, Bob Easton, Pat Egbert, Brice Fuller, Mike Garrigan, Steve Godwin, Rita Hamilton, John Iurino, Ronald Ives, Keith Kaback, Pat Kelly, Pat Krausman, Becky Laughlin, Joyce Lingel, Lyle Mann, Ken Magoch, Debbie Martin, Kevin Mayhew, Judy McCrary, Rick Nentrup, Jeff Rundquist, Dan Rosenblatt, Tracy Sivitz, Lyle Wamsley, Jim Wheelock, and Ron Zuniga.

Last, but certainly not least, I acknowledge the substantial contribution made by Howard Fisher of Fisher Books. Howard graciously took time from his already busy schedule and guided me through the final critical steps of turning my manuscript into the book you are reading.

POLICE RADIO CODES

The radio codes which appear in the text of this book are explained the first time they are used. For readers desiring a reference list, these are most of the major codes used by the Tucson Police Department.

Code 1	Clear to receive confidential message
Code 2	Urgent response
Code 3	Emergency response (flashing lights and siren)
Code 4	No further assistance needed
Code 6	Out of service for an investigation
Code 7	Out of service to eat
10- 1	Radio receiving poorly
10- 2	Radio receiving loud and clear
10- 3	Stop transmitting (a polite 'shut up')
10- 4	Message received; Okay; Affirmative
10- 7	Out of service (end of shift)
10- 8	In service; Back in service
10- 9	Repeat message
10-12	Completing paperwork
10-15	Prisoner in custody
10-18	As soon as possible
10-20	Location
10-21	Telephone
10-23	Arrived at the scene
10-25	Assignment or information waiting
10-31	Family fight
10-36	Burglary
10-37	Burglary in progress
10-39	Major incident in progress
10-41	Drunk or intoxicated person
10-43	Armed robbery
10-44	Sexual assault
10-45	Meet another officer or citizen
10-47	Lost or missing person
10-48	Runaway juvenile
10-50	Motor vehicle accident without injury
10-52	Motor vehicle accident with injury
10-53	Motor vehicle accident with fatal injury
10-55	Drunk driver

10-59	Ambulance
10-70	Fire
10-72	Paramedic unit (also referred to as "Meds")
10-81	Stop and field interview
10-82	Stop and arrest
10-83	Two or more officers trying to transmit at once
10-84	Backup unit
10-99	Officer needs immediate and urgent assistance
DOA	Dead on arrival
GOA	Gone on arrival
GTA	Grand theft of an automobile
Priority 1	Most urgent calls (crime in progress; shots fired; potential for serious injury or death)
Priority 5	Least urgent calls (barking dog, loud music, etc.)
SWAT	Special Weapons And Tactics Team
Number 1	Hispanic
Number 2	Indian
Number 3	Black
Number 4	Oriental
Number 5	White

Police officers have over the years developed a list of unofficial, but generally harmless codes which manage to remain within the parameters of what can be said on the air without violating Federal Communications Commission or Departmental regulations. Among them are:

Adam-Henry	Asshole (generally a nasty and/or drunk citizen)
COC	Contempt of cop
Double-A	Attitude adjustment needed
Flat Cat	A 'run-over' feline dead on the roadway
SIP	Someone acting stupid in public
UIP	Urinating in public (also called UIP'ing)

ABOUT THE AUTHOR

Stuart Gellman has been a reporter for *Fairchild Publi-cations, The Philadelphia Evening Bulletin* and the Pa-cific edition of *Stars & Stripes*. Now semi-retired, he lives in Tucson where he provides on-site crisis intervention for victims of crime and their families. He has written exten-sively on the criminal justice system, and was nominated for a Jefferson Award in 1984 for public service and community leadership.

CONTENTS

Foreword 12

1   The Road to Hell 17

2   Hell.. 27

3   You Bet Your Badge 42

4   The Stick of God 56

5   Amazing Grace 103

6   The Breaking of a Cop 167

7   The Smile of a Stranger 189

8   Rites of Passage 225

9   Being There 255

10   The Adrenaline Express 268

11   Full Circle 278

FOREWORD

A man assaults his wife, then bolts from their apartment, carrying their four-year-old son as he runs. When an officer catches up with him, he puts the child down, throws himself over the hood of a parked car, screaming, "Look at what the cop's doing to your father! Tighter, tighter! Make those cuffs as tight as you can! Go and cut off my circulation!" After the sobbing boy has been returned to his mother and the father taken to jail, the officer is clearly distressed. "If this youngster gets lost or frightened tomorrow, do you think he's going to ask a cop for help? Can you imagine what he'll think about cops when he grows up? It's really sad."

Another officer kiddingly tells his sergeant that "It's time to go and harass the kids" who are congregating in a shopping center parking lot. The sergeant smiles, looks at him and asks, "But where are you going to tell them to go?"

* *

An observer who spends much time in the tight little world of law enforcement soon encounters several troubling truths:
- Bullet-proof vests are merely bullet-resistant.
- Despite well-intentioned statements by cops and the medical profession, men, women and children who are killed by knives, guns and motor vehicles almost never die instantly.
- There is a thin, sometimes barely distinguishable line between right and wrong or good and evil.

•Most disillusioning of all are the terrible things that people do to other human beings — whether in the name of love, hate or survival.

Crime is as old as Cain and Abel, and public fascination has propelled it into a huge box office success forty years after Jack Webb, as Sergeant Joe Friday, was well on his way to truth and justice by saying, "Excuse me, sir, I'd just like the facts."

Not nearly so successful, however, is how most Americans view law enforcement today. It is still among the most misunderstood and maligned of all professions. Its detractors are so vocal that many do not even credit it with being a profession. Many believe that the average cop is macho, not very bright, and still operating under the Old West 'top gun' syndrome.

Indeed, in the not-too-distant past, qualifying standards *were* lax, sometimes nearly non-existent. Training was minimal. Officers got most of their education on the street (some detractors maintain that they still do), and, for the most part, *they* set the rules in *their* territory. Moreover, the United States Supreme Court was not yet looking over their collective shoulders to see if they were violating a defendant's constitutional rights.

The selection and training of potential law enforcement officers began to change dramatically in the 1960s, leading to the establishment of national standards in 1972. Tough new policies significantly limited the use of deadly force, and police academies began emphasizing the importance of psychology, mediation and negotiation. Over the next fifteen years there was a fifty-five percent reduction in the number of civilians killed by police. This philosophy of restraint cut both ways: The number of cops killed by suspects also dropped by more than half.

A 1985 Supreme Court decision went still farther, prohibiting police from firing at unarmed, non-violent fleeing suspects. The Court rejected the argument that a criminal forfeits his right to live by committing a crime and then disobeying a lawful police order to surrender. It was no longer fashionable — or legally tenable — to be a member of the Smoking Gun Club. Although there were, and still are, exceptions to this standard, the era of brawn over brain was on the way out.

The way we view law enforcement was significantly re-shaped by the movie theater and television screens of the 1980s. While TV helped modify existing dumb-cop perceptions, it created new myths by compressing an inordinate amount of action into each weekly segment. Indeed, statistics gathered in 1986 by the National Coali-

13

tion on Television Violence showed an average of thirteen 'violent acts' per prime time hour, with cops and robbers programs accumulating far more.

Lost in all of the carnage was the message that in real life, bad guys triumph far more often than they're arrested, convicted and sent off to prison. But because there would be few viewers if the rectangular screen showed typical officers working typical days, the fact that police work is seldom glamorous has been largely ignored or glossed over.

*   *

Cops do have extraordinary powers. The uniform, the badge, the handcuffs, the gun — all of them can be quite intimidating.

Given this, it is understandable, though unfortunate, that there is a generally pervasive 'Us Against Them' chasm between citizen and cop, especially in urban areas. Although time and education may have softened a few of the edges, too many people consider anyone involved with law enforcement as the enemy.

The word "enforcement" itself has negative connotations, and officers symbolize the very restrictions people don't want in their lives.

Millions of otherwise law-abiding citizens violate the law simply by driving faster than the speed limit, many of them ending up with costly citations and feelings of resentment. Paranoia sets in at the first sight of a police car through the rear view mirror. There's an immediate increase in the heartbeat which lasts until the officer has either passed by or turned away.

Family and neighborhood disputes also leave nearly everyone dissatisfied. "Why are you arresting my husband? He didn't really hurt me." is heard at least as often as "Why *aren't* you arresting him?"

Why did it take an hour to respond to a neighbor's complaint of a loud party across the street? The neighbor doesn't know — or care — that the cop was probably on an assignment carrying a higher priority. He more than likely believes that the officer was drinking coffee with his buddies or writing a 'chicken-shit' traffic citation. The people at the party are not happy either, suggesting that the officer should be out catching burglars and rapists instead.

Even when an alleged burglar or rapist is caught, there is an understandable, but unrealistic expectation of old-time frontier justice — a short trial and a long rope. At the very least, many victims want the suspect arrested, convicted and sent off to prison

14

for life. And they'd be real pleased if it could all be done by sundown.

Another part of the problem is that cops are generally isolated from the people they serve. As early as 1931, a Presidential Commission concluded that motorized policing was significantly more effective than foot patrol or moving about on horseback. Unfortunately, as one modern-day officer noted, "It's very difficult to establish a relationship with a police car that's driving past at thirty miles an hour."

While cops are obviously able to cover more ground more quickly, the trade-off is substantially less positive interaction between them and the community. Officers find themselves knowing less about the neighborhood they patrol, and residents become uncomfortable when they *do* appear.

Of the new breed of cops, there are still many who are macho or who have inflexible attitudes, and despite the screening and controls, some still misuse their position. One thing that cops *aren't* is dumb. Nearly half of the nation's officers have completed at least two years of college, and getting accepted into and successfully completing an accredited police academy is a major accomplishment.

*   *

With a population of more than a half-million people, Tucson is among the nation's fastest-growing cities. It is representative of most large metropolitan areas in the United States, and its problems are generally similar to those of other urban cities across the country. As preparation for this book began, Tucson had the eighth highest crime rate among the nation's major metropolitan areas and was already one of the country's largest corridors for transporting illegal drugs.

In researching and writing "COPS: The Men and Women Behind the Badge," I followed one class of recruits during a lengthy qualifying process, through more than six months of Academy and field training, and then through their first five years on the street. This book was made possible by the cooperation of the Tucson Police Department, which allowed me substantial access to its facilities, personnel and records. The only conditions established were that the participating officers give me written, voluntary permission to follow their careers and that I not publish anything which might hinder an ongoing criminal investigation.

Police dramas are, in many ways, modern-day Westerns, I

15

realized after spending more than 1,000 hours riding patrol with the nine officers who comprise this book. I went wherever their assignments took them. Now and again, I helped on calls, sometimes because I was there anyway, and occasionally out of necessity. It quickly became clear that the need to project a power demeanor is an integral part of law enforcement, but looking beyond that, I found men and women who — beneath their street strut — love, hate, laugh, cry and bleed like the rest of us as they try to cope with daily scenes of violence and pathos. In many ways, I began to think and act like the cops I was tracking.

All of the events described are real. Dialogues are quoted verbatim from cassette tapes, phone calls to 911 and police radio recordings. There are no composite characters and no resequencing of events.

The names of all officers are real. In most instances, only the first names of suspects, victims and witnesses are used. Some of them are the actual first names, while others have been changed.

These men and women live and work in Tucson, but this is a story about city cops everywhere.

Two brief caveats: Although my intent is to inform and educate, there is often a thin line between accuracy and 'good taste,' and readers may be uncomfortable with situations portrayed in these pages. Finally, the language in this book reflects what is heard on the street, and portions of it are likely to be unsettling to some.

1

The Road to Hell

The road to the Arizona Law Enforcement Training Academy is a long and difficult one. For most of the nearly fifty Tucson Police Department candidates who started their formal training January 6, 1985, that journey began years before with the realization that they wanted a career in law enforcement.

A few are able to pinpoint the moment of decision. They know where they were and what they were doing, just as many of us recall the assassination of John F. Kennedy, Neil Armstrong's walk on the moon or the explosion of the Challenger space shuttle. For others, the lure of police work doesn't have a definable starting or ending point; it evolved with the passage of time from dream to goal.

It's not easy to become a cop in Tucson. During the spring and early summer of 1984, applications are submitted by 886 candidates. Following a selection process spanning nearly six months, just forty-six of them will be invited to enter ALETA Class 102.

Officials of both the City of Tucson and the Tucson Police Department call the qualifying process an "exhaustive" one. To the candidates it is also *exhausting* — physically, intellectually and emotionally — requiring dozens of hours of paperwork, testing and interviewing. Before it ends, each surviving candidate will undergo several written and oral tests, a psychological evaluation, an extensive background check, a polygraph and a comprehensive medical examination. Some drop out along the way and others are eliminated at each test point. Those who survive are truly the chosen few.

*   *

For Pat Batelli, the road to the Academy spanned more than twenty-five years and 2,000 miles. She is one of the original 886

17

who filed applications in time to be considered for Class 102. Women comprise about eight percent of TPD's nearly 600 officers, and their numbers are growing. At thirty-six, Pat is nearly ten years older than the average candidate.

Her interest in law enforcement began during her early childhood in Paterson, New Jersey. It is something of an American tradition for children between the ages of five and ten to want to "grow up" to be a policeman, firefighter, nurse, movie star or athlete. The tradition evolved naturally for Pat. Her paternal grandfather was a street cop in Paterson for more than thirty years. "He was a good neighborhood cop," she recalls. "He worked and lived in one of the toughest neighborhoods, a foot patrolman who really cared about people."

He died soon after retiring, and Pat still remembers "the respect and grieving of the community, the long funeral procession and a twenty-one-gun salute." Years later, she hasn't forgotten the caring and compassion that were a large part of his life.

Pat began going steady with her husband-to-be when she was fourteen. They married four years later ("I don't know whether I was in love or in lust," she admits) and settled in Tucson, where their two daughters were born. Although she had dropped out of high school in the tenth grade, Pat later received a GED and went on to earn a B.S. in the Health Arts from St. Francis College. When her marriage ended in 1975, she became a registered nurse, providing an outlet for her need to work with people.

Twice before, she had tried for a law enforcement career. She failed a Department of Public Safety physical agility test in 1976, and three years later made the Sheriff's Department certification list just before a hiring freeze intervened.

For Pat, the third time will be a charm, but not before she relives — and finally puts to rest — a deep personal trauma.

*   *

The City of Tucson's Personnel Department is responsible for the first stages of the qualifying and selection process. Those who have submitted the initial application are invited to a 'courtesy day' where they are briefed on law enforcement in general and the expectations of the Tucson Police Department in particular. Officers are available to answer questions and candidates may, if they wish, participate in a mini-physical conditioning program.

All 886 are asked to take a written test based on material from a twenty-page pre-test booklet. Among the areas covered are knowl-

18

edge of law enforcement language and techniques, appropriate police conduct, the criminal justice system and city geography.

Many candidates take themselves out of the running following their 'courtesy day' experience. Some have lost interest or found other jobs, and still others reconsider their commitment after glancing through the pre-test booklet. Although all 886 are eligible to take the written test, Pat is one of only 517 to do so.

Very little screening is done at this stage. Only those who are unable to grasp basic instructions and situations are eliminated. Pat and 427 others will remain candidates, but only ten percent of them ultimately will be accepted into the Academy.

During the next few weeks, she and the others view a series of training films showing police responding to typical calls. They take extensive notes while watching how officers handled each situation. Next, they will appear individually before a Learning Potential Board.

Two officers who have seen the same videos greet Pat. They attempt to put her at ease by asking non-test questions: When did she begin thinking of a career in law enforcement? What has she done to prepare herself? Pat is dressed casually, but appropriately, and carries herself well. She responds in a low, clear voice.

Pat, like each of the others, is shown excerpts from three of the training films. She is told that after each film clip she will be asked to explain whether the police action was correct or incorrect, and why. Written notes are not permitted.

Officers must learn and follow specific procedures for dozens of situations. As the first video begins, a female officer, working alone, confronts a man breaking into a home through the rear patio door. She orders the suspect to "freeze" and then proceeds, gun extended, to approach, search and handcuff him. The officer in this video is female, but the procedures would be identical for a male. The overriding issue is minimizing risk and maximizing safety.

Pat has two minutes to comment. She notes correctly that the officer stopped at least arm's length from the suspect and instructed him to interlock his fingers and place his hands on his head. The officer conducted a visual search of the suspect from both front and rear. Pat has remembered this, too, along with the reasons for these actions.

Now the suspect is instructed to spread his feet farther than shoulder width apart with his toes pointed out, minimizing the possibility of any sudden movement while he is handcuffed and searched.

It is by far the most demanding of all the videos. There are seventeen specific points which can be made in two minutes and Pat is given credit for ten of them. She scores nine of ten possible points in the other two video segments.

Police officers are often required to testify in court, so Pat is escorted to a simulated courtroom where she undergoes both direct and cross-examination concerning a man who, in another video segment, was stopped, field-tested and then arrested for driving under the influence of alcohol. She is rated not only on the content of her testimony, but on her appearance, voice, eye contact, body language and her overall accuracy of the facts of the incident. One officer gives her fifteen of a possible sixteen points; the other awards her fourteen.

Many candidates are visibly anxious despite efforts of the officers to help them relax. "We still get nervous when we have our own Promotion Board interviews," a veteran confides. Some know that they've blown it. "Is there any way I can do that again?" one asks. He can't, but an officer tries to reassure him by asking what he thought he did wrong. "Everything," he responds.

A few show little grasp of even rudimentary law enforcement concepts. One has good credentials on paper, but they disintegrate when he opens his mouth. He speaks haltingly and indecisively, using valuable time second-guessing some of his own answers. "Almost a total disaster," a rating officer observes to his partner when the candidate has left and their written evaluations have been completed.

Phil Carlin works for the City of Tucson's Personnel Department. He was given the assignment of police testing in 1978 and was responsible for eliminating multiple-choice testing and replacing it with the job-related training films. The newer techniques are identifying better potential officers, he says, especially among ethnic minorities who are often negatively affected by multiple-choice examinations.

Of the 428 men and women eligible for the Learning Potential Board, 355 keep their appointments and only fifty-nine fail to achieve the minimum score for further consideration. Pat has the seventy-sixth highest score of the 296 remaining candidates.

*   *

The road to the Academy passes to the control of the Tucson Police Department. Those who have filled out standard single-sheet job applications in the past are in for a shock. They must now contend with a questionnaire that begins with a table of contents and runs sixteen pages. It asks for the usual personal, family, educational, financial and reference information, but wants it in substantial depth. Detailed information is required about all family members (including in-laws), whether living or deceased. Similar information must be provided about everyone the candidate has lived with in the past five years. Education records begin with grammar school, while job history must go back to age seventeen and include names of supervisors and co-workers. All debts and charge accounts must be listed, and all motor vehicle accidents and traffic citations must be itemized.

There are dozens of other questions. Among them: Have you ever been suspended or expelled from school or denied admission to one? Have you ever been discharged or asked to resign from any employment? Have you ever been arrested, detained by police or summoned to court? Have you ever taken any hallucinogenic drug? Have you ever used marijuana? All "yes" responses require additional explanation.

An applicant who can answer "no" to most of the personal questions, has never married, comes from a small family, hasn't changed residences or jobs frequently and has no debts or charge accounts will still have to provide 150 to 190 pieces of information. For most candidates the number will range upward from 300. Simply *gathering* all of the information takes several days.

Although disciplinary action by former employers, motor vehicle violations or the use of illegal drugs will not necessarily eliminate candidates from further consideration, lying about it probably will. The application makes it clear that "any misstatement of fact or omission of material information may disqualify you." Candidates are also advised that their responses will be the basis for a thorough background investigation during which officers spend two to four weeks contacting past employers and co-workers, neighbors, friends and family members.

*   *

An Oral Board consisting of two officers and a sergeant now begins screening Pat and the remaining candidates. The Boards are structured to the extent that everyone is asked the same questions, with followup queries based on the initial responses.

After brief introductions, Pat is asked to describe the personal characteristics she feels will enable her to handle the job. She's also asked several 'what-if' questions, including whether she could enforce an existing law she didn't believe in. Pat replies that she thinks the fifty-five mile per hour speed limit on the open highway is unrealistic, but "could and would" support it if it were her job. Other candidates cite prostitution, gambling or possession of small quantities of marijuana as laws they would enforce even if they didn't agree with them. "Breaking the law in small ways is still breaking the law," one candidate observes.

The officers are looking for insights into the candidate's thinking rather than "perfect" answers. Some give conflicting replies or opinions, or become defensive when pressed or challenged. Others leave the testing officers with an uneasy feeling. Pat's interview lasts nearly fifty minutes, and Board members rate her "highly recommended," the best of four possible rankings. She is one of 122 still in the running.

The remaining candidates will complete the Minnesota Multiphasic Personality Inventory, an evaluation tool consisting of 566 true or false questions. The MMPI has been widely used for more than forty years to identify potentially serious psychological problems. Many of the statements are — or appear — bland: "My hands and feet are usually warm enough," "I like mechanics magazines." Some refer to daily living: "I work under a great deal of tension," "I am happy most of the time," "I would rather win than lose in a game." While the majority of questions deal with careers, feelings, relationships, health and lifestyle preferences, some appear strangely out of place: "Evil spirits possess me at times," "I see things or animals or people around me that others do not see," "I believe I am being plotted against."

*   *

J. Michael Morgan, a clinical psychologist, evaluates each candidate's file prior to an extensive interview. He asks Pat why she wants to leave a Tucson hospital where she has been an emergency room nurse for three years. She responds that she's not dissatisfied with nursing, but wants to work in law enforcement. Pat has done about a dozen ride-alongs with officers and deputies, and Dr. Morgan asks about those experiences.

She leans forward now, animated and verbal as she warms up to the interview. "I saw officers doing good things for the most part," she says, but also remembers being upset by the actions of one White cop who was "unnecessarily physical" with an Hispanic suspect. "Being a cop is an opportunity to work with people, help them and really feel you're contributing. I like people and I don't think there's anything wrong with giving a damn about them."

Dr. Morgan asks about her family. Pat's father was a crane operator who went to work "sick or not." There is love in her voice and her eyes seem to reach back into her memories as she recalls the times they spent talking or fishing. Her mother "always seemed to be busy" raising Pat and her five brothers. Her parents are dead now — her father of emphysema and a stroke in 1973 and her mother following a coronary a few months ago.

He wants to know about her stress as an emergency room nurse. "It gets to me most when I feel I can't do enough," she responds. Pat says she deals with it by debriefing with co-workers and "bitching a little" to help wind down. Could she, a woman whose career has been dedicated to helping save lives, *take* one if it became necessary? "I don't know for sure, but I think my basic instincts would take over if my life or another life was threatened." And how might she feel about it afterward? "Bummed out, I think, even if I felt there was no other choice."

Dr. Morgan will submit a written, confidential evaluation. His options are to recommend, marginally recommend or not recommend. When Dr. Morgan speaks, TPD generally listens. "He has a good track record with us," says Police Chief Peter Ronstadt.

Pat and sixty-four others — just over half of those who took the psychological evaluation — are asked to return for a polygraph examination. It will be the final major hurdle.

*   *

The often misunderstood and maligned polygraph is to its supporters a combination of art and science. Generally referred to as a lie detector, a more accurate description would be a detector of *truth*. The first working model was introduced in 1921 and modified several times over the next quarter-century.

Controversial from the first, it gradually gained acceptance, although it is still generally banned from the courtroom except in cases where both sides agree to its use.

Jim Mofford, President of Southwest Polygraph Service, is one of about 2,800 practitioners certified by the American Polygraph Association. In the hands of a skilled examiner, he calls the polygraph "the mirror of the mind" and claims that its reliability and

23

validity are at least ninety-eight percent.

He has already reviewed Pat's job application, Oral Board and background investigation. Acknowledging to Pat that there are many misconceptions about the polygraph, he takes more than fifteen minutes to explain the procedure. When someone lies, the body sets up automatic defense mechanisms against detection, he tells her, emphasizing that no such action is needed when the truth is told.

There will be no "trick" questions, he says. He'll go over each question in advance. He will rephrase any question if Pat feels the wording might present a problem. The primary goal of the examination is to make certain there are no unresolved deceptions. He reminds her that lying about a past action is more likely to disqualify her than the action itself.

*   *

Pat was accused of theft by a former employer, read her Miranda rights and told that there would be an investigation.

The weeks that followed were the most traumatic of her life, worse even than the breakup of her marriage. There was a newspaper report of the incident, and in her mind, *everyone* knew. Falling asleep was difficult at best, and often impossible. Her last thoughts in the evening and her first thoughts in the morning were of anger, fear and embarrassment. Her appetite all but disappeared, and she started seeing a therapist in an effort to hold her dissolving world together.

Pat has made full disclosure of the incident in her TPD application and, although the charges were dropped due to a lack of evidence, she knows it will come up in the polygraph testing. She wants it brought up, dealt with and buried, but still she's nervous in anticipation. Listening to Mofford explain the procedure, she can't get the dark thoughts out of her mind. "What if my nerves produce a false result? What if the polygraph makes a mistake? *What if they really think I did it?*"

She's again aware of his voice. "It's normal to be nervous," he assures her. "I've taken more than a dozen tests myself and I was as nervous the last time as the first." He begins reading her the questions he intends to ask. One of them will be, "Have you ever stolen from an employer?" Pat tells him that she has taken pens and pads of paper. He asks how much they were worth and she estimates "not more than a couple of dollars." He will change this question to

24

"Other than up to fifteen dollars, have you ever stolen merchandise from where you worked?"

He looks at her and says, "The polygraph tells the difference between a lie and the truth, but not how *much* difference. It doesn't distinguish between two Bic pens and a box of gold watches." He turns back to his notes and goes over each question with Pat, rewording here and there to make certain that her answers won't be clouded by irrelevant details. He warns her not to withhold information. "If it's in your head it will almost surely show up on the polygraph."

Now he seats her in what might pass to the casual — or nervous — observer as a modified electric chair, and attaches several discs for the test that will probably determine if she'll have the opportunity to become a police officer. With the exception of control questions ("Are you now in the state of Idaho?") which are used as a base for analyzing the other answers, she has heard them all before. "Do you intend to lie during this test?" "Do you have health problems that might interfere with your work?" "Other than the minor traffic violation we discussed, have you been convicted of any crime?" "Other than up to fifteen dollars, have you stolen merchandise from where you worked?" "In the past five years have you used any illegal drugs or narcotics you haven't told me about?" "Have you taken part in any serious undetected crime?"

At one point, Pat is taking only about seven breaths a minute, compared to a normal sixteen. Mofford stops the test, giving her a few minutes to relax. "I know the intensity of what you're doing," he says. "I really do." He is obviously sincere and she relaxes. The questions are repeated; only the sequence is changed so she can't affect the results through anticipation.

More than an hour after she seated herself in the chair, Mofford shuts off the equipment. The pens that have been recording minute physiological changes in her pulse, heart rate, galvanic skin responses, blood pressure and respiration stop tracing the scribblings of her past.

For this test, Pat won't have to wait days or weeks for a verdict. He turns to her, smiles and tells her what she's known for years: "There are no unresolved deceptions," he says softly. "You had nothing to do with the theft."

*   *

It's three weeks later, December 10, 1984. Chief Ronstadt has received summaries on the remaining sixty-five men and women,

25

and their complete files — each more than two inches thick — are available for his inspection. With him in the conference room are Assistant Police Chief Dean Taylor, Training Division Commander Lieutenant Tom Patterson, Internal Affairs Commander Lieutenant Elaine Hedtke, TPD Personnel Supervisor Linda Kegerreis and TPD Personnel Administrative Assistant Becky Laughlin. Progressing in alphabetical order, Ronstadt listens to a brief summary of each candidate. He refers to the folders and asks questions. He has the final decision.

The recommendation to hire Pat is made at 9:54 a.m. Less than two minutes later, Ronstadt nods. Pat won't know it for three days, but after years of thinking about it and six months of paperwork, interviews, testing and waiting, she is on her way to the Academy.

2

Hell

Now the hard work begins.

The Arizona Law Enforcement Training Academy trains police recruits from around the state. Located on a forty-acre site eight miles west of downtown Tucson, it is part boot camp and part graduate school. The physical and academic requirements are rigorous and recruits are subjected to intense levels of stress as they seek to earn their certification.

"You won't all make it through," Tucson Police Department Lieutenant Tom Patterson tells the group two weeks before they enter the Academy. "Some of you will drop out and others will be asked to leave. You're going to a strict and rigid environment where your decisions will be made for you. They'll yell at you and scream at you and you're not going to like it. They'll try to stress you out physically and mentally, because if you can't take it there, you won't be able to take it on the street where some people will try to hurt you. You're not a failure if you change your mind. If this is absolutely, positively what you want to do in life, you'll probably make it. If you've made a mistake, you'll know it soon."

*   *

ALETA Class 102 begins with eighty-eight cadets, the largest group in the Academy's four-year history. Tucson cadets comprise half the class; the rest come from seventeen other Arizona law enforcement agencies. It's the first Sunday of 1985 and there are seventy-five men and thirteen women at the 1 p.m. roll call.

Forget "Police Academy," the movie. *This* is the real world.

"The fun's over!" announces Pima County Deputy Richard Pettitt. His job description is Physical Training Instructor, but it

27

could just as easily be Designated Screamer.

"You're in for eleven weeks of hell," he asserts, his voice level already rising as he scans the lines of cadets, all of whom are dressed in business clothes. "You don't fucking impress me so far; you look like a damn bunch of misfits."

Within minutes they've learned their first command: "Class attenHUT!" Pettitt, a square-jawed former Marine, walks slowly, ominously down the front row. "Eyes straight ahead!" he screams as he approaches one nervous cadet.

Now they're nose to nose.

"Don't look anywhere, don't wiggle your ass, don't move a fucking hair on your head! Is that clear?"

"Yes."

"Yes, WHAT?"

"Yes, sir."

"I don't hear you!"

"YES, SIR!"

All eighty-eight are ordered to hit the ground and do their first push-ups.

Sergeant Dan Abbate jumps in, his voice crackling with intensity. "You people think you can do what you damn well please. That's the trouble with this permissive society. We don't have time to wait for you! When someone says do it, you DO IT!"

More push-ups, then the cadets are shown how to jump to their feet and line up to the person on their right using peripheral vision. The first attempt is sloppy.

"Is lining up that fucking difficult?" Abbate shouts.

"No, sir" comes the fragmented response.

"Are you trying to piss me off the first day?"

"No, sir."

"Is there any doubt in your mind that I fucking mean what I'm saying?"

"No, sir."

"I don't hear you!"

"NO, SIR!"

Eighty-eight cadets drop to the ground for more push-ups.

Next, they begin to learn the drill and ceremony commands. They're shown left, right and about face and how to open and close ranks. Dozens more will follow in the coming days.

Pettitt and Abbate move through the ranks, confronting cadets. "What in hell's taking you so long?" "Don't you understand simple English?" "Don't fucking look at me; keep your eyes straight

28

forward!" "You're not going to make it here!"

There are more drills, more push-ups, a ten-minute break and then to the classroom for the first time. A neatly printed notice on the blackboard greets them: "Welcome to ALETA! Find your name tag. Sit down!! Don't talk and don't touch anything!"

Sergeant Gary Richardson outlines the Academy's rules. They fill six typewritten pages. He explains academic performance standards, telling cadets that they'll be evaluated on classroom participation, written and reading assignments and spot quizzes. There will be a major examination every Friday. A cadet who fails an examination by scoring less than seventy-five percent goes on automatic probation. The result of a second failure is immediate dismissal. Questions are either true/false or multiple choice. Marking and grading are done by computer.

Physical conditioning standards are also formidable. Cadets are timed in both a one-and-a-half-mile run and an agility sprint which reflects how quickly they can change speed and direction. They are also tested for vertical jumping ability and for the number of push-ups and sit-ups they can do in one minute. Up to 100 points can be earned on each of the five tests, and anyone who doesn't accumulate at least 375 of the possible 500 points won't graduate.

A twenty-six-year-old cadet — the average age of this class — would meet the minimum requirement by doing twenty-four push-ups (the Academy record is ninety-seven) and thirty-nine sit-ups a minute; jumping nineteen inches vertically from a stationary position; completing the agility sprint in eighteen seconds; and running one-and-a-half miles in thirteen minutes. A strong performance in one area may be used to offset weakness in another. Women must meet the same standards as men.

Cadets will receive forty hours of firearms instruction, each firing about 1,500 rounds of ammunition. They will learn to shoot from distances up to seventy-five feet and from standing and kneeling positions, using both their strong and weak hands. Cadets must score at least 260 of a possible 300 points.

There are also standards to meet in first aid, search techniques, felony stops and defensive driving. Again, failure to meet ALETA guidelines will result in dismissal.

"I don't ever want to hear that you're trying," Richardson says. "Getting the job done is all we're willing to accept."

The cadets, still in street clothes, are ordered outside for more drills, more push-ups, more stress. One young man is confronted for the second time: "If I know your name the first day, you're in serious trouble, and I fuckin' know your name!"

No one budges. The physical training instructors, who one day may be the cadets' saviors, are simply demons now, already feared or despised by most.

For all of the trainees, it's the beginning of a test of their determination and perseverance. For many, it's the start of a twelve-week trip through Hell with a monthly stipend of $1,205 to help ease the pain.

Two of them resign before dinner and head for home.

*   *

Scattered lights of a mostly-sleeping Tucson can be seen to the east, and, in the desert below, a coyote choir welcomes the approaching dawn. It's 5:15 and still dark when the remaining eighty-six cadets are awakened for their first full day. Before the sun pokes through the clouds over the Rincon Mountains, they will have showered, dressed, cleaned their dorms, eaten breakfast and lined up in the chilly morning air.

"You look like a fucking herd of sheep!" Richardson explodes. "Can't you remember what you learned yesterday?" They do push-ups, review commands, then stand at attention while their tormenters walk slowly through the ranks, finding fault with nearly everyone. There are chewed fingernails, boots not sufficiently spit-shined, lint on clothing, a hanging thread, a cap resting at the wrong angle.

One cadet makes the mistake of moving his head.

"Do you understand the instruction?" screams Kevin Danaher, a West Point graduate with a non-stop scowl emblazoned across his face.

"Yes, sir."

"Are you trying to defy me?"

"No, sir."

"Do you want to stay at this Academy?"

"Yes, sir."

"Then get your head out of your fucking ass and do as you're told!"

After forty minutes of confrontation and inspection, it's time for class. It's not yet 8 a.m.

*   *

Captain Steven Gendler, a graduate of the FBI National Academy, has been the Commander of ALETA for two years. He is gentle

30

and soft-spoken, almost fatherly, as he addresses the cadets and has them introduce themselves. He takes time to ask each a question or two and he banters easily with them. They are relaxed for this brief period and there is even laughter in the room. Reality quickly returns as he reminds them that their training is based on discipline, stress and regimentation.

"You will be thoroughly tested emotionally, intellectually and physically," he says, adding, "We owe it to every cadet who has graduated previously that you have the same training and skills that they have."

Cadets will spend at least forty hours a week in class, and sixteen-hour days will be the rule rather than the exception as they tackle a curriculum which includes more than ninety academic subjects.

Following a full morning in the classroom, thirty minutes is allotted for lunch. One line serves nearly 100 people, and most mid-day meals are eaten quickly. Later, when afternoon classes end at 4:30, cadets have eight minutes to return to their dorms, change into physical training gear and line up in formation.

The daily physical training lasts a minimum of one hour. It starts with a series of stretching exercises, followed by jogging on the hilly terrain adjacent to the Academy. Cadets begin with short runs of a mile or so and will be grinding out three or four miles a day by the fifth week, often led by Gendler, who is still trim despite years behind a desk. Their bodies already ache, lungs and legs screaming to ease up.

Jogging mercifully ends, giving way to more stretching exercises, push-ups, sit-ups and strength training. There are grunts and groans, much of it primal-sounding, as cadets push to keep going. A few take shortcuts when they think they're not being observed.

Dinner is more leisurely than breakfast or lunch. It is followed by a mandatory study period and equipment preparation for the next day. There aren't enough hours to do everyhing.

Another cadet packs and leaves. It's still the first week, but the pressure is already taking its toll. For many, the dream they share in the middle of the desert has become a nightmare. Virtually everyone feels the stress and some show it. "Several of them look smooth on the outside, but below the water line they're already paddling like hell," observes one instructor.

Cadets may leave the Academy for the weekend. Four of them announce their resignations when they don't return by Sunday evening curfew.

*   *

Monday morning lineup begins badly. Cadets aren't reacting to commands crisply enough. "Bullshit! Bullshit, people!" screams Pettitt, his words hitting as hard as a fist. "This is your second week. You'd better wake up, people. How hard can it be to line up to your right? How fucking hard, people?"

There is no response. The cadets have taken this short diatribe as statement rather than question.

"I'm listening!" he shouts.

"Not hard, sir!"

"I CAN'T HEAR YOU!"

"NOT HARD, SIR!"

"We're gonna have to draw little lines on the ground so you'll know where to stand. And you want to be police officers? BULLSHIT!"

*   *

The academic pace picks up rapidly now. There are classes in report writing, constitutional and criminal law, patrol and observation, laws of arrest, search and seizure, and defensive techniques. The lesson plans for the first week filled 219 pages, and this week's load isn't much less. Despite the pressure to absorb huge amounts of data, the classroom has already become a sanctuary of sorts — a haven where they can flee the physical and emotional tension for a few hours.

They do what they must to hang in, but many fantasize about leaving, complaining privately that so much stress and humiliation aren't conducive to learning. "I'm so paranoid I'll be screamed at that I spend more time shining my shoes and taking care of my equipment than studying the day's material," one cadet grouses. Heads nod, and Robert Garcia, who celebrated his twenty-eighth birthday a few days before beginning the Academy, adds, "All one of them has to do is walk near me and my heart starts pounding."

Another cadet — an emergency medical technician for four years — knows what it's like to live with stress. Nonetheless, he walked to the perimeter of the Academy campus late one evening during the second week and stared at the flickering lights of Tucson in the valley below. "I was cold, hurting and tired and was real tempted to pack it in and head home," he recalls, but convinced

32

himself that "I had to look at it as three months toward what I want to do for the next twenty years."

Derek Campbell, twenty-seven, looks like the football player he was in school. He is one of the very few who seem to thrive on the virtual non-stop stress. "I'm having a good time, a lot of fun," the ex-Air Force security policeman and former Chicago cop maintains. "Fuck that stress shit; most of these people don't know what stress *is*."

Pat Batelli does. She's developed a shin splint injury and lags far behind in the afternoon runs, quickly becoming the target of verbal abuse from the drill instructors. At the end of a three-mile run near the end of the second week, Pat struggles up the final hill, half jogging and half walking as everyone stands waiting for her. The D.I. plays it for all he can. "You've been under fire, you're wounded, lying on the road in the heat, waiting for your backup to arrive," he says to them. "You're thirsty, you're dying, wondering if she's ever going to get here." Finally, derisively: "Here she comes, your backup's finally here."

"That really hurt," Pat remembers months later. "I was in pain and really doing the best I could."

No one resigns the second week.

*   *

Les Beach, a Navy veteran and now forty-five, is one of the oldest rookies ever hired by the Tucson Police Department. He failed the physical that would have enabled him to become a New York State Trooper nearly a quarter century ago because he had flat feet and because a statute dating back to the era when officers rode horses had not yet been rescinded.

He remained in New York as a certified flight instructor, and later was a lieutenant in charge of nuclear security at a state facility. Les and his second wife, Sharon, moved to Tucson in 1984.

Sharon, who is writing a daily journal while he's away, recalls the morning he left for the Academy:

"He was oh so methodical. Checking and re-checking his lists. Going over in his mind, as he had so many times before, all he had to remember to bring. They call it necessary equipment. I'd call it camp gear! The look on his face was reminiscent of how my children looked the first day I sent them to summer camp. 'Will I have fun? Will I like the kids? Why is Mom trying to get rid of me?' Only in his case it will be 'Will my body hold out? Will I be able to get back

33

in a school atmosphere after all these years? And most importantly, will I realize a life-long ambition of being a police officer?'"

Sharon has lived in Tucson for less than six months. With family and friends thousands of miles away, her daily journal becomes a form of therapy. Writing it each evening brings her closer to Les, but the time alone also has a dark side when her thoughts take her places she doesn't want to go.

"Would he like to call, or does he feel the young guys would laugh at him if he called home every night?" she writes. "Is he relishing this time away? Does he feel like a single man again, less constricted by a wife?"

On a particularly bad night, she has "this horrendous thought that I would lose him to some young girl cadet who would think of him as her protector, and they would have more in common now, and ride off into the sunset in a squad car."

Sharon knows better. "What is it about a woman's psyche that lets her mind think these thoughts when she truly knows how much he loves and adores her?" she wonders.

Les — the oldest cadet in the group — doesn't have time to wonder about *anything*. All of his energy is focused on getting through days that begin before dawn and don't end until late in the evening. He doesn't particularly like the Academy, but as ex-military he knows what it's like "to keep your nose clean and your mouth shut." This has helped him cope with the discipline and the mind games.

He receives a major setback in the second week when another cadet lands on his chest during defensive takedown training. The pain is almost constant, but he makes it through the week.

The weekend is not as easy.

He is still in pain, and Sharon writes, "When I caught a glimpse of him, he would be grimacing. We went first thing Sunday morning for X-rays. I sat in the waiting room praying that he would be all right, but as soon as he walked through the door, I knew something was wrong. He had three fractured ribs!

"He put on a stern face, but I knew it would not last. The words were hard coming out of my mouth. I knew the anguish he was going through. He worked so hard to get there. He wanted this so badly.

"I tried to comfort him, but I could see I was not succeeding. Then he broke down and wept. All the years of dreaming of becoming a police officer had come down to one moment: Would they let him continue? My fear is that they will be unbending and ask him to leave."

34

Back at the Academy, Les considers not telling anyone about the fractured ribs, but realizes that he must take the chance. He's allowed to remain, but will wear a rib brace for several weeks.

He phones Sharon and she is ecstatic. "Did Alexander Graham Bell realize when he was inventing the telephone how just one phone call could bring sunshine into one's life?" she writes.

Les is now more determined than ever.

"I've waited most of my life for this opportunity," he says. "I'm just telling myself that I have to do it, that no one is going to do it for me, and that even though I'm old enough to be a father to most of the people in the class, I'm not going to get any special break because of it."

*   *

Title 13 deals with Arizona's criminal laws. In the next two weeks, cadets will learn the statutes, procedures, language and elements of a broad range of crimes. Included are homicide, assault, kidnapping, sexual offenses, criminal trespass, robbery, burglary, theft, arson, forgery, bribery, perjury, credit card fraud, drugs, gambling, prostitution, organized crime and more than a dozen others. The full statute book contains more than 250 pages of small print.

Most of the remaining cadets appear more relaxed, perhaps feeling that the worst is over. They have begun to develop rapport among themselves and are providing encouragement to each other. There is more laughter, some of it unplanned. One incident in particular will take its place in ALETA folklore. Two cadets attempting to subdue six-foot, four-inch, 240-pound Derek Campbell during a street survival exercise, reach for his shirt, but relieve him of his shorts as he squirms away. He sits on the floor, bare-bottomed and red-faced, while everyone howls. Pat Batelli begins wearing two pairs of shorts to class.

By the end of the fourth week, the Designated Screamers are letting up a bit, one of them even addressing recruits as "sir" or "ma'am" when acknowledging their questions. As the cadets leave for the weekend, one has been terminated for a rules violation, and three — having failed a weekly exam — are on academic probation, hanging by a thread.

Rene Gomez, twenty-eight and a native Tucsonan, is one of those on probation. His father left the family when Rene was two, and his mother raised him along with his eight brothers and sisters.

35

"She did just an awesome job being both mother and father," he says of his mom. "She worked all her life and the only thing she had to show for it was the love and respect we had for her. In that sense I guess she was a really rich woman."

Rene's father remarried and rarely visited. "I didn't understand why he wasn't with us and I wasn't ready to show any love when I did see him. I tried to hate him, but I couldn't. I just learned to live with it."

After graduating from high school, Rene started classes at Pima Community College, hoping for a degree in art, but soon decided to work in his mother's Mexican restaurant where many of their customers were police officers. Most cops are marvelous story-tellers, and fascinated by their experiences, he decided that law enforcement would make a challenging career. Sylvia, his wife of six years, didn't share his enthusiasm at first, but became supportive when he made the decision to apply in 1982.

Although Rene scored well in the written examination, he didn't make it past the Oral Board. For the next two years, he "ate, slept and thought police," he recalls. "I think if you want something enough you can get it."

His mother is now terminally ill with inoperable cancer, and, Rene often lies awake in his dorm wondering what it will be like after she dies. He also understands the reality that one more failed test during the next two months will result in automatic termination.

Rene's upbeat manner and ready smile are contagious, all the more so in this setting where cheerfulness and serenity do not come easily. Several female cadets take him under their collective wings. "He would come into the women's dorms in the evening and we would tutor him," Pat Batelli remembers. "It was all of us and Rene. I'm sure that other people knew he was there, but nothing was ever said, and there was nothing going on except tutoring and an occasional back rub to relieve some of the stress."

Rene believes they helped him make it through. "They encouraged me. They'd give me little quizzes on the things I was having trouble with. They were giving up some of their study time to help me. They told me I could do it and that they'd kick my ass if I flunked."

*   *

The fifth and sixth weeks provide a change of pace. Cadets spend forty hours learning and practicing firearms techniques.

There are specific methods to learn and time limits for executing each new skill. "We want to give you the greatest possible chance to survive a shooting," they're told. "It's almost 100 percent cast in concrete that you'll have the best chance for survival if you know the rules and follow them on the street."

Family fights have a significant potential for injury or deadly violence, an instructor emphasizes. The bloodied woman who screams for help sometimes attacks the officer who shows up to restrain or arrest her husband or boyfriend. And while most vehicle stops are routine, there is always the potential for a driver or passenger to open fire on an approaching cop.

The cadets learn that family disturbances and vehicle stops have accounted for nearly half of all officer deaths in the United States in the past ten years, and that more than seventy percent of those killed by firearms were shot within a ten-foot range. "Always assume that suspects will respond violently," an instructor tells them. "If they don't, you've lost nothing. If they do, you may gain everything."

Classes in mental preparation are a recent addition to the curriculum. An officer may fire only if his or someone else's life is in imminent danger, and jeopardy is present only if it appears that the suspect has the intent, ability and opportunity to kill.

"Someone who wants to blow you away has a basic advantage because he doesn't have rules and procedures to follow," Sergeant Ed Vesely says. "We'll teach you to turn the odds in your favor through knowledge and common sense."

"Your technical skills will be high, but mental preparation is absolutely essential," Lieutenant Jack Harris adds. "We can teach you *how* to shoot, but you must teach yourself *when* to shoot. You need to have your mind made up long before you get into the situation, and the time to make that decision is before you go to bed tonight, not when you join the force or holster your gun or respond to a call."

Harris tells of a fellow officer who encountered a man with a gun and ordered him to drop it. Instead, the man raised his weapon and pointed it at the officer who momentarily froze. Fortunately, the suspect was disarmed by a second officer. Discussing the incident later, the first officer said, "I've told at least a dozen people to drop guns and knives and they always did. When this guy wouldn't drop it, I didn't know what to do."

The 'shoot-don't shoot' decision needs to be made in advance, Harris says, "by anticipating situations and telling yourself that if he does such-and-such, I'll have to shoot."

Sergeant Bill Hurguy talks about the aftermath of a shooting: "Most officers fantasize what it's like to have to shoot someone. They create the scenario and they're a hero for saving a person's life." In reality, he says, most shootings don't leave the officer proud of himself. "He still second-guesses himself even if he's been absolved by a Board of Inquiry." Hurguy talks about the post-shooting trauma which almost all officers experience.

Peers, trying to be helpful, often make matters worse. "It was a good shooting," one officer was assured over and over. After several days he was ready to explode. "Damn, it was *not* a good shooting," he finally screamed. "I killed someone! He was a criminal, but he had a wife and kids and parents. Maybe there was another way."

To Derek Campbell, it's just part of the job. "God willing, it won't happen, but if it does, you do what you have to do."

*   *

While most of their education has been in the classroom, it's now time for the cadets to practice and hone their skills in a series of Stop and Approach exercises. They search buildings, intervene in family fights, make traffic stops and arrest suspects. Officers play the roles of offenders, and cadets 'die' each time they make a serious mistake. The highly structured simulations represent the most job-related training they'll receive at the Academy.

To ensure maximum benefit, a coach meets with his non-cadet 'players' prior to the start of each exercise to establish objectives and limits. Only the basic scenario is divulged to the cadet before the exercise unfolds.

Today, a cadet is told that he'll be following a car matching the description of a vehicle believed to have been used in an armed robbery in which a convenience store clerk was critically wounded. He's told that a witness reported that two or three people were involved.

When the cadet drives up behind the suspect vehicle there are two people in the front seat. A third man, unseen, is hiding on the floor in the back. While his ability to find and secure the third occupant without being shot is the most vital part of this exercise, the cadet is also graded on his overall control of the situation, including how he positioned his patrol car, his foot approach to the vehicle, and his skills in removing, handcuffing and searching the suspects.

In another exercise, the cadet is told only that he'll approach a car with a flat rear tire and determine whether the motorist needs assistance. The driver appears nervous, but this may simply be his reaction to police officers in general. If the cadet is observant — and this one is — he'll see that the car has been hot-wired. He pretends not to notice, and instead asks the driver to check the trunk for a spare tire. "I don't seem to have a trunk key," he responds. Asked if the vehicle is his, the driver stammers momentarily, then says it belongs to a friend whom he can't immediately identify. The arrest is made without incident.

In yet another drill, a cadet observes a car enter a no passing zone, forcing another vehicle off the road in order to avoid a collision. The violator is initially pleasant and cooperative. After listening to the cadet's concern over what occurred, the violator promises that it won't happen again and turns to leave. The cadet calls him back and begins writing a citation.

The driver now becomes verbally abusive. He refuses to sign the ticket even though he's told it does not constitute an admission of guilt. He says angrily that he'd sooner be arrested than sign. When he persists in this position, he's told he's under arrest and hand-cuffed. Now he changes his mind and insists that he be allowed to sign the citation.

In this exercise, the cadet is evaluated not only on how he handled procedural and safety issues, but on his ability to control a deteriorating situation, maintain composure under verbal attack and stick to an appropriate decision once it's been made.

There are a dozen basic scenarios, each with seemingly endless variations. The common denominator is that officer safety depends on training, planning, caution and common sense.

Between exercises, cadets view videotapes showing cops being blown away as a result of their mistakes. "These are lessons that have been learned over the bodies of hundreds of law enforcement officers," the narrator intones.

Every eye is fixed on the screen.

*   *

As training begins to wind down, cadets are introduced to Title 28, covering Arizona's motor vehicle statutes. A working knowledge of laws covering traffic movement must be demonstrated. The investigation of accidents has become a science, and cadets learn how to keep the mishap from getting worse while handling emergency needs of the injured, securing the scene and gathering information and evidence.

Still to be absorbed are classes in defensive driving, crowd and riot control, suspect identification, domestic disputes, bomb threats, disaster response, liquor laws, rules of evidence, traffic control, fingerprinting, social psychology and mental illness.

Pat Batelli, who has wanted to be a cop since her pre-teen years, has done well academically and has toughed out most of the physical demands despite the injury to her shin. Suddenly, less than two weeks before graduation, she fails an accident investigation examination and is dismissed from the Academy. Too angry, embarrassed and devastated to face her fellow cadets, she loads her belongings and dreams into her car. Doing her best to function in a state of semi-shock, she turns east on Trails End Road and slowly heads home.

Les, Derek, Robert and most of the others make it through. Rene does, too, but the hour or two after each weekly exam have been excruciatingly long as he paces the Academy grounds, a lump in his throat, waiting for test scores to be posted, and wondering how he'll face his family if he fails.

Seventy-three of the original eighty-eight cadets graduate. As they line up in the uniforms of their individual agencies, even the Designated Screamers seem impressed.

■

For the thirty-nine new Tucson Police officers wearing their badges for the first time, it is both an ending and a beginning. Following two days of celebration and unwinding, they report to their own Academy for four weeks of advanced training. The atmosphere here is relaxed; there is no screaming, no confrontation. Academics are intense, but now the pressure is self-imposed. Having earned the right and responsibility of motivating themselves, they go home at night.

To adapt to specific Tucson Police Department rules and procedures, they must now unlearn some of what they were taught at ALETA. A portion of each day is devoted to paperwork as they begin to identify and process the dozens of forms they'll be using on the street. They must learn city geography and memorize nearly 100 radio codes. Physical training is still a part of their workload, but now it's scheduled just three times a week.

Most of the time is allocated to fine-tuning practical skills in defensive tactics, high risk traffic stops, crimes in progress, building searches and arrest procedures.

Their monthly salary has increased to $1,771, and suddenly the new officers are only days away from their first shift in a patrol car.

3

You Bet Your Badge

Sergeant Max Davis, a Tucson Police officer for nineteen years, still hasn't forgotten his transition from the classroom to the street. Although a small portion of his Academy schooling included ride-alongs, there was virtually no training or monitoring after graduation. A rookie was often considered an intrusion, and there was a sink-or-swim attitude on the part of many veteran officers. "I rode with a senior officer just two days," Davis recalls. "On the third morning, he handed me a set of keys and pointed to my patrol car. I can still hear his words as he turned and walked away: 'Son, if I need you I'll call you; if you call *me*, you damned well better *need* me.'"

*   *

While the value of field training seems quite logical, it didn't exist in Tucson until the mid-1970s. The Academy's dozens of field exercises, however well simulated, can't duplicate life on the street. Now, based on a structured, comprehensive and standardized evaluation system, field training gives instruction, direction and guidance. Rookies patrol with experienced officers to demonstrate their knowledge of hundreds of laws, policies and procedures and to show they are capable of making appropriate decisions under stress.

They must pass weekly tests and a final comprehensive examination, and be evaluated once a month by a Phase Board. The thirteen-week program is intense, and the pressure now is to perform on actual calls. Knowledge is obviously important, but it is useless if it can't be applied to what is happening on the streets.

"When you look at new officers, it all boils down to their ability to learn, adapt and follow procedures," according to Captain Michael Ulichny, Eastside Operations Commander. Ulichny, with a college degree in law enforcement and nearly twenty years with the Tucson Police Department, was among the first of the new breed of cops spawned in the 1960s. He rose quickly through the ranks, and as a sergeant helped establish the forerunner of the current field training program.

Although most of his time is spent on administrative matters, he is still street-shape trim and he actively monitors his new recruits. "I need to feel comfortable on many levels," he emphasizes. "Does he recognize danger when it exists and know how to react appropriately? Can he do several things at once, often under stress? Can he plan ahead? Does he demonstrate good officer instinct?"

Ulichny knows that some otherwise capable cops crave excitement so much that they become adrenaline junkies, anticipating the next big call. To them, a bad day on the job is when nothing happens. He says it's important that his officers realize that most of each shift is routine and that they're not going to stop a bank robber or rescue a baby every day.

■

Four months at the Academy teaches basics, but it doesn't make a good cop. Only time and experience can do that.

On the streets where you don't always get a second chance, Robert Garcia became a better officer after being 'killed' by a suspect he was questioning. Fortunately for Robert, the man with the knife was also a police officer and the 'stabbing' was an unscheduled part of his education. Trainer Harry Johnson took him behind an eastside Village Inn late one night, playing the role of a suspect while Robert conducted a field interview.

"I was taking notes at waist level with only partial eye contact," Robert recalls. "Harry pulled a knife on me so fast I didn't have time to react. He looked at me and said, 'You could be dead!' Now I write field interviews at shoulder level."

"Sometimes you feel stupid. There's so much going on and you're supposed to know how to do everything, do it right and do it fast. It's a lot of pressure, even when your training officer is patient and supportive."

Robert was born in Santa Fe, New Mexico, the youngest of six children. His parents separated when he was a toddler. Although raised primarily by his mother, he was influenced by an uncle who encouraged him to become a Search & Rescue volunteer during his early teenage years. Robert participated in several mountain rescues, once helping to carry an obese woman more than three miles to safety.

He moved to Tucson, graduated from high school in 1975, and served in the Army for three years. He worked for Learjet as a technician before going back to school to earn a real estate license. Although Robert was recruited and hired by Merrill Lynch Realty, he soon realized that he wanted a career in law enforcement. He returned to Santa Fe, working briefly for the Sheriff's Department before applying for a Tucson position.

He and his wife Tammy have known each other since her foster brother brought him to their home during her junior year in high school.

"I wasn't exactly swept off my feet," Tammy remembers, but Robert was smitten. They dated for a few months, broke up and then began dating again. This time, it took. Robert joined the Army after graduation. They corresponded — Tammy still has all of his letters — and he proposed when he returned home for the Christmas holidays. Married for nine years, they have two sons and a daughter.

Bushy eyebrows are the most prominent feature of Robert's face, and his thick black hair is tipped with gray. It's quickly apparent that this slim, soft-spoken young Hispanic man likes people. "You have to care and you can't be prejudiced," he says. "Every person is a human being. I believe that people are basically good and that you can accomplish a lot more talking than yelling or fighting."

As he straps on his police-issued .38 caliber revolver and begins his shift two weeks after the 'stabbing' incident, Robert spots a motorcycle without visible rear lights. He uses his roof-top speaker to instruct the driver to pull off to the side of the road, gives the dispatcher his location and focuses his spotlight on the cycle.

A law enforcement officer may not arbitrarily stop a vehicle. He must either observe a statute violation or be prepared to document reasonable suspicion that the driver or a passenger had committed a crime. At the same time, a motorist who is questioned briefly in public view is not in custody and therefore not protected by the Miranda rule.

"I stopped you because you have no tail light," Robert tells the cyclist. A computer check of the driver and motorcycle plate is now

44

legal and automatic. Nationwide, thousands of felons are caught each year as a result of such inquiries. There is nothing outstanding against the young man and Robert waves him on after advising him to repair the light. After they leave, Johnson asks Robert why he handled the situation as he did. "It wasn't a serious infraction." Johnson pauses briefly. "I'd have written a faulty equipment warning, which gives him five days to make the repair," he suggests.

Cruising their beat, there's a report of a patient threatening a doctor who is attempting to treat him at a nearby hospital emergency room. Although they're not assigned the call, Johnson suggests they also respond because of the possible volatility of the situation and the close working relationship officers have with medical personnel.

Police policy restricts the use of Code 3 runs — officers driving faster than the posted speed limit — and dictates that the siren and flashing lights must both be used.

Robert accelerates a bit as he moves easily around the light traffic, opting not to activate either his lights or siren. Officers call this Code 2 1/2, and Johnson observes, "There are times you're going to do this. I call it 'you bet your badge,' but sometimes you need to take a chance."

Police Chief Ronstadt acknowledges that many cops deviate from written policy in an effort to respond more quickly, but emphasizes that the practice is not acceptable. Collisions have occurred during unauthorized balls-to-the-wall runs, and there's significant potential for legal action against the city.

"They don't help anyone if they get into an accident," Ronstadt asserts. He opts for the use of 'silent light' in these situations — officers turning on their overhead light bars, maintaining the posted speed limit, and using intermittent siren bursts when needed to clear the way.

The patient in this call, a stubble-chinned man in his thirties, turns calm before they arrive He declines treatment and walks haltingly into the night.

Later in the evening, they attempt to sort out a family fight. A middle-aged couple, married just six weeks, have been drinking and arguing, apparently heeding the advice of a poster taped to their refrigerator: "Never go to bed angry; stay up and fight." The issues are clouded by too much alcohol, and mediation is impossible. She goes to a friend's home.

Just after 2:30 a.m., the radio announces a silent alarm at a nearby restaurant. They're on the scene in less than two minutes, dimming their headlights as they approach. A quick inspection yields broken glass from overhead lights, but no sign of forced entry. Air One, the police helicopter, checks out the roof, spinning blades slicing through the air as its thirty million candlepower searchlights momentarily turn night into day. The chopper circles the area four times, then leaves when the building appears secure. It looks like just another case of an alarm triggered by the wind or an electrical malfunction.

Because there is no indication of a break-in, a police dog is not requested. The owner arrives and fidgets through at least a half-dozen keys before finding the right one. Johnson turns to Robert: "I'll go low, you cover high." Robert unfastens the strap from his holster, his right hand poised in limbo over the handle of his service revolver. They don't expect to find anyone inside, but nonetheless call out, "Police officers!" as they switch on their flashlights and enter.

Less than a minute later, Johnson's voice breaks the silence: "Freeze! Don't move!" His flashlight piercing the blackness has illuminated a young man crouched on the kitchen floor. For the first time, Robert draws his gun on a suspect. The teenager is handcuffed and read his Miranda rights. Although he's wearing gloves (the temperature is in the low eighties) and carrying a flashlight, he insists he wasn't doing anything.

"Look, don't bullshit us," Johnson tells him. "You don't have to talk about it if you don't want, but don't sit there and lie to us. You're a burglar, a felon."

"I needed money," the suspect responds.

Months later, tonight's lesson has not been lost on Robert. "Now I always assume that someone will be inside."

■

Derek Campbell is another of the rookies who has made the transition from the classroom to the street. Born in Ireland, he was two when his family moved to Chicago. His first exposure to law enforcement was through a high school Cub Scout den master who was also a county sheriff. Derek accepted an athletic scholarship to Southern Illinois University, but soon decided he "didn't want to breathe, eat and sleep football."

He joined the Army and was sent to Thailand. With the Vietnam War winding down, a sniper's bullet smashed into his right knee, but the injury was minor. When his Army stint ended, Derek enlisted in the Air Force as a security officer, advancing in four years to the rank of staff sergeant. He took classes in criminology in his spare time, leaving him fourteen credit hours short of a degree.

Back in Chicago, Derek passed the police officer's examination and spent three months in the Academy there. Two days after he was assigned to the streets, "my wife told me that she didn't want to be married to a cop," he recounts. They were divorced. About two years later, he says he came under pressure after citing an Alderman for a parking violation. "My superiors started coming down on me after that and gave me a lot of garbage assignments," he says. Derek resigned in December, 1983, and marked time for several months before moving to Tucson and applying to TPD.

"Loving it!" is how he describes being back on the street. Although it's still the first week of his field training, he helps investigate a gas station burglary. He uses his nightstick to push open a door so he won't disturb possible evidence, then dusts for prints. Later, he helps arrest three shoplifters, one of them a seventy-nine-year-old woman with two previous theft citations. "I thought I'd kicked the habit," she tells him as he releases her on her promise to appear in court.

He and his training officer also respond to an accident where a car attempting to stop at a Grant Road intersection has skidded sideways and is wrapped around a traffic light pole. There are actually two collisions in every accident. The first occurs when contact is made with another car or object; the second takes place when the vehicle's occupants — still moving at the pre-collision speed — slam into the dashboard or windshield with a force of several thousand pounds. Today, an elderly couple is removed from the wreckage of their car and rushed by medics to nearby Tucson Medical Center.

At debriefing when the shift has ended, a sergeant looks over the accident report. "Who wrote this?" he asks.

Derek (tentatively): "I did."

Sergeant: "Nice job."

The woman dies the next day, her husband a week later.

■

Approximately one of every ten Tucson police officers is female, and the percentage is growing. Anita Sueme, age thirty, is

47

one of them. Her family moved from St. Louis to Tucson when she was six. She attended the University of Arizona where she earned a degree in microbiology. Working part-time in TPD's Records Section during college, she developed an interest in law enforcement. After graduation, she successfully tested for the position of radio dispatcher, and spent the next five years telling officers, mostly male, where to go and what to do.

"I had to learn to do that," she reflects. "I was a shy, quiet kid, and you just didn't give orders to men."

A career as an officer became increasingly appealing as she sat facing her computer screen, orchestrating the movements of up to thirty cops at a time, tracking where they were and sending them where they were needed. Early in 1983, she decided she'd had enough of the high technology and high stress atmosphere of the communications center, and applied for a TPD position.

There was an even more important reason for the career change: "I came to the conclusion that I probably would never marry, and had better find a good paying job so I could afford certain things I wanted, primarily a house and maybe a family," Anita says, adding that she wouldn't mind some day having "a houseful of adopted kids."

She failed the psychological examination and was told her personality was too passive, she recalls. More determined as a result of this rejection, she tried again and was accepted. "Despite days at ALETA when I wanted to pack and leave, I learned how stubborn and determined I could be."

Anita stands five feet, nine inches, but appears even taller in her contrasting light and dark blue uniform. She seldom wears makeup, even away from the job. She has scant interest in jewelry or trendy clothing, but owns a significant collection of string bikini lace bras and panties, most of them red or black. Anita wears them off duty and also underneath her police uniform. "It's how I remind myself of my femininity when I'm working," she says.

Anita is also wearing a wraparound bullet-resistant vest. Officers who opt for them — and most do — pay for their own. Hers cost $319. It's nearly a half-inch thick, and while it provides a degree of added security, it is also somewhat constraining. "Now I know what Victorian women went through walking around with corsets," she observes, a smile lighting her face.

Her field training begins April 21, 1985. Following team briefing, training officer Wayne Jacobs helps her select some of the more than thirty forms she'll need to carry and shows her how to organize

48

them. After some initial nervousness, she's ready to go. "I slept well last night and got up this morning and jogged," she says. "I was fine until I started putting my uniform on. Then I asked myself, 'What am I getting into?'"

They check out their 1984 Chevy Caprice and go into service at 12:41 p.m. with Jacobs behind the wheel. Cruising toward their beat, they drive past the house on Second Avenue where gangster John Dillinger was captured by Tucson police officers on January 25, 1934 without a shot being fired.

They'll spend the next three weeks in a four-square-mile area. "Do just what you're comfortable doing for the first few days, as little or as much as you want," Jacobs reassures her. "You're going to make mistakes and this is the time to make them."

Fifteen minutes later, they receive their first assignment. A sobbing woman — wadded tissues clutched in her left fist — wants to retrieve a water bed from her ex-boyfriend's apartment. The young man refuses to give it up. There's no proof of ownership, and the woman is advised to file suit in small claims court.

Anita writes the case report. She has observed and recalled most of the necessary information, including the description of the former boyfriend. After years of dispatching, she reaches for the microphone for the first time as an officer and gives the computer clearance code.

Next, they stop a vehicle with an unreadable license plate and issue a citation. As they prepare to leave, another car pulls up. The occupants are looking for a Kiwanis barbecue. Anita looks at the date on the invitation and tells them they're a week early. Embarrassed, they apologize and drive off, laughing.

A burglary has been reported at a nearby hotel. Anita leaves her nightstick in the car until Jacobs advises that "It's a good idea to get into the habit of carrying it. You never know what can happen."

Four young people visiting the city have returned to their room and found $150 missing from a purse left in the room. Anita and Jacobs take the information, but there's not much they can do since no identifiable property was taken and because many employees and former guests could have had access to a room key.

A family fight is reported by a neighbor. A young couple has been arguing over money, a situation made more volatile by the husband's heavy drinking. There's a lot of talking going on, but not much listening. It's just another ride on their roller-coaster relationship between love and hate; they don't get anywhere, but it's a hell of a trip. There are no signs of physical violence and Jacobs advises the wife and kids to stay away until things cool down. She thanks them and drives off with the children.

Later, they join two other officers on special assignment in Reid Park where there have been complaints of illegal drinking. In just under two hours, they cite nine people for City Code violations, a fine of $10. One young man is extremely hostile. Wearing a tangle of gold chains around his neck and with a cigarette dangling loosely from his mouth, he baits officers with a volley of angry obscenities, challenging them to do something that anatomically cannot be done. Although he's trying real hard to be arrested, the officers avoid escalating the situation and he eventually calms down.

Anita and her training officer pull into the police station just before 8 p.m. They've driven forty-four miles this first shift.

■

Greg Strom, a big-boned man with expressive eyes, has lived in Tucson since he was a young child. Although he's just twenty-four years old, Greg has already worked for a construction company, installed stereos, painted automobiles and made cash pickups for an armored car company. Unlike many new officers, a law enforcement career had not been a long-time goal. Greg won an Academy spot on his first try and made it through with "lots of support and understanding" from his wife. They married early in 1984 and have an infant daughter, Jennifer.

He's feeling "nervous and with a lot to learn" as his field training begins. As he and training officer Mike Bannister drive to a traffic accident at the end of his first week, Bannister asks if Greg wants to take the lead. He does.

There are no injuries and one vehicle has sustained minor damage. Greg identifies and interviews the principals and witnesses and obtains information for his report. His only mistake, Bannister tells him, is failing to have the damaged vehicle moved from the roadway to prevent the accident from becoming worse.

Greg is fearful that he's not progressing quickly enough, but three weeks later he passes his initial Phase Board. His new assignment: "Don't be so hard on yourself."

He spends the next four weeks with Keith Hensley. At his second Phase Board, Greg waits in another room while Bannister, Hensley, Ulichny and Sergeant Richard Miranda discuss his progress.

50

Hensley: "He knows his material, but he worries too much. He questions himself more than anything and sometimes tends to be complacent with officer safety."

Ulichny: "Is there any pattern with the bad days?"

Hensley: "Possibly a lack of sleep; his daughter has been ill with a high fever. He just needs to be more observant sometimes and use the skills he already has."

Miranda: "How can we help get him over that hurdle?"

Hensley: "I think it's mostly that he's a perfectionist and is being too hard on himself. I think he'll get over it with our help and support."

Ulichny: "Is something at ALETA causing this? It seems to happen frequently."

Miranda: "It's possible that some of it is that decisions were made for them for so long that they're afraid to make a mistake now that they're on their own. I don't see any major problem with Greg. It's a matter of time and confidence, and what he's going through is not unusual, especially for someone who doesn't have a lot of life experience."

Ulichny: "That's why we have a field training program."

Greg is called into the room.

Miranda: "How do you see yourself out there?"

Greg: "Still a little green. I need to work more on assertiveness."

Miranda: "How are you going to do it?"

Greg: "Concentration while I'm on duty and role-playing when I'm not on duty. I think I'm doing better now than in the first phase. I have a habit of asking a question and then stopping, instead of asking a question *on* the question where it would help."

Miranda: "Field training is partly to let you make rookie mistakes. You're going to make them, so make them and learn from them. You have the knowledge you need to trust yourself. Don't let one bad call blow the rest of the shift."

Greg: "I'm trying to relax more and not let a fear of failure or making a mistake get in my way. That's my goal for the third phase."

Ulichny: "How do you define a good day's work? What do you want me to see on your activity sheet?"

Greg: "That I'm taking initiative when things are slow, looking for suspicious activities, checking business security and what's going on in my beat."

Ulichny: "I'm concerned about officer safety. I don't want you to be paranoid, but you need to be able to make split-second decisions. You need to be aware of the circumstances and the

51

potential risks and react accordingly."

Miranda: "Let's set goals. Start to wean yourself from your training officer and work on the things we've discussed."

Greg spends the next four weeks working his beat with a third officer. At the Phase Board, Sergeant Al Nunley reports that Greg's job performance has improved substantially and that he's better able to "make a decision and go with it." Greg, joining the group, says he's feeling more comfortable and competent making decisions and having the confidence that his decisions are correct.

"You've been on the street for less than eleven weeks," he's reminded. "You're doing well."

For his fourth — and final — phase, he'll be back with Bannister, his Phase One training officer. Greg will function on his own. Bannister, not in uniform, will appear to be a civilian observer, intervening only if Greg does something illegal or potentially dangerous.

As the hot days of July give way to the even hotter days of August, Greg successfully completes field training and prepares to go out alone for the first time.

■

Tucson police officers must be at least twenty-one. Although there is no maximum age, most recruits are in their twenties and just a few are over thirty. Les Beach, the forty-five-year-old who survived three fractured ribs at ALETA, is excited to finally be on the streets

Deep blue eyes are the dominant feature of his face, and they appear even larger and brighter when he smiles, which is often. He's allowed his dark blonde hair, though receding at the forehead, to curl down over his ears. Age lines are beginning to appear, but they take nothing away from his sturdy good looks. Just under six feet tall, Les lifts weights and has little of the flab associated with middle age.

"I'm in good physical shape and I don't see any reason why I can't do the job as well as anyone twenty years my junior," he says with confidence.

It's his first week of field training, and he and officer Bill Cook are dispatched to a fight in a parking lot. As they pull up, two men start walking quickly toward a nearby van, and a bystander yells, "They have a gun!" In an instant, Les pulls his revolver from its holster, yelling "Freeze!" He uses his patrol car door as a shield, aiming his spotlight to cut through the early evening darkness. "Stay away from the van and get your hands in sight!" he orders. One of the men continues walking, hands still hidden from Les's view.

"Show me your hands! Let me see them!" he shouts.

The man stops this time, but his arms remain out of sight. Two backup units squeal to a jarring stop a few seconds later and quickly maneuver both men away from the van. A loaded .38 caliber Derringer rests on the dashboard.

"I hope I'm never in the position of having to use a gun on another human being," Les says later, "but I know I won't hesitate if it might save a life."

Cruising slowly now, Les pays particular attention to street names and landmarks. Having lived in Tucson less than a year, he has been driving around the neighborhood during his off hours to become more familiar with the territory. "I'm still a disaster when it comes to geography, but I'm learning," he says, laughing.

He and Cook check the occupant of a vehicle in a park which closes at dusk. Les neglects to advise dispatch where he is and what he's doing, and compounds the error by leaving his radio in the patrol car.

The radio is an officer's lifeline and, arguably, his most important safety device. Most cops go through an entire career without firing a single shot in the line of duty. The microphone, however, is keyed dozens of times every shift, and an officer who leaves his vehicle without it is compromising his physical welfare. Cook makes a point of this lapse: "If I weren't here, no one would have been able to find you if you had a problem."

A few minutes later, they spot a blue sedan with a man sleeping inside. The driver awakens and switches the ignition on as they pull up. "Shut off your engine, please," Les instructs over his loud-speaker, shining his spotlight on the man inside. Les gives his location and requests a computer check of the vehicle's license plate before approaching the driver. Cook approves, reminding Les to "begin to think of yourself as a one-man unit even when I'm here. Even what seems to be a safe situation has potential for danger. You must have a plan of action."

Two months later, Les is working with more assurance and assertiveness and enjoying an easy rapport with the public. Doing a park check, he spots several juveniles congregating after curfew. Les explains the law politely, but firmly, and sends them home without citations.

Just after midnight, he responds to the home of a woman who thought she saw a prowler in her back yard. Air One circles the area, but finds no one. Ulichny, off-duty and in the neighborhood, hears the call on his police radio and stops by. The elderly lady is apologetic, saying she's been "a bother." Les reassures her, telling her to phone the police whenever she sees or hears anything suspicious.

Field training has produced some stress, but Les is confident he'll be able to deal with any situation when he's on his own in a few weeks. "It's been a valuable education, and I believe that I've been well prepared to handle whatever comes along."

■

It's become clear during these three months that several of the new officers can't — or choose not to — handle the stress and demands of the job. Five of the remaining thirty-nine either resign or are dismissed.

As the others prepare to patrol alone for the first time, Pat Batelli, who has wanted to be a cop for most of her life, but was dismissed just eight days short of graduation, gets a second chance. The Tucson Police Department receives unexpected funding to hire thirty new officers. When ALETA, which handles training for almost all Arizona law enforcement agencies, cannot accommodate that many in its next class, TPD decides to temporarily expand its own Academy and train them there.

Although Pat had not met all of ALETA's requirements, Ronstadt observes: "Based on ALETA's reports and our conversations with Pat, we decided that her documented performance in most areas showed the potential for being a good officer."

Pat is rehired, but she hasn't been able to forget the trauma of her termination. "Law enforcement was something I had prepared for and wanted to do for so many years, and then it was just down the tubes."

Starting over represents a new kind of fear. She is, in fact, petrified. "I knew some of the people there would see me as a washout, so there was the obstacle to overcome that my reputation had preceded me."

The three-month Academy goes well. Although cadets are still chastised and punished, Pat feels that she's treated "as a person and not like dirt. It made me want to work harder, to show what I could do." Her shin splint has healed, and running is now less of a struggle.

The icing on her cake comes during the week of graduation. It's the traditional seven-mile uphill run from the grounds of the Academy to the top of Sentinel Peak, a mountain just west of downtown Tucson.

Pat is one of two recruits who move quickly to the front of the pack. "I thought I was going to die," but in what she calls "one of the most rewarding things I've ever done," she leads the way to the top, calling cadence as she jogs.

4

The Stick of God

A cop's day is predominantly routine, and at times, even boring. Although the spurts of adrenaline are only occasional, the reality is that trouble can show up at any time and any place. It's mid-summer, 1985, and the afternoon temperature in the Sonoran desert routinely tops out above 100 degrees. Most days are so hot and dry that trees have been observed following dogs, according to a tongue-in-cheek Indian legend.

The Tucson Police Department has nearly 450 street officers. Before the year ends, they'll be dispatched to 164,790 calls and generate more than 100,000 others in the form of traffic stops and 'on-site' observations. Although a substantial number of these assignments involve volatile situations or citizens with weapons, only three times during 1985 will an officer point his gun at another person and squeeze the trigger. Several dozen cops will be assaulted, but none will be killed.

Greg Strom is apprehensive as he begins his first shift without a training officer at his side. The anxiety is quickly replaced by cold, stark fear.

"I pulled out of the station and the first words over the radio were 'Man with a gun.' It was at a nearby Circle K. I'd been on my own less than a minute, and here I was going to one of the most dangerous of calls. I began sweating. Two other officers got there before I did and the man was gone, but I realized then how alone you can be."

Two weeks later, Greg is more relaxed. "I was real uptight those first few days because I no longer had the security of a training officer," he admits, "but without him I'm more aware of what's going on around me."

His first close-up scare comes three months later. "Another

officer and I made a felony traffic stop in response to a 'shots fired' report. There were two men in the car, and as my partner escorted one of them away from the vehicle, the driver called to me, yelling that he'd been shot. He was reported to have a gun, and yet if he was really hurt, I wanted to help him. My partner was able to approach and cover him from his blind side. The suspect had a 9mm automatic on the seat next to him. There was a round in the chamber and the safety was off. He was ready to fire."

Although Greg knows that traffic stops are almost always routine, "you need to remember that sooner or later one of them is going to go against you and you must be ready to protect yourself by diving to safety or pulling your gun." Greg spends part of each shift playing 'what-if.' "I make up a situation as I cruise, and decide what I would do if it really happened. Hopefully, that will give me a head start when something does happen."

He knows there's a possibility that he might have to shoot someone. "You think a lot about it. You go through the Academy and constantly have it drilled into your head that some people are out to hurt you. I made up my mind a long time ago that if it ever comes down to that, I'd just have to do it. I think about it, not from a worry-type standpoint, but in a constructive way."

Like most officers, he believes that fear is healthy, and that a cop who denies its existence is lying to himself and possibly jeopardizing his life. He thinks about the potential conflict between maximum officer safety and getting the job done.

"Sometimes you must give up a little personal safety to serve the people you're paid to serve. Suppose you're pulling up to a residence where there's been a report of a woman screaming. She runs toward you as you approach. Someone could be chasing her or pointing a gun at her, but you can't just sit in your car and wait for backup units. You just deal with the situation the best you can."

The next few months are routine. Greg's major challenge is learning his territory. "It's more than being able to locate all of the streets," he says. "You begin to know some of the people and problems of the area. It's a more secure feeling when you've been there a while." He's feeling comfortable with the job and sees changes in his style and priorities.

"When I started out, I wanted the calls, no matter what. I was just waiting for them to call me. Even if it was a found bike or a malfunctioning traffic light, I wanted it. Now I find myself thinking more selectively when I hear my designator. I'll say to myself, 'Don't let it be found property or an accident.' I thought it would take me years to feel this way."

■

Trouble seems to have a way of finding Derek Campbell, the burly ex-Chicago cop.

In mid-September, scarcely a month after completing his field training, he has his first close call. It's just before closing time at Cowboys, a large country-western nightclub, where he and Officer Rich Garcia attempt to defuse a fight in the parking lot.

"There were several hundred people milling about, so I asked dispatch for another unit to circulate in the area," he recalls. "Rich saw this guy backing out of the door with a gun in his hand. He grabbed the man, disarmed him and handed me the gun. I put it in my rear waistband and walked up to a dude who was with the first man.

"He was huge, bigger than me. I asked him for some ID. He kept cursing me and I kept asking for the ID. Finally, he started to give me his driver's license, then shoved it back in his wallet, said 'Fuck you, pig!' and jumped on me. I knocked him down and we started rolling around. I yelled to Rich to call for more units, but he'd already done it and they were on the way. It took four of us, including one of Cowboys' bouncers, to subdue him, and all I'm thinking is, 'Please don't let the gun fall out of my waistband.'"

During the struggle, Derek is hit in the back of the head with a bottle and sprains his right thumb, injuries which keep him off the street for two days.

*   *

Several thousand chronically mentally ill men and women live in Tucson. Most are harmless, except perhaps to themselves, and social service agencies simply can't meet their needs. Joe is one of those people moving through life without a road map. He's phoned 911 asking an officer to come to his apartment and "exorcise the devil."

This morning's devil is a visiting acquaintance. Derek, advised by the dispatcher that Joe is listed as a mental patient, attempts a hastily conceived strategy. Pointing to his nightstick, he tells Joe that it's "the stick of God." When Joe expresses doubt, Derek shows him an identification number, saying quietly that "it's a direct line to God." As Joe appears to reflect on this, Derek points it at the visitor and says, "Devil, I exorcise thee, I exorcise thee. Now get out and don't come back." The acquaintance leaves on cue, and Joe is all grin. He turns to Derek. "You're my friend now; you got rid of the devil."

Just after 6:30 a.m. on an unusually cool January day two months later, Derek is dispatched to a suspicious person report. He switches on his overhead light and begins to jot down the call information. Derek is left-handed, and his note pad is a two-inch-wide strip of masking tape on the center of his steering wheel, enabling him to simultaneously drive, write and transmit on the radio.

Pulling up four minutes later, he sees a man urinating on a fence. Randy has sunken eyes and bad teeth, and the upper half of his body is streaked with blood. Brandishing a foot-long knife, he walks toward Derek screaming, "Come on, cop, shoot me, kill me! Kill me or I'll kill you!" Derek unholsters his gun, backs off and radios for help. He keeps moving and talking, trying to avoid a direct confrontation with the young man who appears to be tottering on the edge of madness. The arrival of other officers distract Randy, and Derek is able to disarm him from behind without injury to anyone. What many in law enforcement call the Doctrine of Minimal Force has worked well this morning, and Derek soon receives his first written commendation.

Several months after the incident at Cowboys, Derek responds to another fight in progress at the popular bar. A young woman has been punched by her husband, who says he did it because she was flirting with someone else. Her shoulder-length hair partially obscures fresh bruises over her right cheek. Although she doesn't want to prosecute, her husband is arrested anyway under Arizona's domestic violence law. The woman, sobbing softly, refuses medical treatment and Derek leaves.

As he walks to his patrol car, his thoughts return to the earlier Cowboys encounter. The man who had jumped him later pleads innocent, claiming he was tripped from behind and "fell" into Derek. The judge dismisses the case for lack of evidence, and Derek doesn't hide his displeasure with the decision. "One of these days I'm going to see that dude again," he says, "and hopefully I won't have this blue suit on."

Minutes later, he's dispatched to a hospital where a woman has brought her twenty-year-old son for treatment. She says he was assaulted by two friends, but the young man is abrasive and uncooperative. When Derek asks what happened, he responds, "My fuckin' jaw is broken, that's what happened!" Derek says he has to file a report and asks again for information. "Just put down that I fell repeatedly and broke my jaw," he says sarcastically, raising his head to a rakish tilt.

It sometimes is more productive to ignore the problem than attempt to resolve it. This seems to be one of those occasions, and Derek nods and walks out of the treatment room. As he leaves the hospital, a car screeches to a halt outside the emergency room entrance. A distraught female staggers out and falls on the ground, moaning. She's the same woman whose husband punched her an hour earlier at Cowboys.

*　　*

Though Derek is generally handling people well, animals are another story. When a half-ton bull shows up at a major intersection and begins ambling west in the eastbound traffic lanes, Derek is one of several officers who attempt to corner it. With the battle still a standoff two hours later, the bull goes on the offensive. It charges Derek, who dives into the back of a nearby pickup truck, his hasty retreat captured on videotape by a local television station. The bull is finally shot with a tranquilizing dart and roped by a rancher with expertise at such things.

Derek's encore takes place five months later. Two pit bull terriers, dogs bred for their fighting ferocity, have been roaming an eastside neighborhood and snarling at residents. They are clearly not descended from such fictional pit bulls as "Our Gang's" Pete, or Nipper, who listened with tilted ear to his master's voice.

The man who filed the complaint is wielding a baseball bat for protection. Derek requests that Animal Control respond. While he waits, holding a shotgun and chatting with the neighbor, the dogs approach. They're barking, and the larger one appears to be foaming at the mouth. The neighbor heads to the safety of his home and Derek jumps onto the fender of a truck in the driveway. The larger dog leaps at Derek, who momentarily distracts it with a kick. Now, the animal crouches and growls. As it jumps again, he kills it with a single blast to the head.

The bullet from his shotgun triggers a lengthy investigation. A diagram of the area is plotted, pictures are taken and witnesses are interviewed. All of the information is submitted to a formal Board of Inquiry which will determine if the action taken was prudent.

Seven weeks later, Derek finishes his shift at 7 a.m., puts on a pair of jeans and reports to the office of Captain Michael Leverenz.

Leverenz has read the reports and conducted an inquiry. He asks Derek to describe in detail what occurred, then has him clarify several points. Finally he asks, "Would you change anything and, if so, what?" Derek replies, "No, I don't think I would." He pauses briefly, then, "Well, maybe I would lose a little weight so I could run faster."

The captain's only concern is that the neighbor was in a vulnerable position. "My feeling is that individual was placed in potential jeopardy by being with you," he says. "What would you have done if the dogs had gone after him and were chewing on him? What good would your shotgun have been? If you had a vicious dog situation where you were concerned enough to take the shotgun out of the car, I don't think you should have had Joe Citizen alongside you as long as you did."

"I understand," Derek says, nodding.

Leverenz: "The shooting certainly was within policy. The issue of (danger to) the citizen is what I want you to be aware of."

The captain rises, smiles and extends his hand. "Thank you, sir," Derek responds, turning to leave.

Derek's fellow officers don't let him off so easily. Reporting for his next shift following the shooting, he looks at the briefing room blackboard which contains several anonymous messages. One asks, "Where, oh where has my little dog gone?" Another — a cartoon — shows Derek in his patrol car, staring down at a pit bull and saying, "Go ahead, dog, make my day!" And as briefing begins, Sergeant Al Nunley introduces Derek as "The American Kennel Club's Man of the Year." Months later, he's still catching it in typical police gallows humor.

■

Although he's one of the rookies, Bernard Harrigan is a veteran cop. A native New Yorker, he attended military high school and then served four years in the Marines before joining the New York City Police Department in 1964. He spent his first years on a walking beat in midtown Manhattan — the Eighteenth Precinct, an area encompassing Toots Shor's, Club 21 and much of the theater district. Officers did not have portable radios in the mid-1960s, and when Bernie needed assistance he had to either run to one of the call boxes placed every few blocks, find a telephone or hope that a citizen would phone for help. More than once he commandeered a cruising taxi to chase a suspect or rush someone to the hospital.

61

Bernie was assigned to a Harlem walking beat in 1967. "Even then," he remembers, "most of the adults were good people who didn't want their kids exposed to drugs or criminals. They were generally very cooperative in working with us and protecting us when something came down. Sometimes they would attempt to dispense their own justice and we'd have to literally pull a suspect away from them in order to make an arrest." Bernie was later transferred to the posh upper westside, quickly rose through the ranks and was a lieutenant when he retired in 1984 at age forty-three.

Physical abuse of suspects was not unusual in the early days of his career, Bernie says. "It was never officially condoned, but it happened. I'd see officers kicking the shit out of a suspect who was already in handcuffs. Sometimes a sergeant would have to step between them to stop it. Some of this was still going on in the 1970s."

He and his wife had five children during their eleven-year marriage. A second marriage to a Peruvian woman lasted five years and produced one son.

Timmy, a son from his first marriage, was born brain-damaged. "He functioned pretty well for the first few years," Bernie remembers, going to a traditional school until he was about ten. When it became increasingly difficult for him to cope in a mainstream environment, he was enrolled in a special school. He was a strong swimmer and once ran a six-mile mini-marathon, but by the time he reached his mid-teens, he had to be moved to a group home where he would have constant supervision. Timmy had for years been taking Thorazine, a sedative anti-psychotic medicine. Fearful that he might inadvertently harm himself, doctors needed to periodically increase the dosage, Bernie says. Now nearly twenty-two years old, Timmy lives in a New York City nursing home, a young man among the elderly.

*   *

Bernie has spent the past seven years with Dorothy Siden, a graphics designer he met under circumstances that only a New Yorker would appreciate.

Dorothy lived in an area of Manhattan where people desperate for a parking place have been known to literally kill to get one. Arriving home from the theater late one drizzly evening in 1977, she was circling the block looking for a spot near her apartment when she saw a man walking toward a parked vehicle on the other side of the street. She made a quick U-turn, nearly hitting a fire hydrant in her determination to get there first. She asked him if he was leaving. He smiled, said that he was, then waited while she backed into the vacated spot.

Double-parked now, Dorothy remembers how he rolled down the window and introduced himself.

"Hi, I'm Bernie Harrigan," he said.

"Harrigan?" Dorothy repeated.

"Just like the song: H, A, double-R, I, G, A, N spells Harrigan," he sang as the rain fell on his head.

Dorothy didn't know whether to smile or run.

He offered to walk her home.

"That's okay, I live right over there," she responded, pointing to a nearby building.

"But I'm a policeman," he responded.

She went home alone, but he stopped by to visit the next day and they soon started dating.

"When he said he was a policeman, I guess he thought that was supposed to make it okay," Dorothy recalls with a smile. "Backing into that parking spot I remember thinking, 'Thank you, God, thank you, thank you.' I was giving thanks for the parking spot, not for him, not knowing at the time that I'd go on to spend a chunk of my life with this person."

* *

The day Bernie retired with a lifetime annual pension of more than $22,000, he asked an associate, 'What am I going to do for the rest of my life?' The friend reached into a stack of papers and handed him a Tucson police recruitment folder.

Bernie knew only that Tucson was warm and somewhere in Arizona. A telephone call confirmed that Tucson was testing for new officers, but that the application deadline was only a month away. He and Dorothy drove west, arriving with only two days to prepare for the written test. He failed to qualify by one point and then flunked the physical when he wasn't able to complete the required thirty-five sit-ups in one minute. He passed both examinations on the second attempt.

Because of his twenty years as an officer, Bernie wasn't required to go through ALETA. Instead, he spent eight weeks at the Tucson Police Department Academy before beginning field training. "I had to swallow hard, learn some new methods and accept criticism. It was a good lesson in humility," he says, his accent a giveaway of his

New York roots.

Why would he want to start again from the bottom? "Part of it was to see if I could do it at my age, and part was to be a worker and not a boss. I don't have to bring my job home with me now."

Bernie has dark, curly hair and a ready smile, and his appearance and enthusiasm belie his age. He has a homey approach and is polite and sympathetic whether helping a citizen or writing a citation.

To a young man playing a car radio at rock concert intensity: "I like that music, too, but there's been a complaint." To a youngster who has set off an alarm by bouncing tennis balls against a building wall: "It was nice that you said you did it; why don't you use the wall over there?" And to an elderly couple trying to locate the Knights of Columbus Hall: "I'll help you find it and then I'll know where it is, too."

Mid-evening, he observes a car stopped in a vacant lot. As he watches, it pulls into the street. He follows about a block behind as the vehicle makes a succession of puzzling right-hand turns before parking outside of a neighborhood bar. As Bernie pulls up, three well-dressed women get out. Surprised to see him, the driver explains that they had difficulty finding the place. "We're just three lost women," she says, laughing. Bernie nods and smiles: "Have a good time, ladies."

*   *

There are times when what *isn't* seen can be more deadly than a visible weapon, and though it may border on the paranoid, the best — and safest — cops assume that a tiger lurks behind every door.

It's the start-of-shift briefing on October 4, 1985, and Sergeant Lee Gassaway reads a city-wide memorandum: "Last night at Village Inn, a man pulled a gun on the cashier and walked out with the cash drawer in one hand and the pistol in the other. Seeing two officers walking by, he hid the gun behind the cash box and passed within several feet of those officers, who had basically shut down their reflexes because it was time to eat. When the cashier told them what had happened, the officers ran back outside where they confronted the suspect and convinced him to give up his weapon."

"The lesson to be learned here," he reminds them, "is that they could have been shot in those few seconds. The man with the gun could have been an escaped convict or on the FBI's Most Wanted list, and those officers could have died. It's hard to keep up your guard every moment. You do it automatically at a family fight or traffic stop, but here you're not expecting anything to happen and that's when you can be most vulnerable."

After two decades in law enforcement, this is simply a matter of instinct to Bernie. "You try not to get too comfortable, especially on a quiet day. When it's busy, you're up and alert, but on a slow shift you can be lulled into complacency."

Adapting to the street again has been difficult. "I'll get a priority call and for a moment I may have no idea where it is or how to get there. I do some things well and others not so well, but that's life, too, isn't it? When I was a rookie in New York, a lieutenant told me, 'Knowing the law is the easy part. You know what's wrong and what's not. You know what a robbery is, and if you don't you can look it up.'

"Maybe it's my age. At forty-five and starting over, I guess I'm having some self-doubts, but I know I'm still a good cop," he says, puffing on one of his trademark Jamaican Ascot cigars.

Bernie, who doesn't enjoy jogging, stays in shape by playing racquetball once or twice a week. His most frequent partner is Tommy Knickerbocker, another graduate of ALETA Class 102. Although Knickerbocker is a tall, physically imposing man about twenty years younger than Bernie, they are evenly matched on the court where Bernie's finesse game neutralizes much of his opponent's power.

*   *

A man dubbed "The Prime Time Rapist" because he operates primarily in the early evening, has terrorized the city and is still at large more than two years after his first assault. Nearly thirty attacks have been attributed to him, and they have been growing more brazen. He carries a gun, has held entire families hostage, and has forced at least two victims to withdraw cash from local banks.

Although only a few victims have seen his face, an artist's sketch has been widely distributed by a multi-agency task force working full-time to identify him. The fear in the city is widespread. Business is booming for gun dealers and purveyors of home security systems. More women are taking self-defense classes. Many families are buying guard dogs and one entrepreneur advertises a cassette tape of a canine that randomly barks and growls.

Some citizens have become hostages of another kind. A middle-aged man on the city's far eastside tells an officer that he and his wife now take turns sleeping even though they both work eight-to-five jobs.

More than fifteen minutes of the May 30, 1986 briefing is devoted to a memo from the Task Force. It ends: "Officers . . . who discover a lookalike in a target neighborhood should be extremely careful. The suspect has been armed with concealed handguns and knives and seems prepared to use them. Task Force investigators suggest that any lookalike be frisked for weapons as soon as tactically appropriate. Grounds for detaining a lookalike for a reasonable period of time include unexplained presence in a profile neighborhood, inconsistent and conflicting statements and inappropriate behavior."

It's to be a busy shift. The first real monsoon of the season has come and just as quickly gone, but Tucson motorists react to precipitation by engaging in a form of demolition derby. Beauty has suddenly become the beast, and reports of minor traffic accidents fill the airwaves.

Bernie is dispatched to a hit-and-run. A young woman, a University of Arizona student, is not hurt and her car shows only minimal damage, but she's crying — frustrated and angry that the man who hit her has sped off. While Bernie calms her, most vehicles drive through the intersection at speeds which cause waves of water to cascade ten to twelve feet into the air.

Just as he parks under a shopping center light and begins his report, dispatch advises of a fight in a book store where an employee's former boyfriend is assaulting her new boyfriend. The call is assigned to another officer, but Bernie, less than a mile away, says he'll also start over.

Arriving first, he walks quickly toward a young man lying on his back between two shelves of paperbacks. Bernie works his way down the narrow aisle, sidestepping dozens of strewn books.

"Leave me alone!" the man on the floor screams at three men who are holding him down.

"Calm down and tell me what you're so upset about," Bernie says, moving into position astride him. Josh, a slightly-built young man is identified by witnesses as the rejected suitor. "I'm going to put handcuffs on you and then we'll let you sit up." Bernie tells him.

"You're a cop?" Josh asks, looking directly at Bernie.

"I'm a cop, right," he responds, securing one arm while the man continues to yell and curse. "Calm down a second and lie on your stomach. Everything's going to be okay."

Losing control now, Josh begins to flail. "How can I fuckin'

66

calm down! Fuckin' dumb cop!"

Bernie, ignoring the verbal tirade, turns him on his stomach.

"Good, why don't you kill me? Pull out your gun and shoot me in the fucking face!"

Two other officers rush in just as Bernie has Josh under control. As he's led out for the trip to jail, he walks past his ex-girlfriend working at the front register. "Thanks a lot!" he yells, sarcastically. Most of the dozen or so customers have continued browsing despite the real-life drama in their midst.

*   *

Bernie stops at a fast-food restaurant and again attempts to catch up with his paperwork, but after less than ten minutes he's asked to clear for a collision between an automobile and motorcycle. Despite the noise of surrounding traffic and emergency vehicles, you can hear the cyclist's screams of pain at least 200 feet away.

The thirty-year-old woman who pulled into the roadway from a parking lot keeps saying, "I didn't see him" as the report is taken. She's cited for failing to yield to oncoming traffic. The cyclist's right foot, crushed below the ankle, is amputated later that night.

Bernie spends the next ninety-five minutes on accumulated paperwork. As he's about to end the shift, he's sent to aid an assault victim outside a convenience store.

A large gap-toothed man in his early twenties is bleeding from the mouth, rolls of dirt mingling with the creases in his neck. He says he was attacked by "two Mexican dudes," but seconds later, dispatch says it has received a call from the man's brother who claims the injured man attacked him with a large barbecue fork.

While medics and another officer remain with the injured man, Bernie drives to the brother's home three blocks away. He and two friends are in the living room, a loaded gun within reach. It's past the scheduled end of Bernie's shift, and midnight units are dispatched to relieve him and sort out the situation.

Driving back to the station, Bernie reflects on his life. He doesn't remember playing cops and robbers as a child. His best memories are of the young teenage boy who quickly learned the pleasantries of 'Doctor' soon after discovering girls.

"I still remember the first kissing and the first touching," he says, nostalgia in his words. "I just wanted to do it again and again." Nonetheless, he waited more than five years for his first sexual liaison.

"I was stationed in Okinawa, and it happened in an alley between two bars. A prostitute raised her skirt and munched on an apple during an encounter that lasted about eighteen seconds. In the background I could hear Peggy Lee singing, 'Is That All There Is?'"

■

Like Bernie Harrigan, twenty-nine-year-old Jeffrey Moore is a Class 102 lateral who bypassed ALETA because of prior law enforcement experience and went directly to the Tucson Police Academy. He was born in South Dakota, but spent most of his first eighteen years following his father, an electrical engineer, on assignments in Chile, South America, Venezuela, Brazil, Africa and Ghana.

Settling in Globe, Arizona, Jeff became a fireman, then an Emergency Medical Technician, where he met Nancy, his wife-to-be. Nancy, the first female EMT in Globe, recalls her early impression of Jeff:

"I couldn't stand him. I thought he was arrogant, and he hated me, too. After we worked together about nine months I realized how cool and competent he was. He never messed up and I really started admiring him. When you work with death and trauma you get to see the inner soul."

Their first date was February 6, 1977, and they were married seven weeks later — the second marriage for each of them.

Jeff was soon accepted as a reserve officer with the Gila County Sheriff's Department, and a year later was hired by the Florence Police Department, where most of the population was either incarcerated in the state prison or guarding those who were.

Their first child, Josh, was born in 1980, about the time he began working as an undercover officer. "He was hideous-looking," she remembers with a smile. "He had long hair and a big beard and wore scruffy clothes and metal chains.

"I worried about him all the time. There were no regular shifts. I didn't know where he was working or what time he'd be home. It was such a small community that if word of what he was doing ever got out, he could have ended up lying dead in a ditch. What bothered me most about something happening to him was that I wouldn't be there with him."

Jeff, meanwhile, was gaining the experience he needed to make the move to Tucson.

"Everything I did was in preparation for a law enforcement career here," he says as he begins his shift on February 21, 1986. Jeff is six feet tall, borderline-slim, yet solidly built, and his blue eyes divert attention from an already receding hairline. He exudes command appearance, an added bonus in his southside beat which is generally considered one of the most volatile in the city.

At 10:21 p.m., the emergency tone sounds and dispatch reports a shooting in the desert area behind a neighborhood carnival. Jeff, less than a mile away, pulls up within a minute. As the first officer on the scene, he confirms the shooting and instructs medics to move in.

The victim, an Hispanic teenager, lies motionless on his back, a bullet hole in the right side of his head. Miguel is still breathing and there's a weak carotid pulse, but as Jeff says later, "You can sense the look and the odor of death and I knew he wasn't going to make it."

At least fifty young people are standing around, including Frankie, the victim's fourteen-year-old cousin. An empty, dazed look on his face, Frankie keeps saying, "I know who did it. I know who did it."

While Jeff gathers information on the suspect, two teens reach down to Miguel's bloodied head. "I touched him!" one yells to his friends, extending his hand to show the blood. Others walk over and carry out the same ritual. Medics arrive and immediately start an intravenous line. When time permits, they provide on-the-scene emergency care to stabilize a patient before going to the hospital. Tonight's injuries are so critical that they execute a rapid 'scoop-and-run', lifting the boy onto a litter. Intravenous bag held high, they rush to the ambulance and begin a life-or-death race to the nearest trauma center.

Frankie tells Jeff about the confrontation that led to the shooting. When he begins to break down — blaming himself because he wasn't able to do anything to stop it — Jeff places his arm around him for support and consolation. The young man reaches into his pocket and pulls out a stick of chewing gum his cousin had given him a few minutes before the shooting. His eyes now puddling over with tears, he turns to Jeff. "All I have left of Miguel is this gum and his blood stains on my shirt."

Miguel goes into code arrest en route to the hospital and dies the next day. The teenager who killed him is arrested, pleads self-defense at his trial and is acquitted.

* *

It's a warm early spring evening two weeks later, and Jeff is one of fourteen southside officers preparing to start the Friday tour of duty. Promptly at 6 p.m., as the network news gives way to "Wheel of Fortune," Sergeant Alex Salcido switches off the television which has been mostly ignored anyway, and opens the daily briefing book. He describes several suspects sought for questioning — a local Most Wanted List — and reads policy directives which have worked their way down the chain of command.

As briefing is about to end, Salcido calls an officer to the front and ceremoniously reminds him of his annual physical. The officer has been apprehensive about the rectal examination he'll have to endure. Aware of this, several of his peers slip on plastic gloves and wave them menacingly as he returns to his seat. The laughter fades and Salcido turns serious again: "Be careful out there tonight. Don't forget your backup units and watch the (suspect's) hands; they can hurt you."

A waning sun dips behind the clouds as Jeff eases into traffic, wondering aloud what this night will hold.

He advises dispatch that he's in service and adds that a civilian observer is riding with him. Although this transmission and a subsequent one are acknowledged, something has gone wrong at the communications desk and forty minutes later, he's asked if he's begun his tour of duty. As he meets with Salcido to voice his frustration, the dispatcher asks Jeff if he has an observer.

Street cops depend on the dispatcher to keep track of their movements, and Jeff is angry.

"You hear that?" he says incredulously. "If I get fuckin' hurt tonight because of her. . ."

"She knows you're here *now,* Jeff," Salcido assures him.

Despite the rocky start, the first hours are routine. He checks the parking lot of a country-western bar, looking for a car associated with a rape suspect. The club has a reputation as a shit-kicking place, and strangers are greeted with a cautious eye. The man's vehicle isn't in the area and Jeff drives on.

He stops a car being driven without headlights, and then, cruising slowly, observes a shouting match between a young couple in an isolated alley. He radios his location and drives toward them, but they are oblivious to him until his patrol car is less than fifty feet from where they stand, yelling at each other. The woman has what appears to be blood on her jeans, but isn't willing to talk. She just

70

wants to be left alone and walks off while Jeff calms the squat, square-jawed man.

Twenty-five minutes later, a citizen reports a man and woman arguing and shoving each other. Jeff heads to the area. It's the same couple, now walking hand-in-hand, signaling another rapid shift of emotions. Jeff ignores them and drives away.

He's soon waved down by a man reporting that a neighborhood teenager has been harassing his family at a nearby apartment complex. Speaking in halting English, he says he's tried talking calmly to the boy, but gets hostility in return. "I want to talk to him with peace. I don't want no trouble," he says. Jeff follows him home, but the young man is gone. Before leaving, Jeff approaches other family members, suggesting that they discuss the problem with the apartment manager and phone 911 if the teenager returns.

At 8:50 p.m., Jeff takes fifteen minutes to drink a soda and catch up on paperwork. As he returns to the street, he's instructed to phone an eastside officer concerning an assault which took place earlier in the day. At 9:59, there's a report of two people arguing in a truck parked outside a restaurant. Jeff scribbles the assignment information on his right palm. "It's the best notebook I have, and I never need to look for it," he says, smiling. Although he's at the restaurant in less than three minutes, the vehicle is gone.

At 10:10, he's dispatched to a drive-in theater where the manager says a group of teenagers entered without paying. They've already driven away, leaving behind one angry young man who had walked off to buy a soft drink. The manager declines to press charges, but tells the youngster not to return. Cursing softly, he walks to the street, looking for his friends. Ten minutes later, he's still there, pacing.

An hour later, Jeff drives to the parking lot of a convenience store. A woman in her twenties tells him that she was threatened by several juveniles with sticks. She can't describe any of them, but says she's okay and will head back to a nearby carnival where friends are waiting for her.

*   *

Between assignments, Jeff drives his beat, checking warehouses and businesses and looking for signs of trouble. Despite more-or-less continuous activity, it's been the kind of night that can lull an officer into a feeling of complacency. That changes abruptly just before 11:30.

Officers Jim O'Bright and Terri Andrews are dispatched to

check out a complaint of loud music at a party. When they ask that the sound level be lowered, a young man jumps on O'Bright and a second quickly joins in. Andrews goes to his aid and is also attacked. As she goes down, she keys her radio transmit button: "1-Adam-16, 10-99." She has advised that she needs help urgently and immediately.

Dispatch broadcasts their location, and a third officer already en route to back them up — normal procedure where there is potential for danger — accelerates his response. Three officers at the police substation run to their vehicles. Lights flashing and sirens piercing the silence of the night, they also start up, as do several others already on patrol.

A voice on the radio seems to be advising that the situation is now under control, but the transmission is fragmented.

Dispatch: "I copy it's Code 4 now?"

Eleven seconds pass without acknowledgement.

Another officer asks: "You said it's Code 4?"

Dispatch: "She says to clear the air, but I'm going to wait until we get another unit or two there."

It's been forty-one seconds since the call for help, but because the incident is taking place near the city's southern fringe, most of the responding officers are still several miles away. They need to move quickly, yet not jeopardize their lives or those of citizens along the way.

"The frustration is in not knowing what the hell's going on while you're racing to get there," Jeff explains later. "Even if it takes only a couple of minutes for the first units to arrive, it seems like an eternity."

There is no further radio transmission for one minute and forty-six seconds, and the silence is uneasy. Although officers have begun to pull up, no one has confirmed that the situation is under control. Finally:

"TAC-4, we have about six units. Have the others Code 4."

Dispatch: "10-4; any unit not at the scene, it's Code 4."

To Jeff, who never gets there, it *does* seem an eternity, but in reality, the total time from the initial report to a confirmed Code 4 is less than four minutes. O'Bright and Andrews sustain only minor scrapes, and two men are arrested for aggravated assault.

*   *

At 11:36, a sergeant reports a car being driven at high speed. Two minutes later, Jeff spots a Chevrolet which generally matches its description. He follows for a few blocks and pulls it over. The first officer arrives, but says it isn't the same vehicle. "You really had me worried," says the young man. "I was talking to my girlfriend and I was afraid I hadn't been paying attention to my speed."

Eight minutes elapse, then:

Dispatch: "1-Victor-21, what's your location?"

"Sixth and Irvington."

Dispatch: "10-4. 1-Adam-25."

"Missiondale and Calle Garcia."

Dispatch: "1-Victor-21, you're just a bit closer. Priority one, call 127, reference shots fired at U-Haul, 32 West Ajo. Complainant indicates she heard shots and that she saw people in the parking lot yelling. Call received at 2349."

Jeff, less than two blocks away: "1-Adam-75, Sixth and Ajo, approaching."

Dispatch: "10-4 at 2350. We'll be 10-39 (possible emergency situation) until we get a Code 4."

More information is available as Jeff pulls up.

Dispatch: "We just now received another call reference shots fired. The complainant indicated he saw an Hispanic male in his twenties in the middle of the street apparently shooting a gun. He was last seen northbound, however no description was obtained."

Within fifty seconds, there are four officers on the scene and the police helicopter is overhead, its blades spinning more than 900 times a second as it beats the air below it into submission. Jeff speaks with witnesses, gathering information. One says he was shot at and provides a description of the suspect and the car in which several males sped off.

Another officer comes on the radio with more information: "There have been shots fired, a vehicle has been hit. The suspect vehicle is a gray Cougar. There will be four subjects in the vehicle armed with what appears to be some kind of high-powered hand-gun."

Dispatch: "10-4, and that is a gray Cougar, the suspect vehicle, 10-4?"

"10-4, they're positive it's a gray-colored Mercury Cougar."

Seconds later: "1-Adam-25. I'm going to stop a white-colored Cougar at Seventh and President. It only has one occupant."

Dispatch: "10-4. Other unit for Seventh and President?"

"1-Adam-24, I'm 10-23."

The driver is quickly cleared of possible involvement. Jeff continues circulating in the area and just seconds after Friday night

73

becomes Saturday morning, he spots another car closely matching the description of the suspect vehicle. He keys his microphone and reports: "1-Adam-75. I'm following a black-over-gray Mercury Cougar, north on Sixth approaching Thirty-sixth."

Seconds later, Jeff advises, "It's got about three people in it, but I can't see for sure. It has smoked windows."

"1-Victor-21, that's 10-4. He stated three people for sure, possibly four."

Jeff: "We're north on Sixth at Three-three."

Dispatch: "Any other unit up north for Sixth and Three-three, possible suspect vehicle?"

Several officers report that they're en route.

Dispatch (to the helicopter): "Air One, we have a possible sighting of the shots-fired suspect vehicle, northbound on Sixth from Three-three. A black-over-gray Mercury Cougar."

Jeff, continuing to follow at a distance of about sixty feet: "North on Sixth, passing Two-nine."

Dispatch: "I copy Sixth and Two-nine now."

Jeff: "10-4, still northbound on Sixth."

Dispatch: "There's a couple South Tucson units who are gonna back that up."

Jeff: "Still northbound on Sixth, approaching Two-two."

Dispatch: "At 0002." (Two minutes past midnight.)

Jeff: "We're at Sixth and Two-two at the red light."

Air One: "You want me to light him up?"

Jeff: "Hold off for now; we have backup units coming. We're in the curb lane at this time."

Air One: "Is it the vehicle right in front of you?"

Jeff: "10-4. He just went east on Two-two from Sixth."

Air One: "I have him sighted; do you want me to light him up or wait?"

Jeff: "Go ahead, I think we have a bunch of units now."

Air One: "10-4."

Jeff: "We'll be making the stop at Fourth and Two-two."

Air One: "He's pulling in the parking lot — southwest quad of Two-two and Fourth."

Dispatch: "At 0003."

If the first rule of officer street survival is to watch the hands, the second is that everyone is a suspect, including, in the words of author Joseph Wambaugh, "the old lady in the iron lung."

There are five cops on the scene, three of them with guns drawn, on the strong possibility that someone in the Cougar has a loaded weapon. As it comes to a stop, Jeff, remaining in his car, uses his loudspeaker to give instructions:

"Driver! Turn off the ignition and throw the keys out of the window! . . I want you to exit with your back toward me and with your hands in the air. . . Turn around slowly. . . .Keep going. . . Halt! . . Keep your back toward me. . . Now back up toward my voice. . . Okay, hold it!"

Jeff and the other officers have done a visual search for weapons and now the young man is surrounded and frisked.

He appears confused and scared. Within two minutes, it's clear that although the vehicle is an almost perfect match for the one driven by the suspects, this young man was not involved in the shooting. The driver takes several deep breaths, then sighs in relief as the officers explain, apologize for the intrusion and withdraw.

Nearly seven hours after the start of his shift, Jeff finds time for a bite to eat. Sipping a cup of coffee, he says he empathizes with the young man in the Cougar, and is aware that a complaint might be filed. It isn't, but Jeff and the other officers would be covered because they had sufficient reason to make the stop. Police policy dictates that 'stop' and 'frisk' are separate actions. Reasonable suspicion of criminal activity is necessary to support a stop, and a frisk is justified only when an officer believes himself to be in potential danger and wants to determine whether a suspect is armed.

Indeed, the determination of probable cause — P.C. to officers — is an art form. Often it's not a matter of whether the defendant committed the crime, but whether the officer "played the game right" in catching him. An arrest which results from stopping or searching a suspect can be thrown out of court if the officer can't justify the *reason* for the stop or search, even if it has produced incriminating evidence.

Heading back to the station twenty minutes later, Jeff is dispatched to the nearby impound lot to receive an abandoned late-model white Corvette. The fenced area is the temporary resting place for hundreds of vehicles. Some have been dumped or stolen; others are being held as evidence. At least a dozen of them — little more than grisly chunks of twisted metal — bear mute testimony to accidents which killed or maimed their drivers. Oddly out of place is a *New York Times* vending machine. The paper showing through the window is dated March 23, 1984.

The tow-truck operator arrives at 1:28 a.m. and it takes him more than twenty-five minutes to maneuver the Corvette off the flatbed and into a parking place. Jeff shuts the gates of the lot and resets the silent alarm at 2:02. Debriefing has already ended, but he still must return to the station and complete his reports. He advises that he's out of service.

Dispatch (apologizing for assigning that last call): "Sorry."

Jeff (a twinkle in his voice): "I'll take it out of your next pay check."

Dispatch (trying to suppress a laugh): "10-4 at 0203."

■

It's July 21, 1985, Anita Sueme's second shift on her own. She's working 11 p.m. to 7 a.m. The first couple of hours are unusually slow and she uses the time to make security checks of area businesses. At 1:44 a.m., she observes a male driver 'run' both a stop sign and red light in less than twenty seconds. She stops him and as soon he steps out of his car, his lack of balance suggests that he's been drinking. Smelling alcohol on his breath, Anita asks Edward to perform a series of sobriety tests. First, he's asked to walk eight heel-to-toe steps away from her, pivot and take eight steps to the starting point. Next, he's to extend his arm and attempt to place his index finger on his nose. Finally, she instructs him to raise one leg and remain standing on the other while he counts to ten. Anita explains and demonstrates each test in advance. Edward, who is having difficulty just remaining vertical, fails each one.

Anita arrests him, at which point Edward begins to alternately cry and beg for another chance, saying he has a wife and young child at home and is afraid he'll lose his job if he goes to jail. "I'm not a bad person," he tells her. Anita assures him she doesn't think he's bad.

He tries another strategy: "You should get married; it would make you more compassionate."

Handcuffed, he's driven to the police station where Anita administers a breathalyzer test. He blows a .17, nearly twice the legal level of intoxication. Anita offers to release him on his promise to appear in court when ordered to if he can get a ride home. His wife picks him up, telling Anita as they leave that Edward will be going to Alcoholics Anonymous the next day.

It's been Anita's first 'solo' stop, and she says she wasn't nervous. "The important issue was getting him off the street before he harmed himself or someone else."

76

*   *

Six months later, Anita joins other members of her Academy class to celebrate the end of their one-year probationary status. Because officers work different shifts and in different parts of the city, she hasn't seen most of them since graduation. Veteran cops also stop by. One of them is Randy Graves, a Pima County Sheriff's deputy who encouraged her when things were rough.

She especially remembers an incident during officer safety exercises at the Academy.

"I was demonstrating an after-dark felony stop where I had to secure two suspects by myself. Randy played the role of one of the bad guys. I got him out of his car, handcuffed him and began the pat-down body search. I was a nervous wreck, but I knew I had to get through all of these procedures in order to graduate. I found a gun tucked away in his crotch. I unbuckled his belt, pulled down his trouser zipper, reached in and just ripped out the gun, but I guess I wasn't too careful when I pulled it out because when I mentioned it to him at a party months later, he said that I'd damned near killed him that night."

Anita didn't see Randy much after graduation, but says that he was "a source of encouragement when I did. I could talk with Randy about my feelings, fears and insecurities, and he would listen and give me advice when I asked for it. He really helped me make it through."

They chat a while tonight before Randy heads home to his family. It will be their final conversation.

The next evening, Laurie DeCorte, a staff advocate with the Pima County Attorney's Victim Witness Program, is driving an unmarked police car north on Alvernon Way. At 10:47 p.m., as the mobile Crisis Unit approaches Speedway, its headlights illuminate a man lying almost directly in her path. Braking to a fast stop, she looks out on the rest of the carnage: a moaning woman off to the side, a badly damaged Harley-Davidson motorcycle and a Toyota with three people trapped inside.

"Oh, fuck!" she mutters as her mind begins to process the scene. She activates the emergency flashers and positions her vehicle to protect the injured man from being struck again. As she does this, volunteer Becky Allen reaches for the microphone and advises dispatch of the accident.

Their part of the drama seems to unfold in slow motion. While

77

Laurie walks around assuring everyone that ambulances are on the way, Becky kneels by the man sprawled on his back, motionless except for labored breathing through blood or some other fluid in his throat. He's long-haired and grubby with a straggly beard. To Becky, he looks like a biker, "but they're people, too, and they get hurt and scared, too," she recalls later.

"I wanted to take him in my arms and hold him, but I knew he shouldn't be moved. I just held his hand, touched his face and stroked his hair. I had a feeling he was going to die, but I told him he would be okay and that I would be with him until the ambulance came."

Anita, now working a 6 p.m. to 2 a.m. shift, is one of several officers who head for the intersection to help the victims, 'secure' the scene and begin an investigation. Before she gets there, she's diverted to respond to a child custody dispute. Completing her assignment an hour later, she's dispatched to Tucson Medical Center where the cyclist is on life-support equipment. A nurse hands her two guns found concealed under his clothing, as well as papers identifying him as Jesse Vaughn. Several bikers who show up say they know him, but have no information to help locate his family.

Anita considers entering the trauma room to see the injured man, but doesn't. Instead, she drives to police headquarters to complete her case reports. As she prepares to head home four hours after the normal end of her shift, she's called aside and given shocking news: Jesse Vaughn is really Randy Graves, working undercover as a member of a motorcycle club, and now barely clinging to life.

Although it's soon determined that the accident was not related to Randy's assignment, there's an almost unprecedented thirty-hour news blackout while law enforcement officials assess how the disclosure of his identity will affect the investigation.

Police Chief Ronstadt explains it this way: "We were in the midst of a dangerous and highly sensitive multi-agency operation. Randy was already in real deep. Other officers were at serious risk and we needed time to get them out."

An operation which took months to set up must be dismantled in hours.

Randy dies two days later and Anita is in a state of shock. She begins to face up to the tragedy by serving as an honor guard at his viewing, and later joins family, friends and more than 600 law enforcement officers as her friend is buried on a cloudless, spring-like afternoon.

Anita knows how fragile life can be. "I've had several DOAs, but the youngest was about seventy and they all looked peaceful, as if they'd just fallen asleep. I've had grandparents die, too, but Randy was young and healthy and I'd just seen him the day before. We were talking and laughing together, and now. . ."

Her words trail off; the rest of her thought is unspoken.

*   *

February 18, 1986, three weeks after Randy's funeral. It's 8:26 p.m. when the dispatcher activates the emergency tone.

"Shooting, 2502 East Nineteenth. Two-five-zero-two East Nineteenth."

Within fifteen seconds, Anita and six other units report that they're heading to the scene.

Dispatch: "It's a 10-31 (family fight) situation. Male was shot by his wife. Victim. . ."

Sergeant Tom McNally, cutting in: "Closest two units Code 3."

Dispatch: "10-4. 3-Adam-53 and 3-X-ray-56, Code 3. Female suspect still has the weapon. The victim is on the complainant's front porch at 2502 East Nineteenth. The suspect is inside 2514 East Nineteenth. She should be alone in the house at this time."

Anita pulls up less than a minute later and waits for instructions.

McNally: "Units going 10-23, quad the area and secure it. Do we have a 21 (phone) number for the suspect's residence?"

Dispatch: "We'll try and get it. I don't have it yet."

McNally: "10-4. Once the area is secure, we're going to go ahead and try to make phone contact."

Luis Mariscal, the next officer on the scene, heads for the victim, two houses west of where the shooting occurred, and requests that medics move in. The dispatcher assigns quads — observation stations radiating out from the scene of the incident which provide the best chance of catching a fleeing suspect. Anita is assigned to the northwest.

Mariscal: "Female should be in the house by herself. There may be a dog also. The house is the third house east of Tucson Boulevard on the south side of the block. At this point, there is no activity at the front. Have one unit (meet me) here at the front and have one go to the alley."

It's now been just under four minutes since the call was dispatched.

The staccato beat of the Bell JetRanger police helicopter announces its approach, momentarily covering a wisp of a moon.

Soon, Air One is circling overhead.

Mariscal: "Air, do us a favor and turn the light off. We're going to go around the house."

Air One: "Okay. In the rear is a blue pickup truck."

Mariscal: "10-4. Have all units 10-3 (urgent transmissions only); we're going to be moving to the house."

Dispatch: "All units 10-3."

Air One: "Be advised to the rear there is a dog and I think a shadow on the rear porch. Unknown if that's an officer or a suspect."

The radio is silent for thirty-four tense seconds, then:

"3-Adam-95. Myself and 3-Adam-25 are at the rear of the house."

Mariscal: "10-4. We're attempting contact. There's no answer at the front. Everyone maintain their quads. Anybody just coming in, remain in the street. There's three units at the front door."

Less than 125 feet away from where this drama is unfolding, medics prepare to take the victim to the hospital. Joel has wounds to his stomach and elbow and tells officers that his wife shot him with a small caliber handgun. He gives them his phone number.

McNally relays it to dispatch. "If you are able to make contact, advise her that officers are around the place and have her come out with her hands above her head."

Radio silence for thirty-three seconds, then:

Dispatch: "Units be advised she is not answering the phone."

Air One: "Are we for sure that she is still in the house?"

Mariscal: "As far as we know. There's no indication that she came out."

Kicking down doors with reckless abandon is more a Hollywood response than prudent police action. There are appropriate occasions for such action, however, and this appears to be one of them.

Officers break through the front door and enter. Seconds later, they find the woman dead of a gunshot wound to the head.

Although Anita has witnessed death several times, she has not yet made her first notification to a family member. She drives to the hospital where Joel is being treated in the trauma room. Although he's conscious and his injuries are not life-threatening, she decides to withhold the news until he's been stabilized.

Nearly two hours later, Anita takes his hand. "I'm sorry to tell you this, but after you ran out of the house, she shot herself. She was dead when we broke down the door." Joel screams and begins to pull on the tubes which are sending medication into his blood stream. A nurse helps Anita restrain him for a few seconds. His brief fury spent, he turns calm and they stay with him, talking softly until he's ready to sleep.

*   *

Just before midnight on April 28, 1986, a stabbing or shooting victim — it's not clear which — is dumped in a driveway near Reid Park and the occupants of a vehicle speed off. In a bizarre twist of circumstance, a paramedic responding to aid the victim overshoots his destination and, while making a U-turn, collides with a motorcycle, injuring its driver and passenger.

Anita is one of several officers who respond. Her sergeant instructs her to contact nearby neighbors and ask if they saw or heard anything. She begins ringing bells, apologizing to each resident for the late visit. Two of them recall hearing what sounded like shots or a vehicle backfiring, and one says he called 911 to make a report. Anita documents their names and apologizes again before leaving.

As she briefs her sergeant, there's a report of a young woman crying in the adjacent park. "Why don't you take a walk around the area and make sure we don't have any surprises in the bushes," the sergeant suggests. Anita starts into the park on foot, the beam from her four-cell flashlight showing the way. Suddenly, there is a low hissing sound, followed within seconds by pulsating spurts of water. The park's automatic sprinkler system has turned on. Anita lets loose an obscenity as she jumps out of the way. She walks on, laughing now. Air One flies over. There appears to be no one around.

As she heads back to the street, a man jogs up and says that a young woman is sitting in the alley by his house, crying.

She's hunched up in what looks like a vertical fetal position. "Are you okay?" Anita asks, kneeling next to her.

No response.

Softly: "Look at me. . . I need to see your face. . . What happened to you?"

It's probably the same woman Anita had been looking for in the park, but she can't be certain. Is she connected with the man whose injury began the strange series of events? This, too, is unknown. Anita probes gently, but gets only sobs and grunts in response. After about two minutes, she places a hand under the woman's chin and raises her head. She is young, certainly still a teenager. Several neighbors are outside, even though it's nearly 1 a.m. No one recognizes her. She whines and protests as Anita lifts her to her feet.

81

"Cold," she says. It's her first word.

A young man takes off his windbreaker and wraps it around her shoulders. Anita and another officer half walk, half carry her to a nearby patrol car. Sitting there, she says her first name is Diane, that she's "about fifteen" and that she doesn't know where her parents live or their phone number.

"Something's happened to you tonight and we'd like to help," Anita says.

Diane is tired of the questions. Each time Anita falls silent for a few seconds, Diane nods off in the warmth of the car. Anita radios for an ambulance. Medics report that Diane's right eye is fixed straight ahead while her left eye is wandering off, and that she feels cold to the touch. Not knowing if they're dealing with trauma or a reaction to an alcohol or drug overdose, they take her to a hospital.

Diane just wants to sleep and becomes abusive when Anita tries to question her. "You fucking bitch!" she yells. "I'm going to whip your ass!" Her blood alcohol level is .24, and she's admitted for observation.

The assault victim and both motorcyclists survive.

*   *

After six months on her own, Anita is much more confident. "I remember some days just out of the Academy when I was scared shitless and asked myself, 'What am I doing here?'"

She knows that she's not Superwoman and that fear is part of a cop's life. "I still have days when I ask why I'm doing it, and I know it's okay, even healthy to admit you're sometimes scared." Recognizing that she's not physically as strong as most men, she works out regularly.

She's had no problem being accepted by male officers, she says, but has discovered that many women don't like female cops. "It's generally easier to work with males in adversarial situations," she believes. "The guys can be strong and belligerent, but when I arrest them and put them in the back seat of my car, most of them are sweet as pie. Arrest a woman, though, and it's a different story, especially the little, skinny-assed ones. Boy, can they be bitchy!"

Her job is not without moments of humor.

It's a cold night in February. "It was already down into the thirties," Anita remembers, "and here's this man walking along, wearing shorts and not much more. He has one earphone in each ear and a third one attached to the other two, but none of them connect to anything; they're just hanging in mid-air. His name is Daniel and he's definitely not on this planet. He's friendly, but he doesn't say much that I can comprehend. As he walks away, he pauses to start a conversation with my police car which is parked about 100 feet away.

"Another officer who has responded to back me up switches on his roof-top amplifier and starts whispering in a slow, deep voice, 'This is the car talking, Daniel. Go home, Daniel.' The last we see, he's running down an alley waving his arms up and down. I'm laughing so hard that tears are running down my face. We may have pushed him over the edge."

Her first foot chase is a brief adventure. "It was after midnight and I was questioning a suspect about a wine-skip from a convenience store. He starts running and I take off after him, yelling into my radio that I'm giving chase. I'm hauling ass, but it's hard to run carrying all of my equipment and trying to be coherent on the radio at the same time. He looks back once, probably surprised that I'm still there. He finally goes down an alley, climbs a fence and disappears into the darkness, and I'm thinking to myself, 'I'm not chasing him over a fence for a $2.99 bottle of wine.'"

In a profession where there are many shades of gray, Anita's decision to not pursue was "good thinking," according to Sergeant Phil Corrigan. "The chase sounds like fun, but it can be dangerous, and cops need to weigh the possible consequences. You tell them to work independently, but sometimes you challenge their decisions and most cops don't like it when you second-guess their judgment."

One of Anita's goals is to be the first female on the elite SWAT team. For now, she must settle for a bit part in a narcotics bust. There must be at least one uniformed officer at the front door because undercover officers wear ski masks and disguises.

"I asked what I was supposed to do," she relates, "and was told, 'You're just here for your body. Keep your mouth shut and stay out of the way.' Another officer, also in uniform, is with me at the door. We knock, and when a kid opens it, we say, 'Police!' In an instant, four narcs go running in. I just stand back to avoid being trampled."

■

Rene Gomez, who survived academic probation at the Academy, moved smoothly through the rigors of the field training program.

"It took me two years to get in and I'm doing everything I can to be a good cop. I put a lot of pressure on myself, perhaps too much sometimes, but I've set real high standards and goals," he says as he begins a new shift after three months on his own.

His first call tonight is a dispute in a downtown parking lot. The manager, complaining that a motorist often parks there without paying, has used a metal device to lock the vehicle's wheels. He shows Rene a list of the offenses. The irate man claims it's a "ripoff operation" and that he was told he'd have to pay $50 before the device would be removed. It's a situation that could easily turn nasty, but Rene sorts it out in a low-key manner. When both parties have calmed down, he tells the manager that holding the car violates the law, and suggests that he consider filing a civil suit instead.

As the driver prepares to leave, Rene notices that the car's registration sticker has expired. He checks with dispatch; there are no warrants associated with either the driver or the vehicle.

"Are you going to cite me for the sticker?" the man asks.

"No, you're on private property," Rene responds.

"You'll just get me as soon as I drive off."

"I don't operate like that."

*   *

His next assignment is a motor vehicle accident. There are no injuries and the car that caused it has driven away. Rene takes the information for his report. Back in his car, he observes an intoxicated middle-aged man lying by a bus stop, waiting for a bus that won't come until the next morning. Rene makes sure that he's okay. Next, a prowler is reported outside a nearby residence, but there's no sign of him when Rene pulls up a few minutes later.

As he pauses to update his activity sheet, an armed robber holds up an all-night supermarket and flees on foot. Less than five minutes after Rene begins cruising in the area, a man with a gun robs Pancho's Mexican Restaurant.

"White male, thirty years, five-six, slim build, wearing a gray sweater over an unknown color shirt; last seen on foot out the front door," dispatch reports.

Rene, three miles away, is the first to arrive. The cashier, a young woman, is surprisingly calm, describing how the man lifted his shirt enough for her to see the butt of the gun and said, "Give me all of the money!" Rene radios further information to officers already circulating in the area. He speaks with the cashier and her manager —

both of whom are Hispanic — assuring them in a combination of English and Spanish that robbers seldom return to the same place.

Helping at the scene of a three-car accident, he cites a young man for failing to yield. A computer check shows that his driver's license has been revoked. Rene arrests him, then asks if he wants to call his mother. "Hell, yes!" he responds. "She's got to get me out. I can't handle this."

Later, he stops a driver who has ignored a traffic signal. As Rene walks to the car, he checks to see that the trunk is closed, then shines his flashlight in the back seat in case someone is hiding. He remembers his Academy lessons on the potential for danger on this type of call. "I take these precautions night or day," he emphasizes. "You can't be too careful."

*   *

With the exception of traffic stops turned bad, intervening in family fights produces the greatest number of officer injuries. It's May 28, 1986, and Rene and John Kragnes are dispatched to an 'unknown trouble' call. A citizen has dialed 911. Although the phone connection is broken almost immediately, the address and phone number of the residence remain on the service aide's computer screen. The number is redialed, but now the line is busy. Since it's uncertain what, if anything, has occurred, officers must respond.

A slightly-built woman, tears running down her cheeks, opens the door. While Kragnes takes her aside to talk, Rene approaches the husband — six feet, two inches, and what looks like 200 pounds of pure muscle. He's lying on the sofa, drinking a beer. He's calm for about thirty seconds, then gets up and says sharply, "There's nothing wrong here. Pardon my language, but get the fuck out of my house!"

His wife hears him and walks back into the room. As he moves toward her, yelling, Rene steps between them and tells him to "cool it!" The husband jumps to a karate stance, eyes bulging like goose eggs, and the rest of his face seeming to transform into a fright mask.

"Come on, you're going to have to shoot me to take me!" he shouts.

Rene asks for additional units and stands back, hoping the man will be calmer if he's not feeling challenged. The strategy works and the standoff lasts for two minutes, long enough for three other officers to arrive. Now Rene tells him he's under arrest for domestic violence, moves in and secures enough of a wrist lock to enable the other officers to surround and handcuff him. It's over in seconds and no one is hurt.

Some officers take unnecessary risks and become victims themselves. In his book, *Officer Down, Code Three,* Pierce Brooks calls it "tombstone courage." It's an attitude that frightens Rene. "Common sense is ninety percent of the job," he observes after the man has been taken to jail, "and common sense told me I'd be risking myself and my partner by escalating that situation with just two of us there. I didn't want him hurt and I didn't want us hurt." Incidents such as this also reinforce Rene's belief that most people, even those causing disturbances, react better to an officer who remains calm and shows respect. "You need to be able to put yourself in the other person's position," he says, "and ask yourself, 'What would I want done with me in a similar situation?'"

*   *

At 11:35 p.m. two weeks later, Rene is one of two officers dispatched to a convenience store where a stolen white 1978 Monarch with out-of-state plates has been spotted. The dispatcher, in telephone contact with the victim, reports that the vehicle is on Tucson Boulevard at Speedway, waiting for the traffic signal to change. Ten seconds later:

Frank Delmonico: "He's going east."

Rene pulls in behind Delmonico. The suspect starts out slowly, perhaps testing the water, but soon picks up speed and then makes an evasive and dangerous turn in front of oncoming traffic.

Rene keys his microphone, advising, "He's running, westbound on Speedway."

Dispatch: "Copy westbound?"

Rene: "Westbound and we're at Tucson Boulevard right now, still running."

Both units are pursuing Code 3, and Rene, farthest from the fleeing car, relays the changing locations.

Rene: "Approaching Campbell."

The chase is now entering the downtown area and a sergeant instructs the dispatcher to patch into that frequency so additional officers will be aware of the situation.

Rene: "We're on Norris, southbound from First."

Dispatch: "Southbound on Norris, 10-4."

Rene: "Westbound on Second."

Dispatch: "Team Two units be advised we're chasing a GTA suspect vehicle west on Second from Norris, a white seventy-eight sedan."

Rene: "West on Second, approaching Mountain."

Dispatch: "10-4, Second and Mountain, westbound."

Nine seconds later, the chase comes to an abrupt halt.

Rene: "He lost it at Mountain and Second."

The suspect has run off the road and crashed into an embankment. By the time Rene pulls up, Delmonico has his gun drawn on the man. Rene also draws down, and for a moment the officers are in each other's line of fire.

"It wasn't a picture-perfect felony stop," Rene observes, "but it got the job done."

He remembers an earlier chase which began after he'd stopped for a soda. "I'd just gotten back into my car and was holding the cup in my hand. All I could do was toss it on the floor next to me as I took off after the suspect."

Most officers, Rene included, quickly acknowledge that chases are exciting, but they're also aware of the increased potential for collisions or injuries. "You must sometimes back off to avoid jeopardizing the lives of citizens along the way. Sure, you want to catch the suspect, but you also want it to be a safe run."

High-speed chases are also heady emotional experiences. The adrenaline is pumping and the line separating necessary force from excessive force can be difficult to define in the heat of anger, especially when the suspect appears capable of a good street fight.

"You're ready to kick ass after you've jeopardized your life running after some turkey," Rene says, "Some officers find a way to get their licks or their kicks in and you need to be real careful not to over-react."

How does he handle it? "I'll sometimes release the energy by cussing up a storm, and I've never gone beyond a push or a shove."

*   *

In law enforcement, it's the norm that the hunter — the suspect — becomes the hunted. Occasionally, however, a *victim* may cross a thin line and become a defendant.

It's June 1, 1986, and Rene and Brad Hunt are sent to investigate an incident in which a pickup truck has gone off the roadway, plowed out of control through several rows of dense oleanders and crashed into a large olive tree in the front yard of a residence. The trip through the oleanders has slowed the vehicle and, although the driver and his three teenage passengers are not injured, the front end of the truck and the tree are badly damaged.

An elderly woman who has lived there nearly fifty years comes outside. She looks at her transformed front yard, shakes her head and says, "I don't believe it," then walks to the frightened youngsters to make sure that they're not injured. Her concerned reaction is the calm before an approaching storm. Minutes later, her son returns home from his office. A heavy-set man of about forty, he's out of his car almost before it's stopped, yelling, "Sons of bitches!" He walks toward the damaged tree. "It's going to cost me $5,000 to fix that!" he screams to no one in particular.

With Rene on the street diagramming the accident, Hunt approaches the man to explain what happened. Kevin wants no explanation, nor has he any apparent interest in whether there have been injuries. As he curses and rants, Kevin's face turns bright crimson. In his monologue, the damage has quickly escalated to $20,000. He has a very short fuse and today he's carrying his own match. He's just inches from Hunt's face, screaming in the manner of a baseball manager going chest-to-chest with the umpire.

Hunt backs off a couple of steps, telling him quietly, but firmly, to calm down.

"What are you going to do, arrest me on my own property?"

"I don't want to have to do that, but I need you to calm down."

"Get off my fucking property!"

He's virtually out of control now. "You want to go at it?" he screams. Despite street traffic, Rene has heard the commotion and runs back, pushing his way through the heavy brush. Facing two of them now, Kevin pauses for breath and begins to wind down. The confrontation is over as suddenly as it began. He asks the young people, who had strategically retreated during his diatribe, if they're okay. They nod and he says softly, "That's all that really matters." As the officers prepare to leave, he turns to them and says, "I acted like an ass. I apologize."

Several days later, Kevin writes a letter to Police Chief Ronstadt, commending the officers for their handling of the situation. "I just want you to know that these men are doing a fine job and are a great help to the community," he concludes.

*   *

Nearly twenty years after Rene's father left the home and remarried, a chance meeting has brought them together. Enjoying an afternoon in Kennedy Park with friends, Rene sees him at a nearby picnic table. He waves instinctively and his father motions him over.

"He said hello, introduced me to his wife, then the two of us left and had a couple of beers. I guess the beer made it easier for me to open up a little. I told him that no matter what had happened between him and my mother, I had never really stopped loving him. He put his arms around me and started crying."

His father didn't explain his long absence from Rene's life, and Rene didn't ask. "At first, I think I was afraid that if I brought it up I'd say things I might regret. It's a shame that I couldn't grow up alongside him and that he wasn't there to show me that love, but he's trying to show it now the best he can. I realize that I've forgiven him and I'm just grateful to have him back in my life."

His mother has been dead nearly a year, but Rene still senses her presence: "Even after she passed away I felt her there with me, encouraging me to hang on and do my best."

■

August 2, 1985. Robert Garcia has been on his own for three weeks, working the 6 a.m. to 2 p.m. shift. As most of Tucson awakens to a new day, he is sent to an intersection where a light has malfunctioned. He appraises the situation and advises that traffic engineers are needed. Twenty minutes later, he meets a detective to get information on a child custody dispute. Next, he stops two young men on a motorcycle and cites the driver for speeding. He's dispatched to a traffic accident, but both vehicles are gone when he arrives. All of this has happened in less than two hours.

Just before 8 a.m., there's a report of a silent alarm at an auto parts store. After checking the rear for any sign of forced entry, Robert cautiously approaches the front door. A middle-aged couple is inside. The man says he's the manager and was not aware that the alarm had been triggered. "Who do you call to cancel the alarm?" Robert asks. Dispatch has already given Robert the name of the security company and the manager establishes his identity by answering correctly.

After this early flurry of activity, the shift turns quiet. Three hours later as Robert prepares for a lunch break, dispatch reports a bank robbery in progress. It's a Priority One situation — defined as an emergency in which death or serious injury are possible. The national goal on Priority One calls is that an officer arrive within five minutes. In Tucson, this standard is met three-fourths of the time.

Although he's more than seven miles away, Robert is the closest available officer and he drives Code 3 most of the way. The ebb and flow of the siren encompass the vehicle as he moves easily around traffic. Although many motorists seem unsure what to do when an emergency vehicle approaches, there is an eerie sense of calm as he proceeds and the experience is more exhilarating than frightening.

Less than thirty seconds from the bank, he's advised that there hasn't been a robbery after all. Robert slows to normal speed. As he pulls up, an employee waiting outside says that a teller opening a cash drawer accidentally tripped the alarm. The adrenaline shuts down now, but Robert must still gather information and prepare a report on the non-incident.

*   *

Three months later, he's comfortable with his beat and his ability to stockpile information. "I realize now how much I missed when I was a rookie," he says. "My training officer would ask, 'Why didn't you see the passenger in the back seat?' or 'Why didn't you notice the broken vase under the table?' I didn't see them because I was scared to death trying to learn everything at once. Ideally I'd like to remember everything that's happened before and be able to connect it all up, but it's surprising how much you *can* train yourself to retain. It's mostly a matter of using the knowledge we've been given in our training."

Robert knows that the most important part of putting on the uniform is shifting mental gears so that all non-job-related issues and concerns are put aside. He never allows himself to forget that no situation is predictable. Two recent experiences have reinforced this.

In the first, a burglary is reported to be in progress at an apartment complex. While another officer guards the door, Robert hugs the side of the building as he works himself toward an open window. "You don't know where to look first — where someone could be hiding. I was nervous, but expecting the worst, I was prepared for it." There's no confrontation this time; the suspect had already fled.

Two weeks later, a distraught man calls 911 to report that his wife didn't arrive at work and isn't answering their home telephone. He says that she's been depressed for several weeks. He'll head for their apartment and wants an officer to meet him there.

"Marv (McEwen) and I walk up to the open door and the husband is leaning against the living room wall. He seems to be in a state of semi-shock.

'She's dead,' he tells us, pointing to the bedroom.

90

"I walk in and, sure enough, she's lying on the bed, part of her face blown away and blood all around — on the bed, the floor and most of the way up the wall. I have to pronounce her (dead), so I walk to the bed and lift her wrist which is hanging over the side. As I begin to check for a pulse which I know she can't have, a voice whispers, 'Hi.' She scared the living daylights out of me. I got goose-bumps up and down my arm and for a minute I thought I was going to die next to her. I yelled for the paramedics who had just arrived and they came running in. We lifted her onto a litter and I ran Code 3 in front of the ambulance, clearing the way to the hospital."

The woman survives despite a bullet through her temple.

Today, heading toward a burglary in progress, Robert moves into the area as officers already at the scene report on the search for a suspect. Seconds after Robert leaves his patrol car, a young man bolts out of a nearby door and literally runs into his arms. He looks at Robert, mutters, "Oh shit!" and reaches for the sky.

Later, a citizen reports a fight, saying he can hear someone being thrown against the wall or floor of an upstairs apartment. Robert peers into the window. There's considerable noise, but no assault; several teenagers in the room are break-dancing.

The manager of a motel has called 911 to complain about a man exposing himself. Visibly upset, he tells Robert, "I've got young women and maids all around here." As the two of them walk around the complex, the manager points to a slim man in his late twenties, exclaiming, "That's him!"

Robert approaches the suspect. "Sir, please turn around and stand right there with your hands out of your pockets." Robert checks for weapons, cuffs him, then walks him to the manager's office. Donald, passive throughout, says he had only been tucking in his shirt. The witnesses disagree, however, and a computer check shows a previous arrest on a similar charge.

Robert takes him to be fingerprinted and photographed, and then releases him on his promise to appear in court. Removing the handcuffs, Robert turns to face him. "It looks like you have a problem and that some professional help would be a good idea." Donald nods and walks out.

*   *

May 22, 1986. It's shortly after 5 a.m. and the first light of a new day is visible over the Rincon Mountains. Robert has just finished working an accident in which an intoxicated driver ran his car into

91

the back of a street-cleaning vehicle. As he heads to the hospital to complete his investigation and paperwork, the emergency tone sounds.

Dispatch: "Man with a gun," she begins.

She gives the eastside address and one officer immediately offers to start up.

Dispatch "Unit for a 10-84?"

Robert is less than three blocks away, far closer than the first unit. He advises his location.

Dispatch: "10-4. Described as a White male. . ."

There's a pause of nearly thirty seconds while the dispatcher waits for additional information from a service aide who is talking by phone to the reportee.

Dispatch: "Apparently there's been a shooting. There's a subject down. Suspect's a White male, sixty years old. There's an apartment number 923 indicated."

A sergeant and two other units report they're also en route.

Robert reaches the area, rolls his window down and drives slowly past the house, looking and listening. He's confused by the reported address — he can see that it's not an apartment — but before he can request clarification, the dispatcher is back on the air, advising that it's a residence and to disregard the apartment number.

Still the only officer there, he drives down the alley, alert for any sign of activity. There is none.

Dispatch: "There's a female yelling for help and the complainant on the line is indicating that he thinks the suspect has left the residence. Unknown exactly where he went. He got there by a cab; the cab is gone."

Robert acknowledges he's heard this transmission, then drives back to the street and parks about 150 feet from the residence. He begins moving on foot so he'll be in a better position to observe any activity. Seconds later, he sees a man about a block away walking toward him and carrying something in his hand. From that distance, he matches the description of the suspect. Gun drawn, Robert maintains total concentration on the man, still several hundred feet away. Additional information soon becomes available.

Dispatch: "Suspect has curly brown and gray hair, wearing a checked shirt."

The man walking toward Robert is no longer a good physical match. Robert's interest in him drops a bit, but he continues to watch his movement — especially the hands — at the same time positioning himself in an area providing cover.

Officer Tim Jones arrives, approaches the man on foot and concludes that he's not involved. Three other units pull up in the next eighty seconds and they move into position around the house. As they do this, their radios are silent for more than two minutes. To the dispatcher, miles away, it seems an eternity, but she resists the temptation to request an update, knowing that their silence is intentional and possibly necessary to their safety.

Finally, an officer asks, "Do you have contact with the house?"

Dispatch: "We do now. The complainant's quite hysterical, indicating that the female's been shot and the suspect shot himself."

The caller is asked to come outside. Seconds later, the front door opens and he steps out, holding a portable telephone and still in contact with the 911 service aide. Robert's heart is going "a hundred miles an hour."

He walks in with two other officers and finds the suspect dead on the livingroom floor, shattered fragments of his own bullet sprinkled through his head. Officer Sandy Sellers picks up the gun next to the body and they all head for the kitchen. The floor is thick with blood and Robert, starting to slip, reaches out and grabs a counter top. The woman has been shot in the head, chest, arm and leg, but is conscious. Gurgling, she gasps, "Air, air."

Robert asks if an ambulance has been dispatched and is told that it's now pulling up. Medics stabilize the woman and speed off to the hospital.

Officers are now able to begin determining what took place. The dead man, a sixty-one-year-old Tucson restauranteur, came to the home where his thirty-one-year-old ex-girlfriend was renting a room, and they began arguing. As the fight became heated, he drew a gun and ordered the witness, who rented a separate room at the residence, to leave. It was that man who retreated to another part of the house and phoned 911.

Greg Strom, whose first call working alone had been a man with a gun, begins his shift at 6 a.m. today. He leaves briefing early to relieve other officers at the scene and help with the investigation. The dead man is still on the floor. It's a sight that can send a cop's last meal back up through the esophagus and onto the crime scene.

"It seemed that blood and bone fragments were everywhere," Greg relates later. "I've seen accident victims and suicides before, but this was overwhelming. I thought to myself, 'What would possess someone to do that?'"

Despite her injuries, the woman survives. She'll be hospitalized for nearly three months and undergo a dozen operations, most of them for facial reconstruction. She has nearly lost her life, but a year later, her sense of humor is intact.

*   *

In Robert's opinion, a good officer needs to do a lot of attitude-sensing. Sometimes it's the ability to feel when a situation is about to go bad. In other instances, it's having skin as thick as a catcher's mitt.

About three hours into a midnight shift he responds to back up Officer McEwen who is citing a man for urinating in public outside a convenience store. Robert immediately recognizes Larry from an encounter several weeks before.

On that night, he saw him slumped over his steering wheel. By the time Robert came to a stop, made a U-turn and returned, the young man was gone. Cruising, Robert found him a few blocks away, hanging half in and half out of his vehicle. Checking to see if he needed help, it was quickly obvious to Robert that Larry was intoxicated. He couldn't perform the simplest sobriety test.

"I told him I'd cite him for DUI and release him to his dad," Robert remembers, "but he slammed the citation book out of my hand and started punching me. I used the wrist takedown to get him to the ground and cuffed him. Even in my car, he was still combative, kicking at the door and window."

In tonight's incident, Larry refuses to sign a misdemeanor citation. The citation requires no acknowledgement of guilt, but is simply an agreement by Larry to appear in court if he wants to dispute the charge. He says he'd rather go to jail than accept the piece of paper. McEwen writes "refused" on it and hands him a copy. Still hostile, he refuses to take it, then grabs it, crumples it and walks away. They let him leave, not willing to further aggravate the situation by arresting him.

In a profession where the emphasis should be on helping people, it's not necessary to follow the letter of the law on every traffic violation, and Robert tries to avoid what he feels is unnecessary power-struggling.

"A few weeks ago, I pulled a driver over and he jumped out of his car and started chewing me out," he recalls. "He had just had an argument with his wife, and then his car wouldn't start and he was late for work. It was just a bad day all around. I'll listen to their problems or excuses and sometimes let them off with a warning. Maybe it will help turn around their day."

94

Those who continue to escalate the situation get little sympathy from Robert. "Most vehicle stops involve two or more infractions, but I'll usually cite only the most serious offense. If they keep cursing at me and chewing me out, though, I just keep writing citations. They usually get the message after two or three of them."

Robert saw "very little respect" given to officers in Santa Fe. "Cops were nobodies when I was there, but in Tucson you're respected by most people. It makes me feel real good to see that."

■

Les Beach, the middle-aged rookie, is initially nervous as he begins to patrol alone, worrying aloud about getting a call and not knowing what to do, and wondering how he'll handle situations under real, not simulated, pressure.

Like Robert Garcia, he knows that police officers are expected to have a higher level of tolerance to 'fighting words' than the average citizen. He also believes that cops who spend a lot of time defending their egos are not solving many problems.

"When you're out here carrying a weapon loaded with six rounds and a guy calls you every name in the book while you're writing him a traffic citation and then tells you what you can do with your ticket, your car and your job, you have to be able to smile and keep your cool."

Two months later, the butterflies are gone. He sorts things out at a minor traffic accident and cites one driver for not yielding. He responds to the scene of another reported collision, but no one's there.

A nine-year-old boy has been caught stealing a Voltron robot watch and the manager of the store wants to prosecute to set an example for other youngsters. The third-grader is wearing an oversized Chicago Bears sweat shirt, faded jeans and white sneakers. He shows no indication that he's nervous or scared.

"You have the right to remain silent," Les tells him, and then begins reading from the standard Miranda card. "Anything you say can and will be used against you in a court of law. . . You have the right to the presence of an attorney to assist you prior to questioning and to be with you during questioning if you so desire. . . If you cannot afford an attorney, you have the right to have one appointed for you prior to questioning." Les explains each part as he proceeds, speaking calmly as you might to your own child.

"Do you understand?"

The youngster looks down and nods.

Then, firmly: "You've been arrested for stealing and you could go to jail."

The boy is either streetwise or has seen too many television cop shows. When told to empty his pockets to check for possible weapons, he pulls up his jeans to expose his ankles. His parents can't be located, so he's released to the custody of an aunt and will have to appear in Juvenile Court.

Later, Les is dispatched to investigate a possible child molestation. A maid entering an apartment has heard a child's cry and watched a man walk out of the bedroom, pulling up his trousers. She tells Les that a three- or four-year-old girl, wearing only a T-shirt, was lying on the bed and holding her crotch.

After knocking several times on the apartment door, Les unlocks it with a key provided by the manager. He stands to the side and pushes it open with his foot, announcing, "Police officer!" He follows a similar routine at the bedroom door and a walk-in closet, but no one is there.

Les interviews the maid and apartment manager and is told that the couple living there has no known children. He prepares his report and advises the manager to phone 911 if the girl or man is seen. The sex crimes division will be notified for a followup investigation. As he returns to his patrol car, Les, who would rather talk to people and educate them, allows that "it would be a real pleasure to arrest a child molester."

As he heads north on Wilmot Road, a man driving in the next lane calls over, "How fast am I going?"

"Thirty-five," Les responds.

Minutes later, he pulls into a parking lot to back up an officer checking out a van. "I don't like them because you never know what's inside," he observes. The driver, sought for violating a protection order, is arrested.

He stops a woman making multiple lane changes. "I wasn't thinking about my driving," she says.

"You sure weren't," Les responds. He doesn't cite her, although he could have. "I just wanted her to be aware of what she was doing. Sometimes you can accomplish more with a talk than a ticket. If it's an obvious violation, I'll cite." A minute later another woman ignores a red light and is ticketed. Her bumper sticker: "I owe, I owe, so off to work I go."

96

Four months later, Les is feeling "very good, very confident. The last year has gone unbelievably fast. A lot of the pressure is removed now. On some levels I can make a mistake without harming anyone and without being called down. If I make a mistake on a piece of paper, I just rip it up and start over."

He's been in a couple of wrestling matches with drunks who came after him. "I realize I could get hurt, but I don't work in fear of it. It's part of the job." He appears far less paranoid than most officers, who will generally go out of their way to park their vehicles or seat themselves in public places in a way to minimize the chance of being approached from behind.

"I don't have that sense of fear or apprehension," he says. "I try to practice good officer safety and I'm alert and aware of my surroundings, but I feel I need to remain visible and accessible to the public. That's one of the things I'm paid to do. I also believe that anyone out to hurt a cop will find a way to do it no matter what the precautions. Where I'm apt to feel paranoid is on traffic stops, especially after dark."

An officer can carry the smell of a DOA in his nostrils for days. These deaths have a sickening sweet odor that permeates clothing. It's a scent that is never forgotten, and some officers keep a cigar handy which they can light to blunt the odor.

Les has worked several recent DOAs, the toughest one just before Christmas. Two sisters arriving from Michigan to visit their elderly father phone him from the airport and, receiving no answer, go to his home. When their knocks at his door are also unanswered, they use a neighbor's phone to call the police.

Les walks to the front door with them, takes a tentative sniff and says, "I'm afraid I'm going to have bad news for you." One of the daughters breaks a window and Les lifts himself in. Their father, fully dressed, is dead on the bathroom floor. Water is trickling into the sink, and a roll of stamps, a sponge and several Christmas cards beside him give mute testimony of his last moments on Earth. Les expresses condolences and limits his questions to the information he needs for his report.

He stops to help a disabled vehicle, pushing it into a shopping center a half-block away. Just as he clears the roadway, the crime-in-progress tone sounds. A bank has been robbed less than 150 feet from where he sits. He advises dispatch he's on the scene and cautiously approaches the front door, gun drawn. An employee reports that the robber left in a car heading west. Les broadcasts the information and, although quads are set up in less than three minutes, the suspect isn't found.

Reflecting on what might have been, Les wonders how he'd have reacted had he been there a minute sooner and seen the robber run out with money in one hand and a gun in the other. "Would I have pushed the woman's car out of the way and gone after him? What if he had jumped into his vehicle and raced away? Suppose he had raised his weapon to shoot? What kind of background did I have for my safety and the safety of bystanders?" He plays and replays the scenarios, then concludes that it has still been a valuable learning experience.

*   *

May 20, 1986. Sergeant Max Davis, who began his career after only two post-Academy days of field training in 1966, opens the daily briefing at 10 a.m. Asked about retirement, he says he's looking forward to it, but is "still waiting for my ship to come in."

Officer Jeff Stahl: "It's out there somewhere, Max."

"Maybe, but my eyes are going bad staring at the horizon."

As briefing ends, he informs the squad that "On this date in 1509, Christopher Columbus died."

Les: "Does that make this a holiday?"

Laughter, then it's time to hit the streets.

His first two assignments are minor traffic accidents. The next is a suspicious person who has been parking outside a bank the past two days, but is gone when Les arrives. A few minutes later, there's a request to check on the welfare of an elderly man. Sam has arthritis and is a little feisty, but tells Les that he's able to take care of himself. Officers — especially rookies — must learn to ask themselves, "Is this really a police matter?" Les concludes that this one isn't, wishes Sam well and leaves.

He tries for a lunch break just before 3 p.m., but is told he's needed in a shopping center parking lot where a man is slumped over in a car. Medics who arrive first tell Les that the man, a Navajo Indian, is dead. Beverly, the woman who found him was a friend, and between tears and sips of soda, she relates how her husband's family shared their home with the dead man as part of a cultural exchange program in the early 1970s. He had begun to drink heavily in recent years and was estranged from his own family. He was warm and caring when he didn't drink, she says, and was typical of many alcoholics in insisting that he didn't have a drinking problem.

He had recently been staying with Beverly and her husband, but there were also young children in the house and his drinking was becoming disruptive, she tells Les. Earlier in the month he was persuaded to enter an alcohol rehabilitation program, but he walked out after only three days. In desperation, Beverly and her husband tried a tough-love approach, telling him he couldn't remain in their home if he was going to drink. He said he understood and left. He had apparently been living in his car for several days, drinking gin much of the time.

Like the families and friends of most victims of sudden death, Beverly says he might still be alive if she had done a little more or tried a little harder. The guilt will give way to sadness that he's gone and anger at what he did. Her nine-year-old daughter, Stacy, wipes away tears and draws some consolation that "at least he's not hurting anymore." Les returns to the police station and begins writing reports. He won't have time for lunch today.

■

Pat Batelli is now Pat Horbarenko. She met her husband, Steve —also a Tucson police officer—while she was an emergency room nurse. Steve's sergeant brought him in with a cactus thorn in his hand, telling Pat to "take care of this big baby."

"He fascinated me," she remembers, "and he'd stop in to say hello when a call brought him to the hospital. You could say that the early courtship took place in ER."

On October 26, 1985, the first anniversary of the death of Pat's mother, they are married in the chilly woods of Pinetop, Arizona by a Justice of the Peace who wears a black robe over his camouflage duck-hunting outfit.

Pat, meanwhile, has completed her field training. "I knew I had to prove myself once again," she says. "There was still the stigma of having washed out of ALETA." She finds it challenging and difficult.

"There was a lot of stress, but I think it was necessary stress. My training officers were very supportive and I learned from each of them. It was still a teacher-student relationship, but they never made me feel dumb or small. One of them was also female and I thought

99

she was being tougher on me than the others were. She told me later that this had been her intention — that we were women in what is still basically men's work and that we had to be better prepared."

Assigned to a new squad at the end of field training, Pat finds herself working under a sergeant "who told me flat out that he didn't believe females should be cops. He was nearing retirement and said he knew that times had changed, but that was the way he felt and nothing would make him change his mind. Then he told me that two or three officers in the squad were also anti-female. He said, 'I don't want you to get alarmed. It's not that they won't back you up (on a call). They'll do that, but I want to let you know what you're up against.'"

Pat feels she endured "a lot of nit-picking" from him in her first weeks on the street. "I felt he was doing things simply to bug me. Then he turned to me one day in the briefing room and said, 'I don't want a fucking cunt in my squad, especially one that washed out.' Those were his exact words in front of several other officers."

She doesn't make a formal complaint. "I didn't want to make waves, but when there was an opportunity to transfer, I did. My new squad has become an extended family. It's like it should be, everyone looking out for everyone else. I'm not afraid to ask questions. I can just be myself."

*   *

Pat wears her shoulder-length brown hair held down in a tight bun. Working her beat, she has a pleasant, easy manner, even in adversarial situations. "I think you have to help people understand that you're a person, too, and not different just because you're a cop." She sometimes has to remind herself that she's no longer a nurse. Her instinct is to be close to people in trauma and comfort them. Being an officer, however, usually means keeping some distance, both from a safety point of view and to do the job efficiently.

She converses easily with a fifteen-year-old girl who says her stepfather has been sexually molesting her. "Are you comfortable telling me what's been happening?" she asks. They talk, and then Pat contacts Child Protective Services to place the girl temporarily with a relative. Sex Crimes detectives will investigate to determine if there is sufficient evidence for an arrest.

Later, a University of Arizona student driving to the campus passes another car and slams into a third one. There are no injuries,

100

but both vehicles are badly damaged. The young driver is upset, her vision momentarily blurred by tears. Her late-model car was to be a gift from her father if she kept an accident-free driving record until her twenty-first birthday. She turns twenty-one later this week and begs Pat, "Don't tell my father." Pat cites her, then drives her to class.

The emergency tone sounds. Alice, a woman in her late seventies and reported as being ill and depressed, has apparently fired a single bullet into her head.

Contrary to popular opinion, instant death from a gunshot wound rarely occurs unless the bullet has gone directly through the brain stem. Even after a shot rips through skin and bone on its way to the heart, the victim might remain conscious for several minutes while 'bleeding out.' With no blood flowing to the brain, however, the damage would soon be irreversible.

Still alive, Alice is rushed to a hospital, but dies within the hour. A pair of pliers is found on the bed next to her, and her eighty-year-old husband tells Pat that she probably used it for leverage in squeezing the trigger. He says she had been threatening suicide for months. It's Pat's scene, and she and her sergeant are not convinced that the woman could have shot herself in the manner her husband has suggested.

Officers sometimes need to ask ugly questions as they search for the truth. This is one of those delicate situations, and Pat must read him his rights before proceeding.

"You don't need to read that to me."

"I'm sorry, but I'm required to before I ask you anything else." She completes the Miranda warning, and then looks him in the eye. "Did you help her shoot herself in any way?" she asks.

"Oh, no; I couldn't do that."

"I"m sorry, but I have to ask you. Did you have any part in what happened?"

"No, of course not."

An investigation finds no evidence to indicate complicity.

*   *

June, 1986 has been a bad month in Tucson. The Prime Time Rapist is still at large despite the largest, most expensive criminal investigation in the county's history. There have also been seven homicides in less than three weeks, most recently the abduction and murder of a two-year-old girl. Tucsonans are angry and fearful, and

101

officers seem equally frustrated. More than 100 calls come in each week from people hearing strange noises outside their homes or seeing someone matching the general description of the rapist.

It has also been a difficult period for Pat. Although not involved in any of the recent high profile cases, she's had several DOAs, including her first suicide.

A young woman phones 911 to report that her boyfriend has been depressed and called to say he was going to shoot himself.

"I walk in," Pat recounts, "and there he is on the couch, dead from a bullet wound through his right temple. He was still in his early twenties and I'm thinking, 'It's such a waste.'"

Later, she responds to another home at the request of a postman who says that an elderly woman's mail had been accumulating.

The woman is dead and the odor is assaultive. "As a nurse, I've seen death and I've seen them all bloody, but not when they've been dead for two weeks. I'd heard stories about the 'floaters,' but I'd never seen one. Her body had literally burst and fluids were all over the floor. What wasn't decomposed had turned black. It was difficult to look at her and realize that she had been a human being. I went to several neighbors and no one even knew her. It was just sad that she died alone and no one had missed her."

A few days after that incident, Pat is called to the home of another elderly woman who also slipped from life unnoticed. Although she's been dead for several days, her dogs, dehydrated and hungry, still guard her body. They won't let Pat near, so Animal Control is called to tranquilize them and make them give up their loyal vigil.

Soon after, Pat drives to a manufacturing plant where a woman's head has been crushed in a punch press. Pat must begin the investigation, handle the paperwork and arrange to have the victim's family notified.

Pat saw trauma and suffering as an emergency room nurse, but in that career most of the people survived.

"What I'm finding now," she laments, "is that I walk in and so many of them are already dead, and I haven't been able to do anything to help. I look at them and try to think of them alive. It's a new experience, something I'm learning to deal with. There are a lot of procedures to follow, so I keep busy, but I just wish I had ten quiet minutes alone with them, to think about who they were, what kind of life they had and the people who will grieve that they're gone. It may sound weird, but it's what I wish I could do."

5

Amazing Grace

The incidence of divorce among cops is high, and officers must learn to cope both with the built-in stress of the job itself and with a changing work schedule that plays havoc with family life. As they begin their second year on patrol, several of their marriages are in crisis.

For Jeff Moore, 1986 suddenly becomes the worst year of his life when his wife tells him she's fallen in love with a mutual friend. "My brain said it was happening, but my heart didn't want to believe it," Jeff says, trying to make sense of the situation. Nancy has moved out of their house and Jeff is the walking-wounded, his mind far from the job.

"I wasn't being effective," he admits later. "I'd sit in a shopping center parking lot for hours, waiting for a motorist to run a light. It was stupid stuff, something I don't normally do. What I was saying was, 'I'm angry, I'm hurting inside and I'm going to make you have a lousy day.' And that's just what I did, day after day. I spotted them, drove after them, cited them and then went back to wait for the next one.

"They were legitimate tickets, but the way I did it wasn't fair. I must have written thirty-five or forty citations before I started seeing the human beings behind the wheel and realized I was short-changing the public and other officers who might have to count on me in an emergency."

Two months later, after counseling and a temporary transfer to a desk job, he has begun sorting out the emotional debris. "I made some mistakes in the marriage, but I know what happened wasn't my fault. I took too much for granted, especially the love of another person. My sixteen-month-old doesn't really know what's happen-

103

ing, but the six-year old understands that mommy doesn't live here now. Nancy comes over to visit the kids, and we talk a little."

In his initial anger, Jeff started divorce proceedings, but now he's holding off. "I need time to work things out and see if we can get back together and have a normal life. I'm also prepared to go through with the divorce and carry on without her. Her leaving was the most traumatic thing I ever experienced, but if it hadn't happened, a lot of things within me wouldn't have changed. I've learned to cry, to talk about feelings, to survive pain and see life a lot more clearly. I had to decide if I wanted to remain hurt and disabled, or pull myself up and get on with life. There's still the need to be loved by somebody and to be held at night, but it's in a different perspective. It will come in time, with Nancy or someone else."

*   *

November, 1986. Two days after local elections, a man is using his van to knock down signs placed on behalf of political candidates. Jeff gets out of his car and walks up to him. "You bet I did it," he says.

Jeff reads the twenty-one-year-old University of Arizona psychology student his Miranda rights, then: "You want to tell me about it?"

"Sure," the blond-haired six-footer replies cheerfully. "The election's over. There's no reason for them to be up, I'm tired of looking at them and I'm here to run them over."

"Are you upset because your candidate didn't win?"

The young man is an equal-opportunity destroyer.

"No, it's nothing personal."

"Are these the only two?"

"Oh, no! I've knocked over a whole bunch of them, about twenty-five, I guess. I drive a route and when I see 'em, I run 'em over. I don't pay any attention to the little ones; it's the big ones I'm after. I think they're obnoxious."

Jeff agrees that the signs are obnoxious, but says he has to cite him for criminal damage because candidates are given thirty days after an election to remove them.

In mid-month, Jeff is involved in two foot chases. First, officers spot a fourteen-year-old runaway who is also a suspect in a burglary ring. As the youngster runs from them, Jeff and two other officers watch for a few seconds, looking at each other as if to ask, "Who is going to chase him?" Then, in the same instant, all three begin pursuit as the boy sprints across the street and down an alley. Jeff knocks him off his feet with a flying tackle. The boy's face momentarily eats asphalt, but he wriggles free and pulls himself over a fence before Jeff catches up again. The arrest 'clears' several neighborhood burglaries and aids in recovering some of the stolen items.

Two days later, a neighborhood fight is reported. The suspect has a series of tattoos which cover most of his exposed skin. A dirty baseball cap rests precariously on the left side of his head. A computer check shows he's wanted on two felony warrants for aggravated assault.

Told he's under arrest, he immediately takes off. He hurdles a fence, races several hundred feet into the desert and then back out, ripping his shirt on barbed wire. With Jeff and another officer still in pursuit, he runs through a resident's yard, down a parallel street, and skitters up yet another fence, momentarily disappearing over the edge. Jeff had just finished lunch when the call came in, and the meal is bouncing in his stomach as he keeps up the chase. The man is finally cornered three blocks away.

A little later, an hysterical woman runs into a convenience store to report that her estranged husband has locked himself and their six-month-old daughter inside her apartment. She's afraid he'll harm the baby.

Jeff and two other officers go to the home, identify themselves and tell him to come to the door. There's no response. With a child's life possibly at risk, Jeff splinters the door with one well-placed kick, and they walk in, guns extended. The man is lying quietly in bed, one arm under the baby. Without a word, Jeff scoops up the sleeping infant from one side of the bed as the other officers move in from the opposite side and pin him down.

*   *

It's just after 9 a.m. two days before Thanksgiving. An eighty-six-year-old woman skids her car through a railway crossing gate and it comes to rest at the edge of the tracks. Seconds later, a Southern Pacific Railroad engine pulling thirty-three loaded freight cars slams into her 1987 Chevrolet. The train's speed at impact is less than fifteen miles an hour, but it weighs 3,493 tons — more than seven million pounds.

Although the car is dragged nearly 400 feet as the train brakes to a grinding halt, the woman is coherent and stands without assistance after workers from a nearby business pull her from the wreckage. Medics arrive, place a brace on her neck and take her to a hospital for observation. Jeff interviews witnesses and helps direct traffic at the crossing while what's left of the car is disengaged from the train's engine. The woman dies four weeks later from lung injuries and a lacerated liver.

*   *

As the holidays approach, Jeff — still dealing with his ambivalent feelings — has invited Nancy to move back into their home temporarily. She's found a job and plans to share an apartment with a female friend in January.

"We're friends now, at least most of the time," Jeff says. "Our time together is generally pleasant, and even when we argue, we're still communicating." They've been sleeping together, and Jeff is surprised to hear that this is not unusual for people who once had a close marriage. "I thought it was crazy that we're doing it."

They're both holding on in some ways as they move toward what might be an emotional closure of the marriage. Meanwhile, their time together has removed much of Jeff's loneliness.

Jeff hasn't yet confronted his friend, but the anger is not disguised. "If he were to die today, I'd throw a party. I'd celebrate. I'd toast his death. It would be like *The Wizard of Oz*: Ding, dong, the witch is dead." A short pause, then, "I guess I need to get back into counseling."

Although he generally seems to have separated police work from his personal problems, there are occasional signs of impatience when he's dealing with the public. Tonight he's in a parking lot citing a driver for speeding. His patrol car is blocking another vehicle, whose driver politely asks, "Can I get my car out of here?" Jeff responds testily: "When I'm finished."

*   *

February 20, 1987: It's one year to the day since Miguel was shot dead in the carnival confrontation, and the mention of his name still triggers a rush of emotion. Jeff has handled nearly 2,000 calls since that night when a young man died on the desert floor while strangers knelt to stain their hands with his blood, but the scene remains as vivid as a flash of lightning. "You never really get used to death, especially a child's," he says, sadness in his voice.

He has the ability to retain a staggering amount of information.

106

He remembers names, addresses and detailed circumstances of calls he worked months ago. Most officers carry pads filled with notes for future reference. Jeff does this, too, but appears to have much of it tucked away in his head.

Just after midnight, a driver in a blue Datsun attempts to run down a group of young people. They scurry to safety and are able to get the vehicle's license plate number. They tell Jeff that the driver appeared to be in his early teens. A computer check shows that the plate is indeed associated with a Datsun matching the description provided by the witnesses. Moreover, the car's owner lives less than two miles away.

Jeff drives to the house, but the Datsun isn't there. Lights are visible inside and a woman responds to his knock. Her thirteen-year-old son was able to take the car without permission by going to his bedroom, closing the door and turning up the volume on a tape player to cover the noise of his departure. This isn't the first time he's lifted the keys and taken off, she says. Jeff asks her to phone 911 when the boy returns.

A few minutes after going back on the street, Jeff spots a blue Datsun parked to the side of a road. He pulls alongside and shines a light in the front seat. A man and woman, half seated and half reclining, are locked in an embrace. Jeff accelerates and drives on, laughing at the recollection of a similar incident several days earlier. While responding to a woman's complaint that a car had been parked on her property for nearly an hour, Jeff found a young couple sprawled across the seat in mid-act. "Can you wait 'til we're done?" the man asked, barely looking up at Jeff standing outside with a flashlight in his hand.

*   *

Two men with a gun rob an all-night convenience store at 1:57 a.m. Although Jeff and four other officers are there within minutes, no one is found.

At 2:54, the emergency tone sounds. "Sector One units, we have a gun shot victim at 541 South Santa Paula."

Jeff knows that Santa Paula is an east-west street. He questions dispatch and the correction is made.

Seconds later: "We're now getting information that there's a rust-colored Camaro involved, possibly a seventy-two or seventy-three, last seen going east down the alley."

Jeff drives aggressively — to an observer it sometimes borders on white-knuckle motoring — but his propensity for speed hasn't yet come back to haunt him. He reaches the house in less than two minutes. Several people are milling around outside, and he strides toward them.

"Where's the person who was shot?"

"They're gone," a man says, referring to the suspects and ignoring Jeff's question.

"Was anybody shot?"

"No, no one got shot; they just took off down the alley."

"Did they fire any shots?"

"Yeah, a lot of shots."

Several others who had been partying in the house begin to drift outside and now there are several people talking at once. Two more patrol cars pull up, their red flashing roof-top lights playing across Jeff's face. Air One flies overhead and begins a series of ever-widening circles.

A thin, well-dressed young Hispanic woman bounds out of the house and approaches Jeff. She tries to speak, but she's crying so hysterically that her words are lost. Finally, pointing to the house: "He's hurt." An ambulance screeches around the corner as Jeff follows her inside. A young man is bleeding from the lower arm. As the medics begin treating him, Jeff and the other officers question witnesses and broadcast additional information on the suspects.

The shooting has followed an evening of drinking, and the details are fragmented. What appears clear is that one young man, described as six feet, six inches tall and weighing nearly 300 pounds, became combative.

"He began pointing around the room, yelling, 'I'll take on you and you and you,'" one of them tells Jeff. Told to leave, he stalked out, but soon returned in the Camaro, accompanied by two or three other men. "He just stepped out and began firing. I saw a flash, heard a pop, and then I just started pulling people down on the floor."

Nearly an hour after the brief volley of shots, the Hispanic woman is still sobbing as a friend attempts to comfort her in the beautiful cadence of fluent Spanish. The shooting victim — just grazed by a bullet — says he doesn't need to go to the hospital. He stands over the kitchen sink dousing his wound with 100-proof tequila.

Soon, it's approaching 5 a.m., and the city sleeps. Jeff spends the next hour cruising, hoping for a sighting that might resolve something, "*Anything,*" he says, in this night of loose ends. It isn't to be. As dawn begins to light the eastern sky, no one has been arrested in the robbery or the shooting, and the thirteen-year-old has not returned home.

*   *

Friday, May 15, 1987, and Jeff is working early evenings. Teenagers, reported to be snorting cocaine behind a vacant house, are gone. A pickup truck is stalled at an intersection. Jeff pushes it off the road, then drives the stranded motorist to meet friends at a restaurant three miles away. A young couple complain that kids in their apartment complex are congregating under their window and yelling profanities. All Jeff can do is suggest that they speak with their property manager.

Next, a husband and wife accuse each other of drinking too much and then threatening physical harm. Both agree they're sometimes that way, but that's all they'll concede as they play off of each other with a series of putdowns. The man pushes a change of clothing into a suitcase and leaves, at least for tonight.

A traffic stop. The driver has fictitious plates, an expired registration and no proof of insurance. He picks up more than $200 in citations. A man is reported to be sitting in a woman's car and refusing to leave. She doesn't know him. He runs into the desert about thirty seconds before Jeff pulls up. Two officers search on foot for fifteen minutes, but the suspect is gone. A group of teens is behaving suspiciously outside a movie theater. Several of them run off before Jeff arrives, and those remaining deny that anything happened.

Two officers mediating a family fight don't answer when the dispatcher does a radio check on their welfare. Jeff starts up in case they're in trouble, but seconds later they advise they're okay. Next, there's a traffic accident, with a fight brewing, in front of a nearby convenience store. The driver of one of the vehicles is gone by the time Jeff arrives. Jeff cruises the neighborhood without success. Just before the shift ends, a pregnant woman swallows most of a bottle of sleeping pills and her boyfriend calls 911. Conscious, she's taken by ambulance to the hospital for observation.

It's been a slow Friday night. No chases, no arrests, no one dead or dying.

*   *

Nancy would like to come home and resume their marriage. Carrying a big torch, Jeff has been unsuccessfully chasing her for

109

months, and now is unsure of her motives or sincerity. Despite his obvious brains and good looks, he wonders if other women will find him attractive. He's recently begun dating a woman ten years his senior. She's attractive, bright, exciting and caring. Jeff doesn't know if the relationship has a future, but it's what he's been needing. For the first time in a year, he has the appearance of a man emotionally fulfilled.

■

Despite the risks faced by law enforcement officers, few are killed in the line of duty. Nationally, ninety-six died in 1986, and the number of fatalities has declined sharply in the past decade. Other on-the-job hazards, although seldom fatal, are far more pervasive.

Investigating a report that two teenagers are firing weapons in a desert area, Anita Sueme joins another officer already searching on foot. As she works her way down the rocky terrain in near-darkness, something gives way and she turns her ankle. Doctors diagnose a bad sprain, forcing her on crutches for nearly a month.

With the Prime Time Rapist still at large, Anita is assigned to help with the investigation while her ankle heals. Law enforcement officials receive dozens of tips and possible sightings every week, and each must be checked out, processed and filed. Working at the Task Force headquarters, Anita helps organize the mass of paperwork. She also takes telephone calls from fearful women and those offering leads.

A few facts relating to the rapist and his method of operation have not been made public. One of them is that a specific portion of his lower anatomy has been described by several victims as unusually large.

"Some women call in saying they think their former husband or ex-boyfriend might be the rapist," Anita relates. "I'll be taking information on the basis for their suspicion and, of course, I ask for a complete physical description. Eventually, I say, 'Ma'am, I need to ask you one more thing: Was he well-endowed?'" The responses range from silence to giggles to "How would I know?"

Anita is back on the street in August, still uncomfortable with the lack of flexibility in her ankle. Midway in her first week, she's dispatched to the Mountain Bell parking lot where another Prime Time Rapist lookalike has been seen "lurking behind a truck." Anita checks the area, then turns her attention to the young man who phoned 911.

Brandon is a precocious six-year-old with a full head of curly blond hair and the ear-to-ear grin of a kid who has just found the hidden cookies. He tells Anita that "me and my friends have sticks and we're going to catch him."

Anita kneels to thank him, but warns that the rapist often carries a gun. "Just call us again if you think you see him," she says. Brandon's possible sighting will be passed on to the Task Force.

As the summer winds down, she's having more ankle trouble and running has become impossible. "I was limping around so much, it looked like I was the victim," she says. An orthopaedic surgeon finds that ligaments have been stretched and are not keeping the ankle in its socket. Anita is again taken from her beat and placed in a ten-week rehabilitation program.

She misses the streets. "I've become so much more outgoing. I feel good out there meeting the victims and sometimes even the suspects, and I get a lot of personal satisfaction helping people. Sometimes I wish I could help them more, especially young women who are stuck in a bad relationship with kids to take care of and no money and no real job skills. I was in a situation once where I got kicked in the ass by an affair I blundered into. I would have gladly gotten pregnant at the time. I realize now that not many Prince Charmings exist, and you have to be self-sufficient first and able to make it on your own."

*   *

She resumes patrol in November confident that her ankle has finally healed. The first real test comes three weeks later. A chronic runaway has been located and Anita is dispatched to pick her up. Denise, a feisty fifteen-year-old, begins screaming as soon as Anita says she'll be taken to Juvenile Court.

She sprints from the house, Anita and another officer on her heels. The second officer runs a few steps, pulls a hamstring in his leg and falls to the ground in pain. Anita slows momentarily, but he waves her on, then gets into his patrol car and pulls ahead of them. She resumes the chase, and Denise is quickly caught and hand-cuffed.

"Calm down, you picked the wrong day of the month to mess with me," Anita tells her. Denise has an answer for everything, and

Anita finally stops talking to her.

It's her week for teens on the loose. Three days later, a middle-aged man calls police to report his fifteen-year-old son missing. He says that Tom has a history of discipline problems, that he ran away after an argument, but returned to burglarize the house. Questioned by Anita, however, he says that the only missing items are bedding, some of his son's clothing and two bottles of liquor.

The man says that Tom's Juvenile Court case worker wants him brought in for violation of his probation terms. Anita attempts to confirm this, but the case worker is at lunch, so she drives to the high school where Tom is enrolled.

The pure and simple truth, according to Oscar Wilde, is rarely pure and seldom simple. Tom immediately claims that he was kicked out of the house.

"Your father tells me that you broke in and took some stuff."

"It was mine," he says, denying that he took any liquor.

"You say your father kicked you out?"

"Yeah, but I'm staying with someone right now."

"Okay, I know where you're staying. I didn't tell your father, though. I won't do that. The reason I'm not arresting you right away is that I'm trying to give you the benefit of the doubt."

"What are you going to arrest me for?"

"Well, if it were anything, it would be as a runaway."

Tom, a plump young man not much more than five feet tall, is teary-eyed.

"You've been real cooperative so far. I appreciate it," she assures him. "I'll put that in my report, and in the future I can testify that you did everything I told you to."

A few minutes later, Anita reaches the case worker.

"She's emphatic about taking you down there, Tom. I'd prefer to not have to handcuff you when I take you out to my car. I know it would embarrass the hell out of you in front of the other kids. We don't want to do that, do we?"

He shakes his head and uses his forearm to brush away silent tears.

"I don't want to have to chase you if you run. I already had to do that once this week, and I run pretty fast."

"I'm not going to run."

The bell sounds for change of class, and Anita decides to wait until the halls have cleared so Tom will encounter fewer students.

Tom vents his hurt and frustration as they drive to Juvenile Court. He says he has a grandmother and a married sister in

Michigan, but that his parents won't let him live there. He admits that he ditches school with his friends a couple of times a week. He claims his father told him he had to pay $175 rent by the end of the month or be kicked out, and that's why he left. "Just because my parents don't want me, how come I'm going to jail?" he asks.

"I know you're getting stuck in the middle of a real unfortunate situation."

Tom's anger surfaces as soon as his case worker walks into the interview room. "He kicked me out of the house."

"I understand that, I know that," the case worker retorts. *"Why* did your dad kick you out of the house?"

"Because I didn't pay rent."

"Why didn't you pay rent? Why did you have to pay rent, Tom?"

"Because I was getting calls from school."

"Why?"

"Because I wasn't attending."

"Are you supposed to attend school?"

"Yes."

"That's it. That's the bottom line."

"And you're filing charges against me for breaking in my own house?"

"Your parents are filing charges against you for breaking into your own house."

"Isn't it against the law to kick me out?"

"You're right, but it's also against the law for you not to go to school. So where do we start? Do you want to start way back when you were six years old in Michigan? Do you want to start way back then? You can keep blaming and blaming and blaming and blaming, but you are going to be the one in jail unless you decide to change the way you act. *You* decide whether you want to live in jail or not!"

"No, I don't!"

"Well, then you'd better start showing that you don't want to. Right now, you're not showing that, and right now you're gonna be in jail."

The case worker contacts Tom's parents and advises them to be in court the next morning for a hearing. Tom asks to speak with his dad. He's crying as he asks, "Why are you filing charges against me? . . Does mom feel the same way? . . Then why don't you let me go back to Michigan and live with grandma?"

Anita feels bad for Tom and would like to stay and offer encouragement, but she has no jurisdiction now. She says goodbye and leaves.

*   *

All Tucson Police Department officers, regardless of rank, attend periodic field training to maintain and enhance their skills. It's the week before Christmas and fifteen of them are taking three days of driver training. Anita, less than two years out of the Academy, is part of the class. So is Deputy Police Chief Leonard Dietsch, a cop for nearly thirty years.

Most of the first day is spent on the pursuit course, a series of figure eights, half-circles and hairpin turns, with a few short straightaways mixed in. Three or four to a car, they drive around the course to feel its layout. For today's practice, there's a nine-foot thruway between the plastic cones. Tomorrow, it will be narrowed to seven feet, just twelve inches more than the width of a patrol car.

From a tower above the course, instructor Ed Lee runs the show. "Car ready? Timer ready? Go!" He scores officers on a combination of elapsed time, the ability to negotiate the track without knocking down cones, and on their steering, acceleration and braking techniques. The odor of burning rubber and the sounds of acceleration and squealing tires belie the otherwise tranquil desert setting. They each do two runs and then gather for a critique.

"The screeching tires mean you're going too fast," Lee tells them. "The tires are losing traction; they're starting to skid and slide. They can only do so much. Your steering wheel will turn the rim, but the rubber itself is flexing. It's trying to play catch-up. You're turning the rim, but the wheel is still going the other way. Movie and TV scenes of police vehicles sliding around corners and going sideways are just for drama. It's poor technique and unsafe driving."

Following the general comments, officers are given individual feedback.

"The first run was a little jerky," Anita is told. "There's a tendency to panic when we miss one turn. Our hands begin to shuffle and we're thinking, 'Oh, no, here comes another one!' You were more in control the second time. The handling was smoother. Just try to relax a little more."

Next, officers drive along a 1,000-foot straightaway, gradually picking up speed as they bear down on a series of plastic cones which block their way. Lanes to the left and right of the barrier are lined with two rows of cones, providing a twelve-foot roadway between them. As they're about to topple the barrier, an instructor in the passenger seat calls out "Left!" or "Right!" There is less than seven-tenths of a second to veer as directed, and when this maneuver

114

is immediately and properly followed by two additional sharp turns of the wheel, the vehicle remains in one of the parallel lanes and all cones stand intact.

Instructor Mark Thomas provides perspective: "That barrier you're driving toward can be a box that fell from a truck in front of you or a child on a bike who just pulled in your path. Panic stops often come too late to avoid collisions, and this exercise is to show that you can evade rather than brake."

"Don't touch the brake," he tells them. "If you start to fishtail after you've made the lane change, snap the steering wheel a little bit to straighten the car and regain control. If you hit the dirt, try and keep the wheels going straight. If you find yourself headed for the fence, try to straighten your vehicle and bring it to a slow stop. Be careful to avoid sharp steering. That may cause you to start digging into the dirt. If you dig in too deep, you'll cause an abrupt stop and that's what makes a car flip over."

From a safe distance on the sidelines, Anita observes more than a dozen runs by two other officers and helps replace their flattened cones.

Dietsch, finishing his exercise: "Sorry about all those cones you had to pick up." Laughter.

It's Anita's turn, and she seems tense as she drives with Thomas to the head of the straightaway.

"Get your front wheels centered. . . Heel on the floor at the accelerator. . . Hands on the wheel at three and nine (o'clock). . . Remember to keep your shoulders square. . . We're going to start out at thirty-five (miles per hour). I want you to clear your mind, listen for your cue and react. Go ahead."

Anita accelerates. She's at the barrier in thirteen seconds.

"RIGHT!"

No cones have been touched. Her maneuver appears clean, but it isn't.

"You didn't counter-steer quite enough, so you drifted toward the right," Thomas tells her.

She U-turns and drives back to the starting position.

"Okay, let's go. Thirty-five. . . LEFT! . . . You're trying to hold on with your fingers and getting (unwanted) shoulder action into it. It slows you down and that's why you got that corner cone there."

"Okay. Thirty-five. . . LEFT!"

Anita, going right instead: "Oh, shit! Sorry about that."

"A little anticipation there." Laughter from both, then: "Don't stare at the cones. Pick up something on the horizon to concentrate on. When you anticipate it's because you're worried about how close you're getting and you figure you have to turn. You not only went the wrong way, but you started doing it before I even gave my command."

"Go ahead. Thirty Five. . . LEFT! . . . See your fingers, how tight they were. That's how you got all that shoulder action in there. You got through the exercise, but at higher speeds you wouldn't have made it. Extend your left leg so it's not in your way. . . Your hands are a little bit low. . . That's better."

"Let's give it a try at forty. . . RIGHT! . . . A little indecision. Your maneuver was fine, but you paused and that's how you got the corner cone. You're doing fine at this, Anita. There's no reason you need to be nervous about it. You're not doing badly. I want you to just relax."

"Okay, forty. . . LEFT!. . . That was good!. . . We're going to continue at forty, but I'm going to change your cue to 'now!' You pick which way you're going to go; just make sure you keep mixing them up. Don't start until you hear your cue, though."

The next run leaves all of the cones standing. "You did okay with it that time and you didn't move your hands around. When I said, 'Now!' you immediately started your body lean. It was easy, wasn't it? Hanging on with your fingers is the only thing you've been doing wrong. Just stay relaxed and believe you'll be able to do it."

Anita smiles, but she doesn't believe.

*   *

Three months later, Anita's ankle has caused no further problem. An hour into the shift, medics respond to a 'man down' report and radio for police backup. A slim young man wearing tennis shoes, socks and slacks is yelling about the fighting in Vietnam, but he's clearly not old enough to have served there. He becomes increasingly combative and it takes Anita and four others to restrain him so that he can be transported to a hospital for a psychological evaluation. When his parents are located, they report that he'd been "a normal kid," but lately had begun acting strangely. They relate how they went into his bedroom recently and found several photographs of him as a child lined up on the floor, each with a bullet hole through it.

Next, Anita is dispatched to a hospital to interview an assault victim. Susan is an admitted alcoholic who lay unconscious for nearly two hours after being beaten by her boyfriend. Her face is cut and bruised, patches of hair are matted in blood and her left eye is nearly swollen shut. She's coming down from the effects of both the alcohol and the beating.

Although the treatment room is warm and there's a blanket over her clothing, she shivers as she says, "I gave up my little girl to be with him." A warrant is issued for her boyfriend, but with hundreds of similar cases on the books, it's not likely he'll be located, arrested and jailed. In any event, she's gone back to him before and there's little reason to believe that she won't do it again.

A man in his mid-thirties drives his month-old Dodge pickup truck into a sixteen-year-old Buick. The truck gets the worst of it and the driver is cited for not controlling his speed. He's angry at himself and not thinking too clearly.

"Don't worry about it now," Anita advises him gently. "Just go home and relax and deal with it in a day or two." He takes a deep breath, thanks her and leaves.

The manager of a drug store reports that a drunken man refuses to leave the business. Anita spots the suspect leaning against a nearby phone booth. She asks for identification and tells him there has been a complaint that he's interfering with customers. He gropes through several pockets before producing a Social Security card. A second officer looks at it, tosses it to the ground near his feet and tells him brusquely that he'll be arrested if he doesn't move on.

Using the metal frame of the phone booth for support, he takes more than thirty seconds to bend over, retrieve his ID and get back on his feet. He mutters a mild protest and begins a staggering walk to the fringe of the parking lot. A young couple sitting in a car twenty feet away has watched the episode unfold. Anita is bothered by the way the second officer handled the incident. "He's had a real tough week," she says, "but I wish he'd handed the man his ID instead of throwing it at him."

Anita is a realist when it comes to her impact on the community. "I don't really expect to make a lot of difference. I know what the judicial system is like and I know I'm not going to make much of a dent in it. I can't change society. Where I think I can do some good is treating people nicely, helping them over the rough spots and letting them know that I care. The drunks we see are people, too. They weren't just born on the street."

She is well aware of the 'Us Against Them' syndrome. "I know a lot of cops end up feeling that way and I don't ever want to get to that. It's true that the lives of many cops revolve around each other both on and off the job. It's real easy to get into that pattern because of the work we do and shifts that change every three months. I see some of that happening to me already and I know I need to find time

117

for other people and activities. Right now I have no outside social life at all."

The uniform doesn't help. "Most male officers look good in it and there are lots of women who see one and begin drooling, but it doesn't do much for me. The guys see me in one all the time, and it's not really very feminine. I get noticed when I come in wearing a dress and heels. That's when guys walk up and realize, 'Hey, she's a female; she actually has a body.'"

Intoxicated males are still coming on to her, though. "One man I pulled over looked at me and said, 'You're not a cop. Everybody knows that female cops are fat and ugly, but you're gorgeous.' I wasn't sure whether to take that as a compliment or not."

She says she feels no pressure in what is still primarily men's work. "We're supportive of each other. They respond to some of my calls to see if they can help and I do the same. They know that I won't hesitate to jump into the middle of a fight."

She's begun wearing contact lenses because "one of these days I'm gonna get popped and I don't want my glasses to go flying." Still, she worries occasionally. "I think female cops need to push to be as good or better than the men. Maybe I'm too hard on myself, but I'm not there yet, and that's why I spend so much time improving my skills."

*   *

It's just after sunrise on June 10, 1987, and an early-summer mist hangs over the Tucson valley as Anita walks to her patrol car. Four hours into the shift, a woman complains that a neighbor in her small apartment complex is mentally ill and threatening to assault her. Anita talks to the complainant, then walks across the narrow courtyard to get the other side of the story.

"Grace, it's the police department. Can I come in and talk to you?"

"You bet you can; just come right in. You'll be a relief from all the others."

As Anita walks inside, Grace slams the door shut on a shocked second officer bringing up the rear. Anita quickly opens it.

"Who are *you?*" Grace screams at the backup officer, though her uniform is a carbon copy of Anita's.

"She's with me," Anita assures her. The small apartment is dominated by rags, papers and clothing. The ample overflow rests in cluttered piles on the floor. The livingroom floor displays twenty-one pair of shoes. The slim woman appears to be in her sixties. She's

118

wearing slacks three or four sizes too large for her, rolled up nearly to her knees. A blue tank top fits better, but periodically slips off of her left shoulder. Her hair is long and in its disheveled state looks like a half-bleached rag mop. Whatever else she is now, it's obvious that she was once a very attractive woman.

"I never open my door to anybody. I'm an old woman and I've taken so much around here I don't know what to do," she tells Anita.

"Okay, Grace, come on and sit down so we can talk."

Grace walks tentatively to the sofa and sits. She begins in a baby-like babble, then, screams, "I'm sick of this city!"

Anita, softly: "Don't scream; try to relax."

"How can I relax? I'm seventy years old!"

"What happened today?"

"I don't know. I can't remember."

"Apparently you hit someone outside."

Shaking her head from side to side: "No, I didn't hit anybody. I wasn't out of the house. How could I hit anybody? I was not out of the house and I don't *hit* people! They make it up!"

"Okay, Grace, just relax."

"Why don't you believe me? Why do you listen to that jealous bitch over there? You don't listen to *my* truth."

"I'm trying to get your side of the story."

"I'm not an evil person; I'm a good person."

"I didn't say you were an evil person."

"Why do you take somebody's evil side against me?"

Anita decides it's time to change the subject: "Do you take any medicine, Grace?"

Softly, almost childish now: "I don't take any medicine, no." Then, voice rising again: "What do you mean by medicine?"

"Do you see a doctor for anything?"

"No! What the hell would I see a doctor for? I'm a healthy human being! I don't know what the hell to do. I'm ready to kill myself I'm so scared."

"What are you scared of?"

"What do you mean! I'm scared of the God-damned people across the way! I'm scared of people doing things to me."

"Grace, people around here aren't going to hurt you. The little old lady's not going to hurt you."

"What little old lady?"

"The lady who lives across the way. The little old tiny lady. She won't hurt you."

Getting up and peering out of the window: "Who? Where's that little old tiny lady?"

"She's not standing outside because we told her to stay inside. You want to sit back down?"

"I've been here all day minding my own business watching television! I don't do anything to anybody! I just sit here and when I need to go to the store, I go to the store!"

"Do you drive or do you walk?"

"I walk! Drive? What the hell would I drive with? I *walk!*"

"I don't know. I was just asking."

"I don't have a car, honey. I don't have anything. I don't have a bedroom. I sleep here. I spend a lot of money for this place and I'm tired of being used and taken advantage of and being all alone."

"Don't you know anyone in Tucson?"

"No, no I don't. I never have."

"How long have you been in Tucson?"

"Well, I'll tell you. I came from New York City. I was a model in New York City and I met people and when I fell and broke my wrist, somebody told me I should come out here to Tucson. I came here and since I came here I don't know where I am and what I'm doing here."

As she relates this, her words again become almost unintelligible.

"Grace, when did you come out here?"

"I don't remember."

"Was it a year ago? Ten years ago? In the 1960s?"

A momentary smile hides the sadness trapped inside as she reaches back to a better time: "I lost somebody in Connecticut. I loved Buck from the first day we met. He had his own business and he died. He died and I was alone and I don't remember anything more. I just don't remember. I was so alone and sick. Do you know what it's like to be alone forever and ever?"

She chokes on her memories. A pause, then: "There was an apartment ad in the paper. It said $135, so I came up here to see it. Next thing you know it was $150, then $190."

"Well, rents do go up."

"In one month?"

"Grace, do you know what today is?"

"No. I don't know."

"Do you know what year it is?"

"No, I don't really know."

"You have no idea what year it is?"

"No, I don't."

"Do you know if it's spring or summer?"

"Well I think it's summer, or something."

"Well, we're kind of all baking, so I guess it's summer."

"It doesn't mean anything to me whether it's spring, summer or what it is." Then, apropos of nothing: "What are you going to do to me?"

"I'm not doing anything to you."

"The hell! Everybody is! The whole damn place is! They're just jealous of me! Don't you understand what jealousy is? I was a famous model in New York City! I've had so much God-damned jealousy around here!"

"Okay, Grace, I'm trying to find out. . . ."

"'Cause I'm a nice person and I'm so good looking."

"You're a nice person, and. . . ."

"And also very good looking!"

"You're also very good looking."

"That's the main problem! It's because I got so much damned sex appeal." Grace looks down and begins an animated series of pelvic thrusts. "I'm sick of this God-damned sex appeal! What the hell's with this damned sex appeal? I wish I could give it to someone! Damn, I wish I could give it away! I wish I weren't so damned good looking, I wouldn't have this trouble. Every day I say to God, 'why don't you take this stuff away from me?' What the hell do you do with so much sex appeal?"

"Grace, I'm jealous, because when you got it. . . ."

"Why? Be God-damned glad you don't have it!"

Again changing the subject: "You also said that you're real scared of being here by yourself."

"I *am!* I'm scared of that damned bitch! I'm scared of everybody in this city. I'm scared as *hell* of this city!"

"I'm going to see if I can get somebody to help you out, okay? But I have to ask you some questions about yourself."

"I know, I don't mind. I'm seventy. I'm from Connecticut. That's where I lost somebody that I loved. He died in Connecticut and I didn't know what to do with myself any more. I was sick as hell. . . ."

Grace spends the next half-hour retelling the story of her life. As the largely one-sided conversation continues, other social service agencies are called in for consultation. The consensus is to take Grace to a hospital for mental and physical evaluations, but she refuses and Anita doesn't feel she can document that Grace poses an imminent danger to herself or others. There's nothing to do but

121

leave.

Grace follows Anita outside, takes several steps in the mid-day heat and topples over backward. Anita now has probable medical cause and radios for an ambulance. The medics are young and good-looking, a reality that doesn't elude Grace. She chats with them for a few minutes, remaining calm most of the time, and then allows them to take her to a hospital where she'll remain while city and state agencies work out a plan to help her cope with life.

■

In a profession where shift changes can produce both physical and emotional havoc, Robert Garcia and his family are coping well, all the more so considering that there are three young children at home. As the summer of 1986 begins, Robert completes three months on the midnight shift and goes to a 7 p.m. start. He'll spend the year moving backward against the clock, cycling next to 3 p.m., then 10 a.m., and finally 6 a.m.

It's July 19, 1986. A woman phones 911, crying that her husband is assaulting her. Robert is one of two officers who respond. Attempts to calm Steve fail, and he takes a swing at Robert's partner. Robert jumps into the fracas, and as he helps wrestle the man to the floor, Steve's wife begins yelling and cursing at the cops she had called for protection less than fifteen minutes earlier.

The officers could easily knock the fight out of Steve with a nightstick, but they're trying to subdue him with a minimum of physical force. Now three young kids are awake, crying and screaming as they see their father being handcuffed.

The house is filthy. Grease in the kitchen appears to have been building up for months, dirty dishes are everywhere and roaches are crawling across the floor and walls. The three-year-old sits on the couch, pulling inch-long insects out of his hair and Robert periodically kicks his feet to knock the roaches off of his boots. It reminds him of a call he had when he was an officer in Santa Fe — "A house so dirty I wiped my feet on the way *out*."

Child Protective Services will be asked to evaluate the youngsters' living conditions.

Just after dusk, Robert is dispatched to a southside home. A slim, sad-eyed woman, who has left her husband and filed for a divorce, has come to remove some furniture, clothing and personal belongings. She says that he can be volatile, "A bull who carries around his own china shop."

Tonight, he is finishing a fast-food dinner which he has washed down with at least three cans of beer. Pausing in mid-chew, he grouses, but tells her to take what she wants. She, her two teenage children and a couple of friends shuttle in and out, removing the possessions that money has bought and the memories that fetched a different price.

Robert: "It hurts me to see kids being torn apart, especially when they're young and ask, 'How come you don't love mommy?' or 'How come you don't love daddy?' I see it and, God, I could almost break out in tears, thinking of my own family if that ever happened to me."

It's 10:24 p.m., and a five-year-old boy is reported missing from a nearby swap meet. Thousands of people are wandering the grounds, and, although the public address system has carried several announcements, the boy hasn't turned up. There have been several possible sightings, but no Bryant. Because of the recent kidnap-murder of a three-year-old girl, there's an air of added concern. Bryant's mother, waiting outside the office, describes his clothing and pulls out a recent photograph.

Robert asks, "Where do you think he would go? Does he like pets or the amusement rides?" Mom says that Bryant would be scared and probably not approach anyone. They had discussed 'stranger danger' just today, she says.

Other officers arrive to begin a systematic sweep of the area, and Robert requests that Air One fly over. Although no one thinks the young boy could find the family's vehicle at night in a crowded parking lot, Robert decides to check it out.

"Can I get you something cold to drink?" an observer asks the mother. She shakes her head. "Please, just get me my son."

A woman walks up to report seeing a boy fitting Bryant's description. He was holding a balloon as he drove off with a young couple in a brown Monte Carlo, she says.

"He didn't have a balloon," Bryant's mother responds, not grasping the possibility that the balloon could have been used to lure him away.

Seconds later, Robert's voice comes over the air: "Code 4; I have the boy. Have the mother come out to their vehicle." She takes off running toward the parking lot, stopping twice along the way to catch her breath. She pulls him to her and stands, sobbing out of control. Tears flow down her cheeks and onto his. They cling to each other, both crying now.

After wandering, lost and frightened, Bryant had found his family's truck and locked himself inside. He wouldn't open the door even after seeing Robert's uniform, radio and badge, and was convinced only when Robert said, "Look, I have your picture. Your mom gave it to me so I could find you."

"I was scared on this one," Robert says. "I thought for sure he'd been taken, and I said a little prayer while I walked toward the parking lot. All I could see was *my* five-year-old."

Because of last month's unsolved child homicide and the continued break-ins by the Prime Time Rapist, Tammy is fearful even when Robert is home. He's begun sleeping with his service revolver under the pillow to make her more comfortable. Knowing it's there, however, weighs heavily on his mind. "I don't sleep as well, not because it's there, but because of *why* it's there."

Seven-year-old Bobby is beginning to verbalize his fears about death. "He'll see something on the news and get teary-eyed, and ask, 'But why did he die?' I'll say, 'He got killed in a car accident,' and then Bobby will ask, 'But why did the car have to hit him?'"

Officers witness a lot of death, and it's never far from the conscious mind. Most cope by joking about it, often in the sickest manner. "It's the way we release some of our emotions and frustrations," Robert observes.

"Sometimes you see so much of it that you have to remember it's a real person who's dead. I had a reminder of that a few months ago after an elderly lady died of cancer at her home. Normally I'll tell the family that I'm sorry and ask what I can do to help. This time, I was just asking the necessary questions about names, birth dates, medical history and next of kin. Then it hit me what I was doing. I stopped and apologized for appearing to be so cold. It reminded me that we need to do more than check the pulse, complete the paperwork and leave."

With Tucson's increase in violent crime, Robert is more aware of officer safety. "I used to go to work thinking, 'Yes, it's possible that I may get shot.' Now it's at the point where the chances of my getting shot are greater than before, and the people arrested for violent crimes seem to be right back on the street. That's wrong, just wrong."

He sees ways in which cops can reduce their vulnerability. "I do my best to stay out of trouble. The (bullet-resistant) vest gives you some security, but it may be a false security. You need to be aware of what you say, your gestures, your body language. If I go into a

124

situation yelling and screaming like they're yelling and screaming, I'm just asking for a fight. When you're faced with a potential life or death situation, you just have to be ready."

*   *

September 24, 1986. After terrorizing a city of nearly a half-million people for three years, the Prime Time Rapist has been identified. Undercover and uniformed officers stake out his residence, then surround it when he comes home. At 9:32 a.m., Brian Frederick Larriva opens the back door and walks out, holding a pillow in one hand and a .380 caliber handgun in the other.

"I'm not going to prison. I'm sorry," he says. They are his final words. He raises the gun to his head and fires a single round.

In death, the thirty-five-year-old Larriva leaves questions to which there will be no answers. While there is an immediate sense of relief in the community, there are also feelings of anger.

Sergeant Tom Taylor of the Pima County Sheriff's Department was in charge of the task force that investigated more than 900 possible suspects. He's glad it's over, but is frustrated by the way it ended. "We would have liked to talk to him and known why he did certain things. We would have liked to have known the mistakes that we made in the investigation and to have learned from this case. My training is to put people in prison, and he cheated us out of it. He screwed us all the way."

*   *

Five weeks later, it's 10:50 p.m. on what has been a quiet Monday evening.

Dispatch: "Sector Four units, we have a 10-43 just occurred, Dairy Queen, 8955 East Tanque Verde." A man in his thirties has vaulted the service counter and confronted a terrified young employee. Pointing to a bulge in his jacket, he snapped, "Give me the money or I'll blow your fuckin' head off!"

Robert is the closest of five officers who head toward the scene.

Dispatch: "Suspect is described as a number three (Black) male, five-six, about twenty-five years old, with a short, stocky build. Was wearing white and brown shorts. He had a weapon in his shorts."

Sergeant Stephen Monk: "Is there a vehicle involved?"

Dispatch: "They believe there was an El Camino. It's unknown what color."

125

Just under three minutes pass and Robert advises he's about thirty seconds from Dairy Queen and will "take the scene." As he approaches the store, he goes back on the air: "I have an El Camino on Tanque Verde approaching Pantano."

An officer several blocks away will wait for the possible suspect.

Nick Aussems: "El Camino eastbound on Tanque Verde at Pio Decimo. He's stopped for a red light right now. It's white-over-brown with a number three male in it. I'm following eastbound on Tanque Verde. I'll wait for a backup unit for the stop."

Other officers begin moving in.

Aussems: "Approaching Sabino Canyon. . . Northbound on Sabino Canyon."

Air One: "We've got him (in sight). Through the intersection at a high rate of speed. . . In the curb lane, lost it, and he's going around and around. Here we go, he's now facing southbound, facing northbound again. . . He got it going again; we're gonna be northbound. . . Westbound on River. . . And he lost it again; he's not doing real well. . . Subject's on foot, running. He's falling down all over the place."

As the chase continues on foot, an officer urgently cuts in: "He has a gun in his hand! Gun in his right hand!"

Eight seconds later, Mary Diaz tackles the suspect and holds him down as two others run up to help.

Air One advises that the suspect is now handcuffed.

Dispatch: "All units shut down. Subject's 10-15." For those who haven't made it to the scene, it's just another adrenaline-popping letdown.

Robert remains at the store, calming the two teenage girls who work there.

*   *

It's a February afternoon and Robert is suddenly surrounded by minor emergencies. He's dispatched to a shopping mall where a security guard is with an elderly man suspected of having attempted to pick up two young girls. As Robert reaches the main entrance, a man runs to him, yelling that his motorcycle has just been stolen. Robert stops briefly to broadcast a description of the cycle. As he again begins to walk into the mall, a Sears employee shouts that a customer is leaving with two pair of stolen slacks. Robert watches as the suspect bolts out of the door, sees him, and quickly turns away.

Robert: "Sir, could you hold on for a minute?"

Suspect: "Who, me?"

It appears that he has something tucked under his arms between his shirt and outer jacket.

"Could you raise your hands, please?"

The man lifts them to chin level, keeping his lower arms flush against his torso.

"Bring them all the way up."

He does, and two pair of Levis drop to the ground.

Robert finally makes it inside the mall to interview the original suspect. There isn't probable cause for an arrest, but a record is made of his name, address and birth date. The shoplifter is arrested and the stolen cycle is soon abandoned and recovered several miles away.

*   *

One week later is Friday the thirteenth, and there will be a full moon tonight. For the majority of cops who are adrenaline junkies anyway, the shift has real potential.

In the first two hours, Robert responds to a service station gas skip, takes a report on a home burglary, stops a truck for speeding, and questions two teenagers he believes are involved in fencing stolen merchandise.

Just after 1:30 p.m., another officer observes a vehicle with expired plates and pulls it over. A computer check shows that the driver is wanted on a felony burglary warrant. As the man is told that he's under arrest, he takes off on foot into an apartment complex. The officer sprints after him as other units come to assist. The area is sealed off in a matter of minutes, but there's no sign of the suspect. Twelve minutes later, he's spotted running between buildings.

Robert, nearly four miles away, activates his lights and siren and starts toward the scene. Cops find it both fascinating and frightening that so many drivers become mesmerized by those revolving rooftop 'gumball machines'. Although most vehicles move quickly out of his path, several seem oblivious to his noisy approach.

"Okay, fella, move to the right, move to the right," Robert grumbles aloud as one car holds its ground in the left lane. "That's it; you got it, you got it," he says when the driver finally gives way, allowing Robert the fast lane. The next obstacle is a vintage Oldsmobile, driven by an elderly man apparently deep in conversation with a woman seated next to him. When he finally realizes an emergency vehicle is behind him, he brakes instead of moving out of the way.

Variations of these reactions are common, and many officers

127

call it the Rectal-Cranial Inversion. "I can't get over some of them," Robert sighs in frustration. "If they jam on their brakes, all I can do is eat their bumper."

As he laughs at the absurdity of his observation, one of the cops giving chase advises that the suspect has left the east end of the complex and is running into a nearby desert wash. Robert, now less than a mile away, advises, "Approaching from the north." Seconds later, the man is caught by another officer. Robert terminates the Code 3 run, takes a deep breath and returns to his beat.

He soon sees an apparently abandoned 1987 Corvette parked in a bus loading zone and arranges to have it towed. Next, a woman reports that a four-year-old boy is often left unsupervised and has been taking mail from neighbors' boxes. The youngster cries softly until Robert assures him that he won't be arrested. He promises not to do it again and his mother says she'll monitor him more closely.

Between assignments, Robert drives through the business and residential portions of his more than twelve-square-mile beat. Preparing to end his day just before 5:30 p.m., he spots a Ford Tempo which groans under the weight of a full load of passengers. He pulls it over, and the ensuing scene is reminiscent of a 1950s circus skit as eleven people — all but two of them teenagers — work their way out of a vehicle that seats five. He cites the driver and, still incredulous at what he's just seen, heads back to the station as the sun slips under the horizon across the sky and the first light of the rising full moon appears in front of him.

*   *

A few weeks later, three men — one of them nervously brandishing a small machine gun — enter a bank and order customers and employees to lie on the floor. They hurdle the tellers' counter and empty the cash drawers.

As they begin their exit, a combination of poor planning and fate conspires against them. The man with the gun leaves first, his partners close behind. A bank guard grabs the last suspect as he reaches the door. Less than 300 feet away, a sheriff's deputy is writing a traffic citation. He hears the commotion, sees the second suspect running toward him and quickly has him in custody.

The third robber fares better, at least for a while. In addition to the machine gun, he's carrying a police radio scanner, enabling him to monitor Robert and other cops surrounding the area. As the officers move in, they hear their own voices on his scanner and the robber's apparent advantage has quickly become a liability. In desperation, he climbs a six-foot fence, only to find a large Labrador retriever waiting for him. With cops bearing down on one side and a snarling dog on the other, he opts for surrender.

*   *

It upsets Robert that so many officers have deteriorating marriages. Although his is sometimes under stress, he can't imagine it ever ending. "We're able to talk things out. I think that too many families just let things build up and build up until they boil over. I know I've changed a lot in the last two years. I'm not as sympathetic as I used to be, especially when it comes to my family. What's strange is that I sometimes seem to show more sympathy for people on the street than for my own family. I'm not as understanding as I should be when there are problems at home, and it's something I'm working on."

He has become more protective. "I keep a real close eye on my kids and make sure Tammy does, too. I always felt you could trust your neighbors to watch out for them. Now I know it's possible that my neighbor could also be a pervert. I'm not sure if I'm paranoid or just more aware that things like that happen."

■

Uncertainty is part and parcel of the job. An officer can — and must — make generalizations based on experience, but had better keep an open mind between those open eyes. That 200-pound six-footer with tattoos could be a teddy bear, while the little old lady with white hair may have a skeleton or two rattling in her closet.

Sometimes, for example, a bank robbery is *not* a bank robbery. It's August 28, 1986, and Les Beach's 6 a.m. to 2 p.m. shift is winding down. A pedestrian flags down another officer and reports seeing two young men in a car, the passenger pointing a gun at the driver's head. The vehicle is soon spotted in a nearby parking lot and a witness says two young teenage males entered the business. A bank official contacted by phone says they are talking with a teller, but that he can't hear the conversation.

The cops have to assume that there's an armed robbery in progress. Les is one of six officers who quickly surround the bank. As the youngsters walk out, several guns draw down on them and they're ordered to kneel on the ground, hands on head. One immediately drops to his knees, and when the other hesitates, Les yells, "Get your hands on top of your head, or else!" He obeys.

A pat-down search yields no weapon and a bank official says there hasn't been a robbery. Jeffrey and Richard say they had been "playing around" with a toy gun which they wisely left in their vehicle before making a deposit. Observes Jeffrey, who didn't raise his hands on the first command: "I was really freaking out. It looked like there were at least fifteen officers." Forcing a smile now, he allows that he was impressed with the cops' quick response.

*   *

It's 12:51 a.m. on November 3. Someone dials 911, but hangs up without speaking. The service aide phones back and hears only an unintelligible male voice. It's dispatched as an unknown trouble call and Les is one of three officers who pull up to the residence. The voice of an elderly man is heard as he slowly works his way to the door.

Joseph Miller, seventy-three years old, is bleeding from a head wound. What is obviously a nicely-kept home shows clear signs that all is not well tonight. There is blood on two telephones, the living room wall, a sofa, vacuum cleaner and photo album. A shattered vase has left glittering shards of glass strewn over the carpeting. Sitting on a chair waiting for an ambulance, Joseph is surprisingly calm as he recounts tonight's attack, adding that this is not the first time his wife has tried to kill him. He says he was hospitalized in mid-September after she used a cleaver to cut an inch-deep gash in his leg.

Hazel, lying awake in bed, initially refuses to come out from under the covers, but slowly gets to her feet after a brief impasse. Although she has no visible wounds, her nightgown is stained with blood. A slight, seemingly frail wisp of a woman with curly gray hair, Hazel turns belligerent, cursing and insisting that they just had "a little spat."

The officers don't want to take her to jail because there are minimal facilities there for elderly people. Moreover, Hazel makes it clear that she won't *go*, and that she'll fight if they try to take her. Les, mulling the results of a confrontation — none of them good —

discreetly moves several knives, scissors and other possible weapons out of her reach. Two sergeants respond for a consultation and decide that Hazel should be hospitalized for a psychiatric evaluation. Calmer now, she agrees to go. Joseph is admitted to another hospital for treatment.

Pausing over coffee while they do paperwork, the officers still have difficulty accepting what they've seen. "Those things just aren't done by people that age," says one, shaking his head. Les: "Can you imagine taking a seventy-two-year-old woman to jail? Can you imagine having to *hog-tie* her if she fights you?"

*   *

Five nights later, Les and officer Layton Dickerson respond to a fight. A man sits precariously on the livingroom couch, bleeding from the head. As they speak with him, Brian, a short, stocky younger man with collar-length bushy blond hair strides into the room and begins yelling. When Dickerson tells him to calm down, he spouts a string of obscenities, then turns to leave. As he does so, he backs sharply into Les who is interviewing a witness. Les uses his right hand to deflect Brian's momentum, but Brian comes back, flailing as he moves in. He continues swinging as Les pushes him toward the carport.

Les fends off another blow and then hits Brian on the side of the head. As his fist connects, Les feels a sharp pain in his right hand. Dickerson rushes outside to help, and it takes both officers to cuff him. While being booked into jail, Brian attempts to kick Dickerson and is charged with a second count of assault.

Medics wrap Les's hand to immobilize it, and take him to the hospital. His first thought is that he's dislocated a couple of fingers and might miss a day or two of work. He asks the doctor to "just push the fingers back in place and tape them up."

X-rays, however, show that the knuckles of two fingers have broken off and splintered. A surgeon looks at the film, turns to Les and says, "Oh, my goodness, Mr. Beach." Three days later, his knuckles are wired together and rods are implanted from hand to wrist to keep the fingers locked in place. He goes home with a cast extending nearly to his elbow.

The usually mild-mannered Les is upset. "I'm angry at Brian because of his stupidity and angry at myself because I should have used some other means to subdue him. If you swing at someone and hit bone to bone, something's going to give, and it was my knuckles

131

rather than his head." Les realizes that he faces a lengthy period of recuperation.

Three weeks later, he's already impatient. With the pain gone, the cure has now become worse than the disease. He hopes he'll soon be cleared for desk duty, but meanwhile he can look forward to enjoying the Thanksgiving and Christmas holidays at home. Although he's frustrated and coming down hard on himself, he knows he can't push the recovery process. "I wouldn't want to go back not being 100 percent and having someone else worry about me."

Les is the Department's second-oldest patrol cop, and even injury-free he knows that he won't spend twenty years on the street as younger cops might. His goal is to work with juveniles. He likes talking with kids, and although getting through to them can be frustrating, he believes he's able to provide direction and strong reinforcement.

*   *

It's December 16. Both Joseph and Hazel Miller have been back in their home since shortly after the November assault. Early this morning there's another argument and another call to the police. Joseph, uninjured, but saying he fears for his life, is taken to a nearby motel. He says that Hazel has fashioned a weapon out of tubing and gravel and threatened to kill him with it. He won't go back to her again, he assures a Victim Witness advocate.

On Christmas Eve, he relents and returns for the last time. Two days later, Hazel phones 911 and says a man wearing a black mask broke into their home. "He beat my husband up and he just now left," she tells the police service aide. "He's laying in there on the floor and I think he's dead."

Hazel is arrested, charged with first degree murder and booked into Pima County Jail.

*   *

Les is still limited to light duty, and the case against Brian has not been resolved. As the year ends, Brian — wearing an Adidas T-shirt, cord slacks and tennis shoes — appears at a pre-trial hearing. His trial is set for January 19, 1987, postponed for two weeks, and then postponed again in an effort to negotiate a plea bargain agreement under which one assault charge would be dropped in return for a guilty plea on the other. In return, Brian would receive

132

a maximum three-month jail sentence. He declines the offer, and a third trial date is set.

Les, who attends the court session, wants jail time. "I've spent almost three months off the street, I've been through a lot of pain, and I want him to pay. Perhaps I'm being vindictive, but it's the way I feel."

Les has found that the way he treats someone, even a suspect, usually determines that person's response to him. "Let's say I'm dispatched to a complaint of an unwanted person. I'm not going to just walk up to him and say, 'You're not wanted here; get the hell out!' If I do, he's probably going to tell me to kiss his ass and the situation will go down hill from there. I'd rather approach him and ask, 'How are you doing today?' Then I'll make some small talk before I ask his name or have him show me ID. I'll do the same thing in a family dispute.

"If the suspect is being cooperative and respectful and not giving anyone a hard time, I'll step back and listen to what he has to say. It doesn't help the situation to come on like Gang Busters when you don't have to. Taking time to build a little rapport usually makes things go better for everyone. Now and then I'll catch myself coming on a little too strong for the situation and back off a bit. Some people will act like dipshits no matter how you approach them, but I like to give them a choice."

Five days later, Les returns to street duty with no apparent apprehension. "I've thought out all of the possibilities: Will I drive slower than I should so I won't be the first officer on the scene? Will I drive faster so I can jump right into the fight? Will I overreact and punch someone out who doesn't need to be punched? I've thought them through and they're just not going to happen. I'm going to go about my job the same way I always have. Obviously I'd prefer not being in a situation where I have to use my fist, but then I've always felt that way. If it comes down to it, though, I think I'll be more inclined to use my nightstick."

He's certain of one thing: "People can say most anything they want, but they are not going to take any type of offensive action against me when I'm in uniform. I just will not allow it."

His first week back is routine.

*   *

Four months later, his hand has held up. He's tested it a couple of times in "wrestling matches" with suspects, but hasn't thrown a punch.

133

Today is slow. He arrests a youthful shoplifter, responds to an ongoing domestic dispute, then pushes two stalled vehicles off the street. About the only excitement has been a brief encounter with a middle-aged man who is selectively pulling out weeds around the perimeter of a bus stop and then carefully placing them in a plastic bag. He doesn't appear to be a city maintenance worker so Les pulls up to check him out.

"I'm just getting my supper," he says good-naturedly. To Les, they're just weeds, but the man assures him that boiled, they make a tasty and nourishing meal. He says he's a transient who lives on the streets and sleeps wherever he can find a safe spot. He continues harvesting while he talks, offering that "it helps keep me from being idle." Les smiles, nods goodbye and drives away.

At 5:27 p.m., he's sent to help at a minor traffic accident. As he arrives to find that both vehicles have been moved off the roadway, the shrill beep of the emergency tone changes what has been an uneventful day.

"Ten thirty-seven (burglary) of an occupied structure, 600 North Pantano, apartment 1114." Les revs his engine, flips on the overhead light and siren bar and, without a word to the puzzled accident victims, heads into rush-hour traffic. He's only a mile-and-one-half away, but he'll need to work his way through two major intersections.

Dispatcher: "Complainant indicates a male subject entered her apartment and is armed with a knife. It's the south side of the complex, third building to the left."

Sergeant: "Is the complainant still on the line?"

"That's 10-4."

"Is she still in the apartment?"

"She's in the livingroom in the front. Indicates the suspect was a White male, about eighteen, wearing no shirt, very tan, dark curly hair."

It takes intense concentration to hear the dispatcher over the alternating wail and shriek of the siren. Les pulls up in just under two minutes, hurriedly straddles a pair of parking spaces and sprints eastward through the courtyard where he's joined by two other officers. As they race through the complex drawing curious looks from other residents, dispatch has additional information.

"She does not believe he actually made entry into the residence. He had a knife and was trying to gain entry in one of the windows when she saw him. She might have possibly scared him off."

Approaching the apartment, they slow to a walk, looking and

134

listening. There are ten or twelve teens in the area, most of them in or around apartment 1113, immediately next door to the complainant. One officer goes to the woman's second-floor apartment and quickly finds that no one else is there.

Les, meanwhile, instructs the male teens to stand at the bottom of the stairs. "And for heaven's sake, don't try to run because I'll get real pissed," he warns them.

The young men are separated and interviewed. One of them admits that he was at the woman's back window, but has an excuse. He claims he's been staying in apartment 1113. When he locked himself out, he tried to enter through a rear window, but realized too late that he was next door. The knife, he said, was to help pry the window open.

Witnesses confirm his story and no charges are filed. The manager of the complex, however, says that the legal occupant of apartment 1113 has been served an eviction notice. A check of personal belongings indicates that at least four teens, and possibly as many as six, are living in the three-room apartment. They're told to pack and warned that they'll be arrested for trespassing if they return. Except for one wisp of a girl with a snotty attitude, the kids play it cool, possibly thankful that they're not in worse trouble. They pile into two pickup trucks and leave.

At 6:26 p.m., Les is dispatched back to the traffic accident. The motorists were told the reason for Les's quick exit when they phoned 911 to ask why he raced off. They are still there waiting for him.

Although his occasional Code 3 runs are a source of momentary stress, Les has one advantage over most officers, having survived what appeared to be a certain high-speed collision. Racing to assist an officer requesting emergency help, Les was accelerating in the outside lane when an older woman panicked and locked her brakes squarely in front of him. With no time to think, training and instinct prevailed.

"I knew I couldn't stop without hitting her, so I took my foot off the brakes, yanked the wheel sharply to the right, then sharply to the left, and then back to the center. In an instant I was in the adjacent lane moving past her. All I could think was, 'Holy shit! It actually works just the way they taught it in the Academy!'"

*   *

Les doesn't appear to have changed much after two years on the street. His home life remains largely unaffected by his new career,

135

and the love and support he and Sharon share is easy to see. They seem content to spend most of their free hours together, quietly at home or motorcycling around Arizona.

He's troubled by at least one change in himself. "On the street I'm less trusting than I used to be. I hear so many lies and half-truths that I'm initially skeptical of almost anything I'm told. I don't like that attitude, but it's there."

Nonetheless, he loves being a cop. "It's close to what I expected. A lot of paperwork and a lot of decisions which affect the lives of others. To some, we're the good guys, and to others, we're the bad guys, but either way there's not much recognition. Perhaps once out of a hundred times a citizen's going to pat you on the back and tell you you've done a good job. I have no illusions about changing the world or eradicating crime, and if I were to die or quit tomorrow, the police department would get along quite well without me, but I feel I'm doing a good job and that my being here has a positive impact."

■

Rene Gomez is another officer distressed by an increasingly prevalent 'Us Against Them' mentality. "A lot of cops talk like that. They'll say, 'There's only two types of people out there: the assholes and us.' At first, you think it's crazy, but when you've gotten into enough situations with nasty people, you begin finding yourself thinking that way, too."

Even after more than a year on his own, Rene doesn't feel in tune with the streets until he's completed the first call of each shift. A routine traffic stop will suffice, even if he doesn't cite the driver. "It gets rid of the butterflies and then I'm ready for whatever comes along."

With the summer of 1986 winding down, Rene has been working the day shift for three months. Today, he and John Kragnes search a building for a reported prowler. They don't find one, but must evade an angry German Shepherd protecting its turf. As they return to service, they're dispatched to a family fight. Before they can take positions and knock, the door flies open and a man strides out. Jim is six-five, about 250 pounds. He says that nothing has happened and that his girlfriend is not hurt. While a third officer goes inside to confirm this, Jim tires of his conversation with Rene, pivots and heads for the front door.

Rene, five-foot eight-inches on a tall day, calls him back, shakes his finger at him like a parent scolding a child and admonishes, "Jim, don't you ever fuckin' walk away from me when I'm talking to you! You come here *now!*" Jim turns around and ambles back. Kragnes has watched the mini-drama in amazement, convinced that an out-of-control Jim would know more ways to make them hurt than the Marquis de Sade.

"All I'm thinking is, 'I'm going to die,'" Kragnes says, laughing now. "That man could have wasted us both with his bare hands."

Just after 4 p.m., two officers respond to a northside apartment complex where a man has threatened a resident. The suspect, apparently drunk, swings at one of the officers and they call for reinforcements. Rene, nearly six miles away, is the closest. Because of the distance and the volatility of the situation, he's told to respond Code 3.

It's the start of rush hour, and he must weave his way through traffic which has already clogged many of the streets along his route. Motorists today are responding well, pulling over to let him pass. Although Rene reaches speeds as high as seventy-five miles an hour, there is no sense of danger. The constant wail of the sirens makes the eight-minute ride almost dream-like.

By the time Rene pulls up, the man has been subdued and placed in the back seat of a patrol car, a trickle of blood visible on his forehead. An ambulance arrives to treat the suspect and an officer who sustained a hand injury in the melee.

Kenneth, who appears to be in his mid-thirties, won't leave the patrol car, and it takes three officers — one pushing from one side and two pulling from the other — to get him out so that medics can cleanse and bandage his head. Typical of many drunks, he exhibits sudden mood swings, alternately yelling at the cadre of cops around him and promising to behave if they'll let him go. Soon, he's escorted to Rene's vehicle and placed in its screened back seat.

Rene attempts to question him. "Where do you live, Kenneth?"

"None of your business, asshole!" he shoots back in a staccato tough-guy voice.

"Do you have someone you want us to call?"

"I'm a citizen of the United States!"

"How old are you, Kenneth?"

"Let me out of here, mother-fucker!"

"What color are your eyes?"

"The same color as your dick, asshole! What's your badge number, fella?"

137

"Officer Gomez, 12774."

"I'm going to find out who you are and come after your family!"

Rene and the others walk away, realizing that talking with him is futile, but they sprint back a minute later when Kenneth attempts to kick out the side window. This time, they push him to the ground, hog-tie his ankles and return him to the car face down. He's charged with criminal damage, aggravated assault on a police officer and resisting arrest. A records check reveals that he has been imprisoned in three states.

*   *

Like most young officers, Rene is aware of changes within himself and their effect on his marriage. "When you're at work you're so hyped up that you're always alert. I'm on that roller-coaster ride, but when I get home I'm coming down off of that and that's the part the family sees. I want to play with my three-year-old, and I don't talk to Sylvia the way I used to. She bends over backward. She does so much and hardly ever pressures me. I feel guilty when I don't respond. Part of me would rather be at work or having a drink with the guys and telling war stories. If my marriage is on the rocks, it's because of me, and I know that it's up to me if I want it to last.

"When we were warned at the Academy that the divorce rate among cops is high, I remember saying, 'Well, it won't happen to me,' but now I can see why it *does* happen. I just don't know what I want, I guess."

*   *

On November 6, 1986, as Rene makes a sharp turn during his annual driving test, he feels a sharp pain in his shoulder. "I think I set a course record for knocking down cones," he'll quip months later. Although X-rays show no break, the hurt remains. Five weeks later, he's in physical therapy, but doctors still haven't found the problem. Rene is frustrated and impatient: "I didn't spend eleven weeks having my ass kicked at the Academy to sit behind a desk answering phones. I'm getting a lot of kidding at work. I know it's in fun, but it's getting to me."

Being off the street is a further strain on his marriage. "I go home in a bad mood. Sylvia knows that it's driving me crazy and she's understanding and good at leaving me alone to snap out of it

138

myself."

His ordeal is to last into late spring while he submits to what seems to be an unending series of medical tests followed by orthoscopic surgery, weeks of trigger-point shoulder muscle injections and months of continuing physical therapy.

Finally cleared to resume street duty, Rene rides two shifts with another officer to reacclimate himself, then prepares to set out on his own. It's May 25, 1987, and for the first time in nearly seven months, he carries his gear to a patrol car, eases himself behind the wheel and heads into the night. He keys his microphone and signs on at 11:21 p.m.

Like Les Beach, Rene wonders aloud whether his injury has healed. "I think about what would happen if something goes down and my arm just doesn't work, and I get hurt or another officer gets the shit beat out of him because I couldn't function properly. I have all of these possible scenarios. Maybe I've been thinking about them too much."

His immediate goal, as always, is to get that first call behind him. Three minutes later, his designator is called. "Here we go," he says, smiling in anticipation as he reaches for the microphone.

"Speedway and Country Club," he reports.

"It's nice to have you back," comes the voice from the Communications Center nearly ten miles away.

"Thank you. Good to *be* back."

The on-air welcome is appreciated, but he still wants an assignment.

At 11:38, he's sent to look for a man walking in the roadway at a nearby intersection. Rene checks the area, but finds no one. He cruises for the next forty frustrating minutes, waiting to be needed. He can't even find a good motor vehicle violation.

Shortly after midnight he checks the welfare of two other officers signed out on a traffic stop. They're okay and he leaves. He approaches a car still in a park three hours after its posted closing time. The two people sitting inside show identification and Rene doesn't cite them. This routine encounter is his first street contact of the evening — and the year.

Fifty minutes later, there's a report of a 911 hang-up call. Rene and Brian Klinger arrive almost simultaneously, park about 100 feet away and approach the house on foot. They can hear conversation, but no yelling.

Rene knocks, and a more-than-plump heavy-jowled woman opens the door. She says that her husband is the problem, that he's

139

been drinking and that he hit her when she tried to stop him from driving off with their infant son.

Rene asks the man to step outside so they can talk privately. Tony is immediately abusive.

"What is this shit?" he slurs, a thin mist of saliva forming in the corner of his mouth. "You wanna take me in?"

"I don't know yet. We just want to talk to you and find out what's been happening."

"I don't care," he says, taking a few clumsy steps toward the street, then coming back, arms flailing.

Rene decides it's time to cuff the increasingly agitated man. It doesn't mean he's under arrest, Rene explains. "What I want to do is talk to you. I'm going to put these on for my safety and yours."

As Rene secures the first cuff, Tony begins to lash out with his feet and free hand.

"Relax. Settle down," Rene orders in vain. Within seconds, all three are on the ground, Rene and Klinger trying to hold him down without hitting him. As the wrestling match unfolds, Tony's nine-year-old daughter comes running out of the house, screaming, "My daddy! My daddy!"

She's headed directly into the confrontation, and is intercepted just a few steps away by an observer who reaches out and places a protective arm around her waist. Though assured that her father, uninjured and now on his feet, will be okay, she cries hysterically for nearly a minute.

Tony, now officially in custody, is seated in the back of Rene's patrol car, where he is alternately calm and belligerent during the ride to jail. Entering the intake room, he refuses to sit, so Rene places his right hand on Tony's left shoulder and pushes him into the chair. Though still handcuffed, he jumps up and confronts Rene. Three jail deputies, watching from an adjacent room, are there in five seconds. They force him back in the chair and hold him there. Tony, his face now beet-red with rage, screams a series of profanities, then refuses to be fingerprinted. Guards escort him to a cell, postponing the necessary paperwork until he's calmer.

Rene had forgotten the shoulder injury that sidelined him for more than six months. Asked what he was thinking during the struggle, he leans back and smiles. "I never thought about it until now. I guess what happened answered all my doubts."

*   *

June 9. It's 1:01 a.m., and officer Herman Salazar reports a vehicle running from him. Nearby units head toward the chase and Air One is overhead in less than three minutes.

Air One: "I'll be calling it. . . Northbound on Third. . . East on Twelfth. . . South on Toole. . ."

Another officer begins transmitting changes in the suspect's direction of travel, but is quickly preempted by an assertive voice from the helicopter: "We have the vehicle. We'll take the radio."

Dispatch: "Units 10-3. Air One has the chase."

Air One: "Northbound between Third and Fourth. . . East on Thirteenth. . . North on Fourth, coming up on Broadway. . . East on Broadway. . . North on First. . ."

Sergeant Steve Horbarenko, moving in the direction of the chase: "What kind of speed do we have?"

Salazar: "A lot of speed."

A dog unit joins the chase and is assigned to go after the suspect if he runs from his car.

Salazar, utilizing the helicopter's searchlights to look inside the fleeing vehicle: "We (also) have a female in the car."

At 1:07, the chase moves eastward from the downtown area where it started. As it crosses Mountain Avenue into Team 3, midtown units are advised of the situation. Rene is the closest. With several patrol cars already involved, Rene initially just follows the general direction of the chase.

Salazar: "He's going sixty-five to seventy now."

Sergeant Lester Arndt, hoping to encourage the suspect to end the chase and run on foot: "Have units back off a little bit if he slows down."

Salazar: "Copy description of the driver. White male, approximately six feet, 200 pounds, blond hair, thirty to thirty-five."

It's 1:14, and Team 4 officers are advised as the suspect continues east, changing direction frequently as he plays out a cat-and-mouse game. At times he slows to under twenty miles per hour, and at others zips along in excess of sixty. Fortunately, there's little street traffic and the officers are going only fast enough to keep the suspect in sight. There are now more than a dozen police vehicles involved, most of them traveling on nearby streets.

At 1:26, a computer search identifies the probable driver of the vehicle, and an officer is dispatched to set up near his last known address. A minute later, the chase leaves the city limits and sheriff's deputies are advised.

As the suspect enters a deserted stretch of highway east of the city, Rene finds himself the second closest unit in pursuit.

Arndt: "Any dead ends on Tanque Verde?"

Air One: "Not for a long time."

The suspect is now fleeing at speeds up to ninety miles an hour. Two minutes later, he turns south, heading back to the city.

He cuts back his speed and, sensing an opportunity, Rene and two other officers attempt to box him in by positioning one car in front, one in the rear and one to the side. Rene gets a good look at the apparent victim. "I couldn't hear her, but it was clear that she was frantic and yelling for help," he says later.

With one officer now in front of the suspect, they're able to slow him to less than ten miles an hour. They try to force him onto the road's dirt shoulder, but he evades their maneuver, cutting ahead of the lead patrol car and again accelerating.

Salazar: "Do you want us to try that again?"

Horbarenko: "Negative."

Air One: "What they did back there was just excellent. They almost had him. I think we should consider doing it one more time before we get back to the city."

The officers in the helicopter are in the best position to make this judgment.

The answer comes back: "Go ahead and try it."

Salazar: "It's going to be a little difficult now. The road has three lanes. If we ever get him out in the sticks again, we'll try."

Air One: "Do you think maybe two or three (vehicles) could shoot past and then block him?"

Salazar: "Negative. He'll hit one of the side streets. He's pretty quick at that. We can try if you like."

Air One: "I think that would be better than busting (through) these intersections. If we could get three abreast in front and just shoot past him real quick, I think we can jam him."

Late-night traffic begins to pick up as the suspect makes a sudden turn and heads west again, and this plan is also abandoned.

At 1:40, the suspect and the lead chase vehicle go through an intersection traveling between forty-five and fifty miles an hour. Rene follows, lights and siren on as they have been for more than a half hour.

When a car driving east enters the intersection. Rene instinctively slams his right foot on the brakes, but it's too late. His patrol car spins and the two vehicles collide, the sound of steel against steel intertwined with the wail from his overhead siren.

Air One: "We have a 10-50 at Fifth and Columbus."

Rene, breathless, sixteen seconds later: "Negative injuries."

Two officers head to the scene.

Horbarenko: "We're going to have the first two units remain in pursuit. Other units start paralleling and resume normal speed."

The suspect slows the pace again and begins a series of turns, not going more than a few blocks in any direction. It's 1:49, and suddenly there's a new development.

Air One: "I have a passenger jumping out. The female's jumped out. Lying in the street. Now she's going into the oleanders on the north side of the street next to a big city dumpster."

Although two officers are there within a minute, a half-hour search fails to find her.

Less than thirty seconds after the woman bails out, the driver loses control of his car. He spins out, but quickly recovers and continues on a circuitous route within a three-square-mile area. Because he's believed to live in this area, Horbarenko advises units to back off, hoping to encourage him to make a run for home. He doesn't, and at 2:10, more than an hour into the chase, the suspect picks up speed and heads back downtown.

Another five minutes pass, and suddenly Air One advises, "He just spun out! He's stopped right now!" The radio is silent for sixteen seconds while the first two ground units reach his vehicle and squeal to a stop. Then: "It's Code 4. Everybody Code 4. They have him."

The driver is arrested for felony fleeing, kidnapping and two counts of aggravated assault. The chase has covered 66.1 miles, and along the way, he's picked up 133 moving violations — methodically tabulated by the helicopter's co-pilot — most of them for ignoring stop signs and traffic lights.

"I didn't know anyone was chasing me," he tells officers. The woman is found two days later. An alleged prostitute, she says she was kidnapped, but fled because there were warrants against her and she was high on heroin.

Soon after the collision, Rene feels pain in his left knee, and is taken to the hospital. He's been back on duty less than two weeks and all he can think of now is that he faces another long stretch of recuperation.

"I'm tired of being called 'light-duty Gomez' and I don't think I could handle sitting behind a desk again," he grouses. X-rays are negative and although he's slightly bruised, Rene will miss only one shift.

It's after 5 a.m., the first light of a new day begins to color the Rincon Mountains, and a tired but happy man is limping home.

Prompted in part by an FBI report that more people are being killed by police cars than by police guns, law enforcement agencies nationwide have been reassessing high-speed chases.

Some officers are so determined to catch every fleeing suspect that they develop a Pursuit Fixation Syndrome. While many chases are clearly necessary, others should never have begun, and differences of opinion are the norm rather than the exception.

Tucson Police Department pursuit policy states that officers may ram a vehicle, surround or box it in, force it off of the roadway, or establish a blockade when it is necessary to prevent a suspect's escape.

Caveats are then listed: "Attempt all other reasonable means of apprehension before resorting to these methods; exercise caution for the protection of the officer, suspect and public; obtain supervisory approval if possible; and be prepared to justify the tactics used."

In a June 11, 1987 memorandum to field sergeants, Deputy Police Chief Dietsch attempts to clarify the Department's policy, emphasizing that "the real key is the use of common sense."

He offers several general examples:

"If an individual is wanted for kidnapping and we believe the victim is in a vehicle being driven at a slow rate of speed, it would be appropriate to box in the vehicle, and it could be appropriate to block the roadway. On the other hand, if the individual is being pursued for a minor traffic violation and refuses to stop, but is going at a slow speed, ramming or boxing the individual in or blocking the roadway would not be appropriate."

Addressing the issue of a continuing pursuit, he writes: "If the individual being pursued is jeopardizing other citizens' lives *prior* to coming to the officer's attention, we have an obligation to try to preserve lives."

He cites an intoxicated driver taking traffic head-on at a high rate of speed. "We realize that unless we stop that individual, there is going to be a very serious accident. On the other hand, if an individual is speeding and begins driving more recklessly due to our pursuit, we are pushing that individual into taking additional chances. It is then appropriate to back off and allow him to escape, as the probability is that he will then slow down so as not to attract the attention of another officer."

Dietsch notes that one sergeant might handle a pursuit in a

144

different way than another. "That does not mean that either decision is inappropriate. You are not going to select the best response in every situation, but if it is at all reasonable, I will not recommend disciplinary action."

He concludes: "The real bottom line is that you're on the scene, you have the best information and your decisions, if at all reasonable, will be upheld."

To most cops, the phrase "if at all reasonable" is not reassuring.

Law enforcement is a tightly-knit brotherhood. Most officers arrive at work early and appear in no rush to go home when the day's shift has ended. While they genuinely need time to unwind from the physical and emotional ups and downs of the job, it appears to go beyond this. They seem most at ease among their own, and spouses often find themselves left out, even at social events which tend to be havens for sharing the latest crop of war stories.

The Tucson Police Department allows and encourages its officers to occasionally invite a family member to ride patrol with them. While most street cops exercise this option, some are reluctant to place loved ones in a potentially vulnerable situation or believe that their presence is not appropriate.

Greg Strom's father has anticipated observing his son at work for more than a year. In the early summer of 1986, George Strom trades the precision of his daily accounting world for the uncertainty of the street. He remembers snapping on his seat belt and suddenly seeing his son as an adult. "I'm thinking he's a grown man now, doing his job and loving it."

It's a routine day until Greg spots two teenage boys on a motorcycle. They speed off and Greg weaves in and out of traffic to keep pace. This is too much for George, and parental instinct takes over: "You're going too fast, son," he chastises. An immediate "Keep quiet, dad," brings him back to reality.

"You don't want to play father, but sometimes it's hard not to," George observes after the teens are stopped and ticketed.

Greg's wife has not ridden with him. Their marriage has become increasingly shaky. Greg knows that the stress and demands of his career have affected his home life.

"I had to learn to be more aggressive to prepare me for life as an officer, and I see some of this decision-making getting in the way," he acknowledges. "The stress that comes with the job itself isn't hard to manage. I feel it trying to deal with family life and I haven't learned how to switch off when I get home.

"We've both changed a lot, and right now we're trying to figure out what we want. She's not sure that she wants to stay married to a cop and I'm not sure that I want to stay married to someone who can't support my job. It's really strange because when I first started she was totally supportive and I know I wouldn't have made it through the Academy without her."

Greg will move into a nearby apartment while they see if the marriage can be rescued.

*   *

It's September 20, 1986, and Greg's squad is at briefing. Sergeant Bob Elash begins the evening on a serious note: "This may sound a little like an ass-chewing," he says as he discusses the aftermath of a recent armed robbery in which so many officers were looking for the suspects that there was an "unacceptable delay" in responding to the drug store to protect evidence and interview the victim. In addition, he says, two men sitting in a car near the robbery scene weren't properly interviewed and were later found to have been part of the team of robbers.

Greg feels he was partly to blame. "Since I was closest to the scene, I probably should have gone directly to the drug store instead of looking for a suspect. You always want to catch the bad guy and that was the first thing on my mind."

Elash reassures them: "This was an instance where communications partially broke down and incorrect assumptions were made. Use it as a learning experience."

Just after midnight, Greg is one of two officers dispatched to a home where a frustrated young couple want a man in his early twenties removed from their property. Bill says that he's "come to Phoenix" to find his girlfriend. Unfortunately, he's in Tucson, 120 miles away, and it's immediately clear that he's been drinking. He is, in fact, *beyond* drunk, and when he attempts to walk, he resembles a leggy foal taking its first awkward steps.

Bill's speech is slurred, but he's coherent most of the time, and apologizes for being "a bother." It's not clear whether he's refusing to leave or simply unable to leave. Trapped in his hangover, he can't take more than a few steps without staggering into or bouncing off

146

of something. At one point, he straddles a twenty-five-foot tall palm tree and then tries to climb it.

Arresting him would not be appropriate, and the available shelters are either full or unwilling to accept a drunk, so Elash is called in for a consultation. Although positioned around Bill, the officers stand several feet away, not knowing the direction of his next lurch. They encourage him to remain seated on a stoop, but each time he starts to talk, he struggles to his feet and the routine begins anew. Finally he comes to rest on the hood of one of the patrol cars. "Okay, now I can talk," he says, acknowledging for the first time that he's not capable of using his mouth and legs simultaneously.

Although the city's parks are closed, the officers drive him to one, reasoning that if they leave him to wander the streets, he'll draw complaints from neighbors or be struck by a vehicle. Bill has two small suitcases, and Greg and officer Rosemarie Cowan each carry one for him — perhaps Tucson's first documented room-service-in-the-park.

*   *

With the year winding down, Greg has two close calls. As he stands in the curb lane while writing a speeding citation late one evening, an approaching car veers to the right, knocking him down. The driver stops, screams a twelve-letter epithet at Greg, then jerks his transmission into gear and speeds off. Greg goes to the hospital with a bruised leg and misses one shift

Three weeks later, he and another officer are asked to escort an ex-convict out of his mother's home. They peer into the bedroom, where Dennis is apparently asleep. It takes only a glance to see that he's huge — well over six feet and more than 250 pounds. Greg backs off until a third unit can respond.

As soon as they approach him, Dennis bolts out of bed and leaps at the nearest officer. Greg takes an all-out forward swing with his nightstick, striking the fleshy part of Dennis' right shoulder. It doesn't even slow him down. All three officers jump him, trying to bring him to the floor. Like buzzing flies on a horse, Dennis shakes them off with what appears to be minimal effort. While the other officers are temporarily reeling, Dennis comes after Greg, who is just pulling himself off of the floor. Greg draws his gun, and Dennis stops in mid-step.

"You can't shoot me; I don't have a weapon," he says, staring directly at Greg. There's barely a blink as four men each wait for

147

someone else to make the next move. Ten or fifteen seconds pass, then Dennis raises his hands and says softly, "Okay, gentle as a lamb." The officers, not sure what to expect, move in warily, but cuff him without further incident.

It's the first time that Greg has come within a heartbeat of taking a life and he is shaken by the encounter. "In my head I was thinking, 'He better buy this, it better intimidate him,' because I didn't feel justified in shooting at that point. I hadn't really decided at what point I *would* shoot, and that's what was scary about it. If you haven't decided to shoot and he's going to fight you, having the gun in your hand can be detrimental because you don't have that hand free to protect yourself or fight back. If I had fired, I don't know how well it would have stood up. It's a fine line because (to shoot) you really need to be in fear of losing your life."

*   *

Greg's dream life has been active lately, moving randomly between his still-new career and the upheaval in his personal life.

"I'm always up against incredible odds trying to save the damsel in distress. There's never a gun involved, just a physical fight. Sometimes I dream that I'm on duty and everyone I talk to wants to fight. Even if I say, 'Good morning,' we get into an argument. I'm sure that coincides with what's happening in my marriage."

On the street where alertness is essential, he tries to limit the distractions. "When things are slow, I sometimes find myself driving along thinking about my marriage and my daughter. I realize I'm not concentrating on what's happening around me, but I try hard not to let my problems get in the way of my job or to leave victims feeling that I don't care about what's happened to them."

It's the day after Christmas, and Greg's squad has been on duty the last two evenings. Given the faltering state of his marriage, work has become a diversion. Greg has spent much of the past two shifts spreading a unique form of holiday cheer by giving verbal warnings and candy canes instead of citations on most traffic stops. Most recipients seem surprised and pleased, but several don't even acknowledge the gesture in their haste to drive off.

Greg's first assignment tonight is to assist nurses and security officers at St. Joseph's Hospital. A man has been found unconscious in the desert. He smells of liquor, and a blood test shows a .40 blood alcohol count, four times the legal limit for intoxication. Awakening from his stupor, he offers a string of profanities and begins thrashing

148

wildly. It takes four people to strap him down, but the situation is under control by the time Greg pulls up. "You might want to keep him restrained until the alcohol wears off," Greg suggests to a nurse who is still catching her breath. She looks up, and not quite suppressing a laugh, says, "I'm not taking them off, ever."

*   *

June 5, 1987. Vice President George Bush arrives in Tucson on Air Force Two. Seventeen months before the Presidential election, he's in town to meet supporters and raise money to qualify for matching Federal campaign funds.

Dozens of law enforcement officers — the Secret Service won't disclose how many — are mobilized to guard the route Bush will travel. Greg and another officer are part of the security detail. They're stationed first at an intersection as the Vice President is driven to a hotel luncheon, whizzing by at what seems to Greg to be at least seventy miles an hour. Later, they're positioned under a bridge as the motorcade heads to a private home for a reception.

They have been assigned to cover another intersection during Bush's return trip to the airport, but they lose track of the time, and when they ask when they're due at the new post, a nervous voice responds, "If you're not there now, we're gonna be in big trouble."

They run Code 3 the rest of the way, arriving about two minutes ahead of the convoy.

"I was thinking that he'd get stuck at a traffic light because we weren't there to close down the intersection and I'd lose my job," Greg says later.

*   *

Greg's marriage is beyond repair and his wife has filed for divorce. Financial details must be settled, but there's so much anger and hostility that each has retained a lawyer.

For the first time in nearly a year, he is working an all-daylight shift. To many officers, it's a time to ease up a bit. "The reality is that you need to have a different attitude at night," he believes. "That means not letting someone have as much leeway in what they say or do. You need to have more of a survival instinct. The thoughts that go through my mind are mostly safety-oriented. On a traffic stop, for instance, I aim a lot of light toward the subject and I'm more verbally assertive. During the day, I'm still aware of officer safety, but it

149

doesn't seem to have the same sense of urgency."

Greg continues to see changes in himself. "What I've found lately is that I don't listen as well as I used to, and that probably goes hand in hand with being less tolerant. Chris (Oaxaca) just pointed this out to me a couple of weeks ago. We responded to an argument over what was strictly a civil matter. I was talking to this one guy, but I wasn't really listening to his side of the story. I knew what I wanted done and I pretty much cut him off.

"Part of it is that you go to a family fight or you go to a burglary, and the people are upset because it may be the first one for them. But I've been through them a couple hundred times and I know pretty much what they're going to say. All I want to do is get the information and get out of there and it's sometimes hard for me to remember that it may be the first time for them. It's something I'm working on — to be more aware of what the victim is feeling."

After two years on the street, he, too, has begun to develop the 'Us Against Them' syndrome. "It's easy to think and act that way. You hear so many lies on the job that it carries over. When I talk to my friends off-duty, I find myself mentally checking on what they tell me, kind of second-guessing them. It's not right. It annoys them and it annoys me to know I'm doing it. I've gotten to the point where I'm not so idealistic as to think I can make a major difference in saving society. It's sure not what you see on *T. J. Hooker*."

■

Mid-summer, 1986. Sunset is approaching as Pat Horbarenko begins her shift. Her work briefcase is more like a suitcase, stuffed with Arizona statute books, binders filled with police directives, copies of recent case reports and dozens of miscellaneous forms. It weighs nearly twenty-five pounds and wouldn't fit under the passenger seat of most airplanes. Little of it will be needed tonight, or any other night — unless she neglects to bring it along.

Three hours into the evening, a young woman folding clothes in a laundromat is approached by a man who unzips his trousers and makes an offer she immediately refuses. Rebuffed, he grabs her purse and runs out. Pat is there in less than five minutes, but the man has disappeared into the safety of the moonless night.

Some of the contents of the purse are found near a trash dumpster about 200 feet away. Pat boosts herself over the lip of the dumpster and drops gingerly into the mass of garbage. Using her flashlight to make short sweeps over the rubble, she soon spots the purse. Except for about $15 in cash, everything seems accounted for. The young woman is delighted. Pat is pleased and appreciates the gratitude of a happy 'customer,' but would prefer a cleansing shower. At this moment she'll have to settle for a fast visit to a restroom.

The dumpster caper reminds her of another recent encounter with grime. Responding to a silent alarm alert at a fast-food restaurant, Pat found that the business had already closed for the evening. Although there was no indication of forced entry, she climbed a ten-foot ladder to check the roof.

"I hadn't realized that the ladder was resting in an area coated with grease. Just as I got to the top, the ladder started sliding sideways and I had to hang onto the drain gutter until it stopped moving. I was thinking how embarrassing it would be if I fell off or if the ladder gave way and left me hanging there. While I tried to figure a dignified way out, a young guy parking his car across the street called out, 'You fucking cops; you couldn't even catch the Prime Time Rapist.'"

The remainder of the evening is busy. A hospital reports that the brother of a shooting victim is hysterical. Pat starts up, but the situation is under control before she arrives. She checks out a nearby pizza place where teenagers have been reported drinking. It's quiet there tonight. She's dispatched to take a burglary report from a man who has returned from a late dinner to find his home ransacked.

Just before 1 a.m., a late-model truck broadsides a car making a right turn, and the impact pushes the car's frame within a few inches of the still-conscious driver. While an ambulance takes the victim to the hospital, Pat interviews witnesses. An hour later, there's another accident less than a mile from the first one. The injuries here also could be life-threatening and she works with traffic investigators for more than two hours as they measure and diagram the area.

Medics are usually on the scene within five minutes of an accident report, and when they're delayed, it's the police officer who must attend to the victim.

A few weeks later, Pat is dispatched to a collision between a motorcycle and a pickup truck. Seeing the cyclist lying on his back in the middle of the roadway, she positions her car to protect him from being hit again, then kneels next to him. There are scrapes on the side and back of his scalp, but not a lot of blood. His left leg is rotated backward and Pat guesses to herself that he has a broken hip.

She suspects that his most painful injury is a bad case of road rash from skidding across the ground.

He looks up at Pat.

"I'm dying, I'm going to pass out."

"An ambulance is on the way and you're going to be okay," she assures him.

His eyes roll and Pat fears he might be going into shock.

"Come on, you have to fight it," she says, louder and more assertively now, not wanting him to lose consciousness.

An ambulance arrives a few seconds later and takes him to a hospital less than two miles away.

Still wondering about the cyclist's condition several hours later, she goes to the emergency room and is told that the injuries are minor.

"How's his leg?" she asks.

A nurse points to the trauma room.

"It's hanging on the wall in there."

A shocked look fills Pat's face until the nurse stifles a laugh long enough to tell her that the leg is a prosthesis resulting from a previous accident.

*   *

As 1987 begins, Pat's relationship with her husband is in trouble. Unpredictable even before they married, it has gotten worse, especially since his recent promotion to sergeant. Now, according to Pat, too much of Steve's life revolves around his job, and he brings home not only the frustrations of his own work, but also those of his squad members.

Pat and Steve work different shifts and this is also a problem. There is no special accommodation for officers married to each other. Policy doesn't permit them to be assigned to the same squad and the scheduling rotation seldom has them working similar hours.

"Sometimes the only way we can see each other is to meet for a meal, and even then, another cop is likely to walk in and sit down with us," she complains. "It's fine to talk about work some of the time, but it never seems to end. I need his whole-hearted attention at least part of the time. We don't have a lot of time together, so the quality of that time is really important.

"Since I'm a cop, I think Steve sees me as less female. There's not much hugging and affection. It's almost like I'm just one of the

152

guys. We've been going to counseling two and three times a week, but that can really drain you. My release is to eat a lot when I get depressed."

She's gained ten pounds in the past three months.

*   *

Responding to search a building after an alarm has sounded is among the scariest of calls, especially after dark. Pat has two of them this evening. She and Anita Sueme — they're working overlapping shifts — are sent to investigate a possible break-in. The northside home is surrounded by a six-foot wall, and portions of the area between it and the home are enclosed by wrought iron fencing. Pat and Anita climb over, then move cautiously, checking doors and windows. Air One circles overhead, its lights projected through the heavy shrubbery casting eerie patterns across the white adobe walls. There's has been no entry, but an apparently faulty alarm continues to cycle on and off.

Several miles away, two young people return home to find their front door partially ajar. They phone 911 from a nearby convenience store. Pat and another officer respond.

Flashlight in one hand and gun in the other, they approach from opposite forty-five degree angles. The door is broken and there are fresh wood splinters around the threshold. They step inside, moving methodically and cautiously from room to room. Their eyes are in constant motion, scanning left and right, up and down, index fingers never losing contact with the cold steel trigger guards of their weapons. No dice. A burglar has come and gone, and the couple can now return to list the stolen items.

To Pat, "It's always scary because you don't know what you'll find. Your mind is active, anticipating. It seems the search is taking forever." She's worked about two dozen open door calls, a few of them alone. Most are false alarms, and the burglar, when there's been one, has always fled before her arrival, but Pat knows that "sooner or later, there will be a confrontation."

■

Derek Campbell and Sharon Deitch have had an ongoing but sometimes strained relationship for three years, and his new life as a cop has made the situation worse. "She says I've changed, and I know that I have," Derek offers. "She says I'm too cold and callous, that I'm unemotional and don't talk. I know I shut down and I don't

153

know why. It's just something I have to work on. I went through that back in Chicago, and my ex-wife said the same thing."

Two months later, on May 3, 1986, they make a "spur of the moment" decision and drive to Las Vegas to get married

As he begins his second year on the street in late June, Derek picks up his first written reprimand. Two drunks angrily shove a waitress and then run from the restaurant. Because of a backlog of calls, the case isn't assigned for more than an hour.

As Derek tells it, "I got there in less than three minutes. As soon as I walked in, the waitress started wailing, 'What took you so long to get here?' I said, 'Ma'am, I just got the call.' She came back, 'Well, I called this in hours ago.' I said, 'Hey, I'm sorry; I just came on the street, and apparently we're real busy tonight.'

"She complained some more, and then I asked her what the men looked like. She said, 'Well, I don't remember.' She gave me a (license) plate number and I put out an Attempt to Locate. I asked if she wanted to press charges and she said, 'No, I don't think you're ever gonna find them.'

"I know we're not supposed to react that way, but her whole attitude put me in a negative frame of mind. It turned out that the guys had damaged the outside of the restaurant, but nobody told me about it while I was there."

When the manager sees the damage the next day and files a complaint, the Internal Affairs Division concludes that Derek didn't conduct a proper investigation and issues a Letter of Reprimand. Of all the possible negative results of an inquiry, this is the least serious, but Derek's vocal displeasure with the verdict brings him an invitation to visit a police psychologist to discuss his "negative attitude."

"My first thought was the stigma of having to see a shrink," Derek remembers, "but I decided to go with an open mind. He told me he thought I was pretty easy-going, but that because of my size, I have to be really careful about body language and tone of voice so I don't come off as too aggressive. I'm more conscious of that now. I had a good session and I'm glad I went. I'd recommend it to anyone. It can't do anything but help you."

*   *

July 28, 1986. Derek generally signs out a shot gun at the start of his shift. Although few officers exercise this option, Derek likes the added security of "a little extra firepower in case of an emergency." He slides in four rounds and places the weapon under the front seat of his patrol car.

It's the end of a busy week, highlighted by his first chase. "It was just after 3 a.m. and the streets were nearly deserted. I was cruising west on Broadway when this pickup truck blew by me like a white streak. I started after him, and at one point he was going over ninety. He almost lost it making a sharp turn, and that gave me a chance to catch up. When he pulled over, he got out of his truck, threw up his hands and said, 'Shoot me, shoot me, I want to die.' He was intoxicated, had no license, no registration, no insurance, nothing."

Tonight, a man reports hearing a gun shot from a neighbor's home. Derek and Greg Strom pull up from opposite directions. As they approach the house, a middle-aged man, his right hand behind his back, walks silently toward them. Not knowing who he is, they unholster their weapons. He stops immediately and says, "Wait a minute, it ain't me. I made the report."

Other officers seal off the area. It's still not clear that there's been a shooting, but an ambulance is parked nearby in case it's needed. Derek, Greg and a third officer edge toward the house and take positions to the front, side and rear.

Derek is just off the partially ajar front door. He has the best view and calls out, "Police Department, please come outside." There's no answer, so he peers through a window and sees what looks like someone on the floor.

Walking in, he and Greg find a man on the bedroom floor, a shotgun partially visible under his body. There's nothing left of his face above the top of the mouth. Blood, brain tissue and pieces of bone are splattered across the room. Later, Derek calls it "the worst suicide I've ever seen, here or in Chicago."

The remainder of the shift is more routine. A young man says that his former girlfriend took two of his pay checks and left town. A home has been burglarized. A suspicious vehicle in a nearby park is gone when Derek arrives. A man is yelling obscenities outside a home. Juveniles are reported to be partying in an apartment clubhouse and destroying property, but the five teens there when Derek arrives are orderly and the night guard says there's been no problem. A tearful woman needs an officer to stand by while she removes personal items from the apartment she'd been sharing with her boyfriend. Two routine traffic stops complete the evening.

*   *

It's the day after Thanksgiving, traditionally the year's most frenzied shopping day. Two of Tucson's four major east-west streets are in Derek's beat. As he signs on at 1:17 p.m., he's dispatched to a food market where a security officer has caught a young man with two cartons of cigarettes beneath his sweater.

He tells Derek he was going to pay for them, but he has only $1.44 in his pocket. Derek: "Come on, man, don't bullshit me. You're not going to get these for less than seventy-five cents a carton." Enough marijuana to make several joints is found in his jeans pocket. He says "some guy" gave it to him. A records check shows he was arrested for shoplifting less than a month ago. Derek takes him to Pre-Trial Services, where he is interviewed, then released to family members. Derek finishes his report and is back on the street at 3:09.

Three juveniles have been throwing rocks at an elderly woman's home. They're gone when Derek arrives. They come back twenty minutes later, but again run off. This time Derek is able to get their descriptions from a neighbor. Cruising the area hoping to spot them, he stops a motorist for speeding.

He pauses to remove his sunglasses before approaching the driver. "I think some people are irritated by the mirrors and the lack of eye contact, so now I either take them off or flip them onto my head when I'm talking," he says. "People seem to listen and respond better when they can see your eyes. The job is hard enough; I may as well find ways to try and make it easier."

Derek likes 'writing traffic.' It ties in with his goal of being a motorcycle officer, a position he'll be able to apply for after completing three years with the Department.

At 3:55, he spots a stalled van at a busy intersection and pushes it into a service station. Fifteen minutes later, there's a report of a man refusing to leave a nearby high school athletic field where he's said to be interfering with the football team's practice. The man has jogged off by the time Derek pulls up.

Just before 4:30, Derek returns to the food market to give the manager a copy of the shoplifting report, and then stops at the police station to label and store the confiscated marijuana.

At 5:12, he's one of two officers dispatched to meet an assault victim at a convenience store. Mindy says she was punched by Larry, her estranged husband, and that he has continued to harass and threaten her. After being treated in the hospital, she returned to her apartment to find her car's distributor cap removed. Derek escorts Mindy and her two young children home.

While he checks under the hood of her car, Larry appears, but speeds off when he sees Derek. In the few seconds it takes Derek to jump into his patrol car, Larry has disappeared, but within two minutes a passerby reports seeing a man hurriedly leave a vehicle and run north.

Derek finds him in a nearby alley. "Stand there and don't move!" he orders, then snaps on handcuffs.

"Did she press charges?" Larry asks.

"She doesn't have to if we have probable cause to make an arrest."

Another officer takes him to jail. It's 5:53.

Nineteen minutes later, three juveniles are reported trying to break into a concession stand. Derek spots them several blocks away. They admit they were in the area, but deny trying to take anything. Derek pats them down, then asks for their names, addresses and ages. They are all under sixteen. "It's not going to go anywhere but in my personal file," Derek assures them. Then, to Dispatch: "It's Code 4 here."

"What does Code 4 mean?" the oldest boy asks.

"It means everything's okay, that you're not giving me any hassle. If you were (hassling me), things would be different."

Pointing to the patrol car: "You mean we'd be in there, huh?"

"Relax."

"I was nervous; I've never been approached by a cop car before."

Smiling, "There's a first time for everything."

*   *

At 7:10 p.m. with his shift winding down, he stops for a snack. He'll have his real dinner — Thanksgiving leftovers with Sharon and her daughters — when he goes home in two hours. As he resumes patrol, his sergeant asks to meet him at the station for his yearly evaluation.

Derek appears apprehensive as he and Mark Kapellusch walk to a vacant office. Kapellusch closes the door, motions Derek to be seated and then hands him a manila folder containing his personal records, including copies of commendations and the July reprimand. Derek scans the sheaf of papers, then signs a statement acknowledging that he's reviewed the file.

Next, Kapellusch hands Derek his annual review — four single-spaced typewritten pages. As Derek reads, his expression becomes strained. He is silent for more than two minutes, then: "Because of one reprimand I'm below standards in compliance with rules and procedures? Because of one reprimand?" He pauses, then: "Well, I

157

don't agree with some of it, but I'm not going to question it."

"Let's talk about it," Kapellusch suggests, aware that Derek is upset. "The whole idea of the evaluation process is to be positive and not negative."

"What are the guidelines for reprimands? I just don't agree with 'falls below full performance standards' and 'below standards in the area of compliance with Rules and Procedures' because of one reprimand."

"Technically, if you have any reprimand or any violation of Rules and Procedures, that is below standards."

"Well, it still doesn't answer my question here, Mark."

Softly, seeing Derek's growing level of irritation: "What is your question?"

"Because of that one reprimand and the circumstances that it entailed, is that falling below standards?"

"I considered that situation (the June restaurant incident) to be fairly serious. It's not a situation where you went in and did an investigation and forgot to take prints or forgot a portion of the investigation. There *wasn't* an investigation; that's the problem."

Derek goes back to the typed review for about thirty seconds, then switches agendas: "I think this is bullshit about submitting a copy of a physician's report for each instance of sick leave. I gotta go see him if I have a cold?"

"It's not as though you had one major illness and everything else was fine. From the time you had six months with the Department, you started using sick leave at a pretty steady rate. For a while there, it was almost double the accepted standard. You'll notice in the evaluation that there's nothing that says anything about abuse of sick leave. I'm not in any way intimating that you're abusing the sick leave privilege. You're not the first to go through this. I will tell you quite candidly that the person on the other side of the desk from you has gone through the same thing."

"How's that going to affect me?"

"I don't anticipate a problem. I've said to you repeatedly. . ."

"Okay, Mark, that's fine, but still because of that one reprimand I'm below standards. One fucking reprimand in the last twelve months puts me below standards. I think that's bullshit; I really do."

"Well, I'm sorry that you feel that way, Derek. Considering the circumstances. . ."

"I mean, because of one reprimand, Mark, and every other time I'm out there busting my nuts. . ."

"I agree with that. I've put in your evaluation that I feel you

158

exceed standards overall in the area of quantity and quality of your work. I recognize the fact that you're always out there working and that you have a good attitude toward the job. I don't have any problem with that. I don't have any problem with the majority of your work. I'm very happy with it, but these are the two specific areas that I think need to be addressed, and I think it's to your benefit that they get addressed early. I'd be a fool to expect you to be pleased with this. I just hope you take it positively."

"All right, fine. What else is there?"

"Just initial all the pages, and sign this one. I'll bring you a copy in a minute."

"I don't want a copy."

"Are you sure? You're entitled to a copy of it."

"I don't want it, Mark."

Derek stands and walks out of the room, visibly angry and hurt.

*   *

Convinced that his working relationship with his sergeant is strained beyond repair, Derek decides to apply for a transfer to the DUI squad. He gathers what he believes are his best drunk driver reports and asks Kapellusch to look them over and choose the best two. Derek is pleased with Kapellusch's encouragement and support so soon after the annual review confrontation. Three weeks later, he is one of seventeen candidates invited to take the city-wide Oral Board examination for a DUI position.

Derek spends several hours researching the impact of intoxicated drivers prior to his interview. He finds that fifty-five percent of Tucson's motor vehicle fatalities are alcohol-related. When the Board's first question is, "Why do you want to be on the DUI squad?" Derek reaches into his briefcase, places several newspaper articles on drunk drivers on the table and says, "I want to stop this." The interview goes well, and Derek has a good feeling about his chances. Although he has less time with the department than any candidate, he's selected for one of the five openings.

Derek begins DUI patrol March 1, 1987, and as he's driving east on Speedway just before 2:30 a.m., a car speeds past him in the opposite direction. Derek makes a U-turn and begins pursuing. The vehicle is traveling at least eighty miles an hour and it takes Derek nearly a mile to catch up. The driver flunks all of the field sobriety exercises and refuses to take the intoxilyzer test. He tells Derek he was speeding because he thought his girlfriend was out with another guy and he was trying to find her.

Derek, arresting him: "Man, you were going too fast to see *anything.*"

Later, a woman speeds away from another officer, and Derek joins the chase. She 'blows' several traffic signals and stop signs and it's fortunate that the roadway is all but empty. When she finally pulls over, Derek positions his patrol car just ahead of hers and to her left. Looking straight at him, she jams her gear shift into drive and plows into his right front door panel.

Derek jumps out, draws down on her and yells, "Freeze! Don't move!" She hangs onto the steering wheel, but is pulled out and cuffed. Linda is in her mid-fifties, short, plump, and, with her hair cut short, somewhat androgynous.

Derek, calm now, asks, "Why did you run from a police officer?"

"I was trying to get home."

"Why did you hit my car?"

"Because you were in my way."

While Derek is doing paperwork prior to taking her to jail, his radio broadcasts the description of a woman in a similar vehicle who raced off earlier in the evening after crashing through a locked gate at a nearby Air Force base. Linda admits that she was also involved in that incident, saying she did it "because the guard on duty wouldn't let me in." There's no indication that she's intoxicated or on drugs, and a computer check shows no police record. She is cited for speeding, felony fleeing, endangerment and criminal damage.

*   *

Most DUI shifts — generally from about 6 p.m. to 2 a.m. — are not only routine, but repetitive and dull.

It's Friday, April 10, and an officer is good-naturedly grousing how slow it's been lately. "I worked North Campbell between Grant and Fort Lowell for a while and the average speed was about thirty-one," he says. "I tried East Speedway and the average there was maybe thirty-six. I headed to North Swan where you can always find someone going seventy, but there was nothing. Finally, I stopped one guy doing fifty-five, but when he pulled over, it was the clerk at my favorite Circle K, and I wasn't going to cite him."

As Derek leaves the station and heads east, there's a report of a fight at a downtown bar. He's only a few blocks away, and swings by in case he's needed, but the situation is already under control. At 9:08, he pulls over a red Datsun which has been randomly accelerating and then coasting. After speaking with the driver, Derek is

160

satisfied that he hasn't been drinking.

A few minutes later, he watches as a woman in a Chevrolet enters the roadway without checking for other vehicles. He stops her, and as she goes through her glove compartment in search of registration papers, Derek has his hand on his gun. "There was something in there that looked like it might have been a weapon. I don't like those kind of surprises." He warns her, but doesn't write a citation.

A man makes a left turn against oncoming traffic, nearly causing an accident. He's wearing a hospital scrub outfit and tells Derek he was day-dreaming. It's quickly obvious that he's not drunk. His bumper sticker warns, "I brake for the hell of it." Tonight, his acceleration earns him a failure-to-yield citation.

At 9:46, a vehicle with glaring headlights approaches from the opposite direction. Derek signals the driver several times without success, then makes a U-turn, catches up, and uses his roof-top speaker to instruct her to pull over. She ignores three requests, then finally coasts into a parking lot. She's a Vietnamese woman driving a new Mitsubishi van with temporary plates. Her knowledge of English appears minimal, but it's clear that she's upset at being stopped.

"Relax, I'm not going to give you a ticket," Derek says. She seems to understand this.

In the next hour, he'll make five more stops and write one speeding ticket and one equipment repair order. "I'm looking for flagrant violations," he says.

Just after 11 p.m., he observes a vehicle being driven erratically, and decides to administer a field sobriety test. He explains the process to the young man who is wearing a tank top shirt, jeans and white sneakers.

"Walk forward, placing the heel of one foot directly in front of the toe of the other," Derek tells him, demonstrating as he talks. "Count off nine steps, then pivot on the left foot and take nine steps back the other way." The driver passes and Derek opts to not give him any of the additional tests, but cites him for an unsafe lane change.

He makes four additional stops before the shift ends, one of them leading to his only arrest of the night. It begins at 1:42 a.m. when he spots a Nissan pickup truck driving without its headlights on. Mike, the driver, is twenty-eight, slim, well-dressed and very intoxicated. He fails three sobriety tests and is taken in for an intoxilyzer.

Derek explains the testing procedure: "Take a real deep breath

161

and blow into the machine long, hard and steady, like you're blowing up a balloon. Do that until you hear the machine click."

The test takes about ten seconds, and the readout shows .147. There are no 'priors' on Mike, and he has been cooperative. Derek completes his report, gives Mike a copy of all the records, including a bottled breath sample in case he wants an independent analysis, and offers to drive him home. Making small-talk now, they discover that they both grew up in Chicago. They spend the next few minutes bantering about their home town sports teams as friends might do over a couple of beers.

Derek seems sincere in his desire to get impaired drivers off of the road. He acknowledges two job bonuses: He earns overtime pay if a case goes to court, and with no specific beat, he has the freedom to respond as a backup unit on other calls. After six to nine months of this, he'll return to routine street patrol.

He has concluded that women are the worst drunks. "Most of them are either nasty or they come on to you, hoping you won't arrest them. One of them nearly broadsided me a few weeks ago and then sped off. When I caught up to her, she pulled down her top, grabbed her boobs and said, 'Here, do you want some of these?' She blew a .31, and I arrested her."

■

It's a late August evening, still hot and muggy, even though sunset was more than four hours ago.

A young man's clothing is stolen from an apartment complex laundry room while he's upstairs talking with a friend. Bernie Harrigan takes the report, including descriptions of each missing item, then walks around, shining his flashlight in the bushes. It's obvious to both Bernie and the victim that there's virtually no chance of recovering the clothing, yet Bernie's doing more than simply going through the motions.

He prefers the day shift because it's generally less hectic and it allows him to chat with people where they live and where they shop. He makes what appear to be effortless connections with most people, including those he arrests.

Three months later, he starts patrol at 4 p.m. He walks through a neighborhood shopping center, bantering with customers and checking the doors of businesses which have closed for the day. He

162

pauses to chat with a woman whose purse had been grabbed by a young man who is also a suspect in another robbery.

As he starts back to his car, dispatch broadcasts the description of a man refusing to leave an apartment complex less than two blocks away. Bernie drives in one entrance and circles around the rear. As he heads out the other side, the suspect comes into view, walking within ten feet of his patrol car. Bernie recognizes him as the purse snatcher, arrests him and begins an eight-mile drive to the Pima County Jail.

A twelve-foot gate topped with razor wire opens, and Bernie helps his prisoner out of the car. They walk about forty feet to a door which leads to an alcove area about five by eight feet. That door closes electronically and another opens, this one into a reception room where the defendant may make a phone call. Next, they move through still another door into the booking area. Handcuffs are removed and he's fingerprinted and processed.

It's not yet 6:30 on this Friday evening, but the booking area is already filled with cops and perpetrators. A cacophony of sound echoes through the room — a tenuous bridge between freedom and at least one night in jail. A woman who appears to be in her late teens is there, arrested for shoplifting. She weeps as her belt, sneakers and personal possessions are removed, listed and bagged for safekeeping. She wants a cigarette, but smoking isn't allowed in this area.

A bearded man in his forties and obviously drunk is talking incoherently. As the arresting officer prepares to leave, the man walks unsteadily to him and shakes his hand. "Take care, amigos," the cop responds. An Indian man with tinted spectacles and a nervous cough won't give his name so he is booked as a John Doe. A few minutes later, he and the accused shoplifter stand in a corner kissing.

Back on the street, Bernie loans a slim jim — a thin metal device which is inserted between a vehicle's window and door lock — to a man whose keys have been accidentally locked inside his Chevy truck. He tries without success to engage the unseen and elusive mechanism. A companion also fails, as does Bernie, who suggests, "What we need here is a car thief."

A young man walks by, hears Bernie's comment and offers to try. He works the slim jim for about two minutes before handing it back. "It's probably just as well; I might have incriminated myself if I'd opened it," he says, laughing as he walks off. Several others make attempts, and one of them quips, "Where are the crooks when you need them?" The growing group includes Whites, Blacks and

Hispanics, and there's a rare sense of camaraderie among strangers as they collectively challenge an unyielding lock.

The owner of the truck walks to a pay phone. He returns to announce that his son is on his way with a spare key, but now it's become a matter of principle among the onlookers that someone must snap open the lock mechanism *before* the key arrives. A short, squat man with a sizable pot belly forgoes the slim jim, using a wire coat hanger to fashion his own device. In less than thirty seconds, the door is open and the growing crowd cheers. Bernie has been there for the better part of an hour, but there have been no priority calls, and his presence has probably made a few friends for the police department.

"The way citizens perceive us is important, and I think we sometimes forget that," he says as he stops for a cup of coffee. "As you get older, you realize the importance of community relations. We come into most lives for just a few minutes. We don't solve many problems out here, but it's nice to think we've touched people who will remember that someone cared enough to spend a little time with them."

The work load begins to pick up now. A woman complains that a barking dog disturbs her sleep and that the owner is not receptive to her request to keep the animal inside until 8 a.m. The neighbor is not moved by Bernie's attempt at compromise, so a report will be made to Animal Control.

An off-duty policeman attempting to break up a fight radios for help. Bernie, at least seven miles away and hearing several closer units start up, remains in his beat.

A neighbor reports a young, unmarried couple arguing in their apartment. The woman's voice can be heard from the bedroom, but it's not clear what she's saying. Bernie walks past the open front door, calling out, "Police officer!" She comes out, slumped over and crying hysterically. It takes her nearly a minute to regain enough composure for Bernie to understand her through her sobs.

"He's leaving me. Oh, God! I can't live without him. I love him so much. What am I going to do? Oh, God, he hates me, he hates me!"

The male friend comes outside, says he needs some time away and heads toward his car. It's obvious that the young woman requires more help than Bernie can offer, so a crisis counselor is called.

An hour before his shift ends, Bernie is dispatched to arrest a man who, earlier in the day, picked up a wooden coffee table and threw it at a friend's teenage son, cutting the boy's head so badly that more than thirty stitches were needed. He and another officer knock at the man's door and ask him to step outside. Bernie confirms his name and date of birth, then says that there's a warrant for his arrest. "I'd appreciate your cooperation," Bernie says softly as he prepares to handcuff him. The man, in his early forties, is docile.

The arrest has gone smoothly. Most of them do, according to Bernie, who finds that suspects are often too cooperative for their own welfare. "Many of the people I arrest can't wait to talk, even after I've read their rights," he observes. "It seems that they all smoke and the first thing they want is a cigarette. I think there should be a pack in every police station. If someone's going to talk, it doesn't hurt me to hunt down a smoke. I tell the suspect, 'I promise you two things: When we get to the station, I'll take the cuffs off and I'll get you a cigarette.' If he's just bullshitting me, what has it cost? Just someone else's cigarette."

*   *

After living together for nearly ten years, Bernie and Dorothy are discussing a trial separation. They survived problems early in the relationship when he was still working for the New York Police Department. "I guess we thought they'd go away," he says, "but I still have hope that our relationship will survive."

Two months later, a message from the past throws Bernie's already tenuous personal life into further disarray. A letter forwarded to him by friends in New York begins, "I hope the years have been good to you. By the time you read this, our son will know who his father is. . ."

It comes back to Bernie in a rush of emotion — a woman he fell in love with while separated from his first wife in 1966. When Bernie went back to resume the marriage, Anne, carrying his unborn child, married a man she'd known for several years.

Bernie saw his infant son just once. When he phoned six months later, he was told that she had moved without leaving a forwarding address.

Bernie rereads the letter, folds it back into the envelope, then takes it out again. There's no anger in the letter, just the matter-of-fact recounting of two decades in the life of a woman and a child. Anne asks for nothing, not even a reply, though she makes it clear that she'd welcome one. Bernie is simultaneously awed, frightened and curious as he's quickly caught up in a dream of what once was,

165

and still might be.

He loves Dorothy, but now can rationalize that a trial separation has been her idea, making him a free agent. He wonders if there can still be a spark among the twenty-year-old smoldering embers. And, if he goes back to another time, will he be risking the pot of gold to chase the rainbow?

Bernie plays and replays the scenarios. It's not a decision to be made today.

6

The Breaking of a Cop

On the last evening of her life, twenty-two-year-old Michelle Tindall leaves the apartment she shares with her boyfriend and drives to a nearby nightclub. Shortly after midnight, she and a sixty-three-year-old male acquaintance go to his trailer in a southside mobile home park. She grabs one of several guns he owns, points it at him and fires two errant shots, then orders him outside. She fires several more rounds as he rolls under the trailer, huddling there for safety. Tindall gathers up two other guns and an assault rifle, jumps into her car and speeds off.

Officers respond, but the frightened man doesn't know Michelle's last name, where she lives or her car's license plate number. There isn't much they can do except take a report and broadcast the limited information they have.

Three hours later and six miles away, a new and deadly drama begins to unfold when the after-midnight quiet is broken by the sound of gun fire. Stephen Villarroel, twenty-eight, staggers from his apartment, blood spurting from his chest.

Several calls light up the 911 switchboard, reporting shots and cries for help. The dispatcher sounds the emergency tone: "Shots fired, Thunderbird Palms Apartment, 1252 South Craycroft. I'll give you further as I get it."

Officers Jeff Stahl and Tony Pappas are barely a half-mile away, having just checked a malfunctioning burglar alarm. They drive their patrol cars to the southeast fringe of the complex, dimming their lights as they approach. Pappas strides toward the victim's apartment while Stahl begins to walk around in the near-darkness looking for either the suspect or a witness.

Dispatch: "So far all I have is a male was shot by his girlfriend."

167

Gene Walker, also in the area, pulls up. Seconds after he eases out of his car, he reports that he has "eyeball" on a female carrying at least two firearms.

Stahl: "Where is he?"

Dispatch: "10-23 at Thunderbird Palms."

Stahl: "I know, but where in the complex?"

Dispatch: "1-Adam-13, where exactly are you?"

Walker: "East side, right off of Craycroft. She's carrying two (weapons) and she's running from me. She's running between the buildings and I also have one weapon on the ground here." His voice becomes increasingly breathless as he sprints to keep her in view. "Number five female, blue T-shirt, white hat and Levis. She's carrying the rifle."

The woman turns a corner and Walker loses sight of her.

Sergeant Steve Monk: "Get as many units (as possible) down there to seal that complex off now. Code 3 is authorized."

Dispatch: "Additional units who can clear, respond Code 3."

Stahl begins moving north in an attempt to pin down her location and block the major exit from the complex. Within a few seconds, two more officers arrive.

George Eppley pulls up and quickly spots the weapon abandoned by the suspect when she began to run.

The dispatcher repeats the woman's description.

Monk: "As soon as we get the apartment complex sealed off, make sure that we get at least two units to respond directly to the apartment to check on the victim." In the confusion of these first few minutes, he's unaware that Pappas is already with Villarroel and that an ambulance is on the way.

Stahl has now reached the northern-most limit of the property. It's been about three minutes since Walker lost sight of the woman. Soon there are six officers taking positions around the complex.

As Stahl begins retracing his steps, he approaches a large dumpster and senses that he's not alone. For a moment, he believes it's another officer, then quickly — though he can't see her — realizes that it's the suspect and that she's hiding behind the dumpster less than ten feet from him.

He jumps back and finds partial concealment behind the slatted fence which frames three sides of the dumpster, then quickly scampers another thirty feet to the far side of a parked car.

"Got a woman with a gun, northeast quad, behind the furniture store," he advises breathlessly.

The next several seconds of transmission are so fragmented that almost nothing is comprehensible.

Pappas, comforting the injured man, asks the dispatcher whether an ambulance is responding.

"One's en route." The stress is showing; her words have a sharp edge.

Walker, trying to determine Stahl's location: "I'm in the rear of the furniture store. Where is he?"

Stahl: "South of the furniture store."

Walker: "I'm directly behind RB Furniture. I don't see him."

Dispatch: "4-Adam-44, give us further."

Stahl: "Get somebody in here."

Dispatch: "Where are you?"

Stahl: "Behind the furniture store, enclosure of (the) garbage dumpsters." His attention is fully focused on the woman and he's feeling frustrated that his transmission is not specific.

Walker: "Where are you from the RV truck that's parked back here?"

Ed Goodwin, working with a rookie officer, answers for him: "We're with him. She's pinned up in a dumpster and she's holding a rifle on us, so we can't see her."

Dispatch: "10-4."

Goodwin: "Directly to the south side."

Dispatch: "South of the RV, 10-4?"

There's no reply. Twenty-one seconds of silence, then:

Goodwin: "She's at the southwest quad of the furniture store."

Jim Coburn pulls up. "I'm approaching from the south. Where do you want me?"

Dispatch asks Monk for guidance, but he's not yet on the scene. "Can you give me some help?" she asks.

No help is offered; the situation has developed so quickly that there are few points of reference and no one has the total deployment picture.

Eppley: "We have a female over here. It's actually behind the store on the other side of the wall."

The dispatcher, alone with her headset miles away, is not getting the facts she needs to help protect the officers' safety. She's quite direct and blunt as she keys her microphone:

"Where do officers need to respond so they don't get shot?"

Ten seconds of heavy silence, then:

Goodwin: "We've got the west side covered. Next unit, have them come to the southeast side of the furniture store."

Walker: "That's where I'm at. If he could just identify which side

169

of the wall he's on so we could determine which dumpster she's at."

Eppley: "She's actually in the first driveway off of Craycroft into the complex."

Walker, less than thirty feet from her, almost in a whisper: "I'm walking up behind her."

Air One is responding from the opposite end of the county, and is now just two or three minutes away. "If you want to have the units hold off and have us advise, it's up to you."

Monk: "I want the units at the scene to keep her under observation. Do not approach until we get Air overhead."

Suddenly the woman breaks her silence. She calls out that she has a young boy with her and that she'll shoot him if officers don't back off.

As the impasse escalates, another officer approaching the scene, reports, "The subject you have pinned down, her first name is Michelle in case you want to talk to her." None of them is aware of the earlier shooting.

In the next minute, a half-dozen cops have her contained in a semicircle of sorts. When several of them illuminate her with beams from their high-powered flashlights, it's immediately clear that she has no hostage. Tindall has lost her trump card.

Now Stahl and Eppley call out, "Tucson Police. Put the gun down!"

"Get that fuckin' light off me!" she screams.

In the frightening seconds that follow, she ignores another order to put down her weapons, yells "Fuck you!" and extends her left arm, revealing a handgun. She points it at Eppley and fires one round.

Stahl squeezes off a single shot, then hears several others. Tindall staggers backward.

Goodwin, urgently: "We're getting gun shots!"

Stahl, almost simultaneously: "Shots fired! Subject's down!"

Dispatch, confirming: "Shots fired."

Walker: "Suspect's down. Have 10-72 (ambulance) respond."

The dispatcher, nearly ten miles away, still has no indication whether the officers are safe.

Walker puts her at ease before she asks:

"The officers are Code 4."

"10-4, thank you."

It's 3:44 a.m.

Eppley, a former paramedic more accustomed to saving lives than taking them, has fired three times; Stahl, a cop for nearly twelve

170

years, just once. Tindall is struck in the waist and chest.

Later, Stahl will remember little about the first seconds after he aimed his gun and fired. "As soon as I knew she was down, I put my gun on the hood of a car, but I have no recollection of doing that. My heart was pounding and everything got blurry. I knew I had shot her, but it was almost as though I was watching the situation unfold without really being there."

Undercover officer Chris Zeller is the first to reach Tindall. She's lying face down and motionless, her right hand resting on the butt of the shotgun. Zeller rolls her over, finds a small revolver clutched in her left hand, and pulls it easily from her grasp.

With both weapons secured, he looks at her for the first time. Her eyes are fixed and dilated, and Zeller, also a paramedic before he joined the police department, sees that Tindall is in a state of agonal respiration — her breathing more reflex than voluntary. He knows that she's beyond help and was probably medically dead before reaching the ground. He raises her T-shirt to her neck. A bullet has hit her squarely in the mid-sternum. "Nice shot; ten-ring," he observes to no one in particular.

Officers, like others who routinely witness death and man's inhumanity to man, often fall back on a dark sense of humor to lighten the load and help maintain their sanity.

"I don't know what possessed me to say that," he observes later. "I wish that I hadn't, at least not just then."

Medics have been standing by, and now they move in. They take a fast look at Tindall, scoop her up and try unsuccessfully to resuscitate her as they race to the hospital.

Stahl had stood almost motionless as Zeller and the others rushed to where the woman lay. "I don't remember analyzing it, but I think there was a conscious decision on my part that I didn't want to go look at her. I didn't want to see what I had done."

Even in a state of semi-shock, he's aware that there is going to be a major investigation. "I knew that they were going to call out everybody in the world and that I didn't need to be concerned about doing police work at that point," he says later.

*   *

Several of Tindall's friends and acquaintances remember her as sometimes volatile and mean-spirited, likely to lash out blindly at anyone who came too near.

Her mother remembers another side of her, "A girl who wrote

171

beautiful poems and would cry when a bird fell out of a tree."

Villarroel is hospitalized, but survives.

*   *

An officer seldom has more than a split second to make the decision to shoot. When it results in injury or death to a citizen, a heavy toll is exacted. In the macho environment of law enforcement, police are generally perceived as ready and even eager to use their firepower. Too many cop shows portray the hero blowing the smoke off of his gun, flipping it back into its holster and moving on to the next assignment.

Not so in real life. The gun is one of the key pieces of evidence and is taken from the officer almost immediately. It will soon be replaced with a new weapon, but meanwhile the cop looks down at an empty holster. He will also be relieved of street duty for several days.

He is probably already asking himself if there might have been some way to have avoided the shooting, and may begin to feel that he *has* done something wrong. There will be questions to answer and sworn statements to make as a full-scale investigation gets underway within the hour.

Tonight's incident has an immediate ripple effect, branching out from the participants to other squad members, and soon touching virtually every cop in the city.

Stahl arrives home at dawn to a real-life episode from *The Twilight Zone*. His wife, Susan, seven months pregnant, is sitting on their bed, crying hysterically after awakening from a vivid dream in which she looked on helplessly as he was shot. Jeff has gone to work more than a thousand times since they've been together, but the nightmare is one she's never had until tonight.

Stahl soon goes to bed, sleeping nearly seven untroubled hours. He begins dealing with the shooting when he awakens, and the mandated days off prove a blessing.

"I was glad to have time to think about what happened," he observes later. "My mind was working real hard, galloping on fast-forward. I relived the shooting and what led up to it over and over, and I really needed that time to let those thoughts burn themselves off."

Les Beach learns about it when he walks into the eastside station at 5:40 Sunday morning to begin his 6 a.m. shift. "I knew immediately that something had gone down. All I saw was brass. I went into the briefing room and saw Jeff sitting there doing a crossword

172

puzzle. I said, 'Hi, how was the night?' He said, 'Well, it got kind of hairy out there,' without really looking up to make eye contact. That's all he said and I didn't pursue it.

"About two minutes later, they took our squad into another room, told us what had happened and instructed us not to talk about it with any of the officers who had been involved. That was fine with me because Jeff and I are real close, our families get together socially, and I wouldn't have known what to say."

*   *

Stahl and Robert Garcia are assigned to the same squad, and sit together at daily briefing. Robert, recuperating from a gynacomastia — the removal of a non-malignant tumor from his chest — had missed Saturday's shift. The shooting took place in his beat and he would have been there. When he hears the news, he immediately embarks on a frustrating series of questions without answers: Could he have talked the woman into giving up? Would he have fired the fatal shot? Might he have found himself in a vulnerable position and been shot?

His wife Tammy is particularly upset by the last possibility. They talk in hushed tones so their three young children won't hear. Many officers acknowledge a reluctance to fire unless fired upon, and Tammy is concerned that Robert might wait too long in a similar situation.

"We'll both be thinking about that for a long time," he says.

*   *

Seven minutes before the start of Sunday night briefing, the mood is subdued. There is none of the usual light-hearted bantering and the room is silent except for brief, almost whispered conversations. If you didn't know what happened, you might think that a *cop* had been killed.

A veteran officer, crouched about 100 feet from Michelle when the shooting began, is asked to describe his impressions of the final seconds: "It took a long time to unfold. I heard one pop, then two, then two more. They didn't sound like gun shots and I wasn't even sure she was hit until she went down."

The officer's perceptions are normal, Sergeant Bill Hurguy assures. "That's what happens under stress. You develop tunnel vision and there's sensory distortion. It can be real confusing. If you

173

were there, you may run it through your head over and over. There's nothing wrong with that, and it will diminish over time. Just remember that you're not in control in that situation. The person in control last night was the woman with the weapons. She was making the music and we were all dancing to it."

Hurguy, who taught a class on the aftermath of shootings when Robert attended the Academy, is asked how officers should approach Stahl and Eppley when they return to work.

"People usually don't know what to say and since they're afraid of saying the wrong thing, they often avoid any form of verbal contact," he tells them. "Most officers think that they'll do just fine if they're involved in a shooting, but when one comes down, the result is usually a lot of self-doubt. What we really want is approval from the people who work right next to us, and the officer who has shot someone is probably most concerned about what his peers are thinking.

"Don't say that it was a good shooting and don't use humor unless they do. The best ice-breaker is a simple 'Hi,' but if you ask 'How are you doing?' make sure you have time to listen if they want to talk. Your rapport with them may be the single most important factor in how they adjust to the street in their first days back.

"The biggest lesson I want you to take from this is to never become lax with officer safety," he concludes. "Questions?"

Silence for a few seconds, then, "It's time for work."

*   *

During a twenty-year career, the average police officer in the United States has less than one chance in ten of ever firing his service weapon except on a shooting range.

Lieutenant Doug Scoopmire, a cop for twenty-one years, has studied and analyzed the use of deadly force by Tucson officers since 1973. In the fifteen-year period through 1987, he found that Tucson Police Department officers were involved in eighty-five shooting incidents, resulting in the death of nineteen suspects. Two cops were killed, both of them plain clothes narcotics officers shot at close range while attempting to make an arrest. In addition, thirty-three suspects and four officers were wounded.

Scoopmire has accumulated extensive statistical details.

A total of 304 shots were fired by officers, eighty of which struck suspects. Sixty-three shots were fired by the suspects, eleven of

174

them hitting officers. Some suspects employed weapons other than guns, including knives, hatchets, screwdrivers, motor vehicles, a machete, a choke-hold and a two-by-four spiked with nails.

Of the eighty-nine suspects, sixty-one were under the age of thirty, but three were older than fifty. Forty-two were White, twenty-six Hispanic, nineteen Black, one American Indian and one of unidentified race. Three were women. Half were unemployed, thirty-eight percent were intoxicated, and sixty-six percent had at least one previous felony arrest.

Eighty-one percent of the shootings occurred between 5 p.m. and 5 a.m. and there were three times more shootings on Sunday than on Saturday. Forty-one percent of the cops fired just one shot. Two officers fired eight times, requiring them to stop and reload.

Their accuracy rate was fifty percent during daylight hours and twenty-three percent at night. The distance between officer and suspect was thirty feet or less sixty percent of the time.

Forty percent of the shootings were the result of officers intervening in family fight or disturbance situations.

*　　*

The Model 66 Smith & Wesson .357 Magnum used by the Tucson Police Department weighs slightly more than two pounds and may be loaded only with .38 Plus P ammunition. Squeezing off a round from the four-inch barrel sends a bullet speeding toward its target at 960 feet per second, the equivalent of more than 650 miles an hour.

When an officer shoots another human being, the result of that split-second decision will be scrutinized at length and in depth by a Board of Inquiry comprised of several ranking police officers, a representative of the City Attorney's Office and a member of the Tucson City Council.

In Arizona, an officer may shoot to kill only to protect the life of someone else or when he perceives his own life to be in imminent danger. Deadly force may not, for example, be used against a fleeing suspect when there is no indication that he poses an immediate danger to anyone. The statute states that "the reasonableness of the force used must be judged in the light of the circumstances as they appeared to the officer at the time he acted."

The Board's mandate is to review the entire incident, identify information available to the officer at the time of the shooting and, ultimately, to determine whether the officer's actions were lawful and within departmental rules and procedures.

The Tindall investigation package consists of 381 pages of documents, statements and reports from more than thirty officers, investigators and civilian witnesses. Diagrams, charts and photographs show the location from which every shot was fired, where each bullet struck and where each came to rest.

Five months after Tindall's August 30, 1987 death, the Board concludes that the shooting was justified.

Stahl says he never worried about the outcome. "They were doing what had to be done and I thought that everyone went out of their way to be considerate, supportive and non-judgmental. It was as painless as the department could make it."

Although he hasn't asked, he's certain that he fired the fatal shot. "Maybe there's something in my subconscious that doesn't want to see it in print. It's an action I took because I felt I had no other choice and I've never really second-guessed myself. Obviously I wish it hadn't been necessary.

"I've never, ever wanted to kill somebody, but there's nothing I can do about it now and there isn't a whole lot of point in beating my breast and tearing out my hair. If I let it do that to me, then maybe I shouldn't be in this job. I can't imagine that there are many cops who haven't thought about whether they could pull the trigger if another life depended on it. I'm sure there are cops who couldn't, but don't know it. At least now I know I can if I have to."

■

It's September 10, 1987. Greg Strom has added a dozen pounds as well as a mustache which is now at the awkward stage, not sufficiently filled in to look good.

At work, it's been a slow summer, except for a string of deaths, including three suicides. Two of them lay undiscovered for several days in the summer heat before gasses from their decomposing bodies attracted the attention of neighbors.

"The paperwork is pretty simple and I don't have any real problem seeing what's there," he says of his first 'floaters.' "What troubles me is trying to understand what drives people to kill themselves. When I'm having problems, I try to get help and work things out. I've just gone through a difficult marriage breakup and the stress of a divorce, but you keep trying."

176

Most rewarding to Greg is an aborted suicide attempt. A woman phones 911, concerned that she hadn't been able to contact a despondent twenty-eight-year old friend for several days. Although Tyrone's car and motorcycle are parked outside, there's no response when Greg and a second officer knock.

Unlocking the door with a key provided by the friend, Greg calls to Tyrone, but there's no answer. They check the first floor and then walk upstairs. The door to the bedroom is closed and a muted groan is heard. Greg tries to turn the handle, but it's locked. The other officer kicks in the door and as it flies open, they see Tyrone lying on his bed, eyes open. A revolver is in his left hand, one finger resting inside the trigger grip.

Using the door for cover, Greg crouches and asks Tyrone to move his hand away from the gun. Tyrone remains motionless; there's no acknowledgment that the officers are there and no indication that he has shot himself. Greg attempts to initiate conversation, saying that friends are concerned about him.

"I'm really in trouble now," Tyrone says, breaking his silence.

"We're here to help you, not to arrest you," Greg tries to assure him.

There's no reply. Tyrone doesn't appear agitated, but maintains a palm-up grasp on the gun as it rests by his thigh.

Other officers are on the way, but in the absence of hostages or threats, the situation calls for calm rather than force. Tyrone has almost nothing to say, appearing to be in another world. After nearly ten minutes, he closes his eyes. Greg doesn't know if he has drifted off to sleep or simply tired of the one-sided conversation.

They decide they'll try to get the weapon from him. While the second officer draws his gun to cover Tyrone, Greg takes the long way around the room, staying out of direct range. Reaching the man's side, he wraps his right hand around the main frame of the gun so that the cylinder can't turn even if the trigger is squeezed. Greg twists it from Tyrone's grasp and it comes away cleanly.

While looking for other weapons, they find books on failed relationships and pictures of Tyrone and an older couple, possibly his parents, torn and scattered on the floor. Tyrone sobs quietly while a psychiatric evaluation is arranged.

"It was one of those situations where everything is so quiet that you're sure he can hear your heart going boom, boom, boom," Greg recalls later. "I didn't think he'd be able to fire with my hand on the cylinder, and if he did, I knew I'd be able to control the direction of the shot.

177

"It felt good that we got there in time to stop him from shooting himself. At the least, we bought him some time."

*   *

Humor can often help defuse a touchy situation. Sergeant Bob Elash joins Greg as they check the welfare of an a middle-aged woman who is reported to be off her medicine and possibly suicidal. They attempt conversation while awaiting an ambulance, but Evelyn is rambling on and not making much sense.

Elash, quizzically: "Do you have your henweigh here?"

She pauses for a moment, as if to consider the question, and then goes back to her monologue.

Elash, at her first pause: "I need to know if you're going to take your henweigh to the hospital."

She's not buying it.

Elash shrugs and tries a new question. "Well, then, how about your piecost?"

This catches Evelyn's attention. "My piecost?"

"Yeah, are you going to take your piecost with you?"

She pauses, dead silent for a moment, then looks up at him. "What's a piecost?"

"Oh, about three bucks."

Greg begins to lose it and has to step outside to regain his composure, but the absurdity of Elash's query brings Evelyn back to reality. She laughs and soon begins a normal conversation.

For Greg, the days of laughter are down to a precious few.

*   *

October 12, 1987. Driving west on Broadway, Greg recognizes a white Volkswagen with black stripes as it passes him. The car had been described by an acquaintance as belonging to a drug dealer. He follows the VW into the parking lot of a neighborhood club featuring topless dancers. Off duty and wearing civilian clothing, Greg goes inside.

"I sat at the bar and ordered a drink," he says the next day. "I noticed two men at a table in the middle of the floor. One guy was real laid back and just kind of relaxing, but the other one was acting strange, kind of uptight, looking around and checking everyone out. I was real suspicious that there was something illegal going down and I decided I would phone for uniformed officers if my suspicions

178

continued.

"The uptight guy nursed his beer and watched everyone walking in or out. He was much too observant for a typical bar patron. Twice, he and his friend got up and walked outside and I followed them a minute or so later to see what they were up to. They used the pay phone and then come back in. I thought I recognized one of them and by the way he was acting I figured it might have been someone I'd arrested."

Greg's actions have attracted their attention and the situation turns into an awkward staring contest. Now, Greg begins thinking that one of them might be a police officer working undercover and realizes that he could be interfering with an investigation.

He uses the phone in the club's office to call the Communications Center. George Smith, the sergeant in charge of the undercover team, soon calls back.

"He was hot," Greg recounts. "I tried to explain, but I don't think it made much of an impression. He said, 'We'll be talking to you later' and hung up. At that point I knew I was in the middle of something that I shouldn't have been in the middle of."

Greg drives home and receives another call from Smith. "When I asked if I had screwed something up, he immediately began playing me for the bad guy, asking, 'Well, did you?' He asked what I was doing there and I told him. He asked why I was able to use the office phone and I told him I had a friend who worked there."

As Greg prepares to end his shift the following afternoon, he's instructed to report to Internal Affairs.

*   *

With the exception of staring down the barrel of a suspect's gun, nothing frightens most officers as much as a telephone call from the Internal Affairs Division, and many cops believe that an administrative investigation is *more* stressful than being on the wrong end of a weapon. Ironically, IAD is also generally mistrusted by those outside of law enforcement, some of whom portray it as a giant washing machine where everything goes in dirty and comes out clean.

In truth, the mandate of Internal Affairs is to investigate all allegations of officer misconduct or criminal activity. The source of an inquiry may be either a citizen's complaint or information developed within the department.

Nearly all of the approximately 950 complaints lodged by

179

Tucsonans in a typical year allege misconduct by street officers. More than two thirds of them have to do with perceptional or attitudinal issues. Rudeness is the most common charge, and because of limited resources, most of the relatively minor complaints were handled through a military-like chain of command until 1986. This, however, resulted in a lack of consistency, according to Lieutenant Thom Hacker, head of IAD.

Under the new system, most are resolved by a cross-education process which attempts to give both cop and citizen a better understanding of the job.

According to Hacker, "a large majority (of citizens) express satisfaction that we took the time to look into their complaints and report back, even when we didn't believe there was a reason to discipline the officer. A lot of times there's no way to either prove or disprove the issue, especially in the area of individual perception. One of the things we're able to do is give the citizen the officer's perception of what happened, and sometimes that in itself is beneficial.

"There's a lot of mental role reversal involved. Many citizens will be able to put themselves in the officer's shoes and come away with a better understanding of what his job is like. We also go back and tell the officer how he was perceived by the citizen and that maybe there was a better way for him to have handled the situation. It's often something as simple as an officer not making eye contact or saying 'Have a nice day' while he hands over a citation. Citizens need to know that their concerns will be dealt with fairly and expediently, and officers need to know that complaints against them will be handled on both a timely and consistent basis."

Each time a cop is named in a complaint, there is a review to determine if there is a pattern of behavior which needs to be corrected. About ten percent of complaints result in some combination of an oral or written reprimand, mandatory retraining or counseling.

Charges of excessive force, brutality, corruption or breach of civil rights require a thorough investigation which begins with formal statements from complainants, officers and witnesses. Where charges are substantiated, the range of disciplinary actions includes a written reprimand, suspension without pay, demotion or dismissal. Of Tucson's more than 700 officers, an average of seventeen are suspended, reduced in rank or fired each year.

Hacker acknowledges that "there's a definite fear factor among some of the younger officers who come in. They're terrified, and I don't want that. I'm not here to intimidate. All I want is to know what happened. If they've messed up in a minor way, I just want them to learn from the mistake."

Although Ronstadt believes that "in their heart of hearts I think they know that IAD isn't out to screw them," he also realizes that cops frequently walk a moral tightrope.

"We are held to a higher standard and we can't lose our temper when someone baits us or yells profanities. The minute a cop lets his personal feelings get in the way, he's not doing what we expect him to do. Inappropriate action cannot be excused. We understand why it happens, but we can't condone it.

"Officers need to remain detached, put up with the verbal abuse and not react out of frustration. If the officer's response crosses the line, I'd rather hear, 'I lost it and I'll take my lumps' instead of a denial. I'd rather hear, 'Whatever you're going to do to me, it was worth it at the time.'"

*   *

Greg, preparing to drive to Internal Affairs, asks Elash what to anticipate. "He said I could expect to be in a little bit of trouble and that they would probably want to know why I was interested in this type of thing off duty," Greg recalls. "When I asked him, 'Are we talking about my job?' he shook his head and said he didn't think it was that serious."

His mind already racing, Greg walks to his car and heads downtown. He's told almost immediately that IAD will conduct a criminal investigation.

"The Lieutenant read me my Miranda rights and that was scary," Greg remembers. "He asked if I understood what he'd just said and if I would answer his questions. I wanted to just lay everything out because from my point of view it was a gross misunderstanding, but I remembered being advised at a Fraternal Order of Police meeting not to make any statement without an attorney present.

"Everything stopped for about an hour until the FOP attorney arrived. I filled him in on what had happened. He said he didn't think there was a case against me and felt it wouldn't be a good idea for me to make any statement until we knew more about what was going on. That was hard for me to understand, but he was the expert and I felt I needed to listen to his advice.

"Lieutenant Hacker then told me that the case would be turned over to the County Attorney's Office to decide if criminal charges would be filed and that I was suspended with pay. The worst part was removing my badge and gun and reaching across the table to hand them to him."

Greg drives home, confused and scared. His mind races, but without focus or direction. Struggling to hold on to his dreams a little while longer, all he remembers is "wishing that I had gone downtown in a police car so I could feel I was still a cop."

Depression set in immediately. "It's scary how important giving up that badge and gun was. I stayed in my apartment for a week and I think I only showered and shaved once. I was a zombie, sitting in front of the TV most of the time."

*   *

A Grand Jury convened by the County Attorney's Office concludes that it doesn't have sufficient evidence for a criminal indictment. Greg is advised of this and also told that it could be up to two weeks before the Tucson Police Department determines its next step. He tries to remain optimistic as he waits for the call that will tell him it has all been a mistake, that he did nothing wrong and that he can rejoin his squad. But as the days pass, he becomes increasingly fearful that what he labels an innocent friendship with the club's assistant manager might be used against him.

"I'd have a drink or two and shoot some pool. We're friends, but my relationship with him has never crossed over my job line. We talk about my work in general, mainly calls I've been on. I have no knowledge or indication that he's involved in anything illegal. If I did, that's where the friendship would stop.

"I keep wanting to go downtown and make a statement on my own behalf and my FOP lawyer keeps telling me that it's not time to do that. Not saying anything bothers me, but I'm at the point where I have to trust somebody."

Most upsetting to Greg is that he feels the entire case is based on accusations of other cops. "If there was an undercover operation going on there, I can understand someone wondering about the possibility of my being involved. What I don't understand is why someone doesn't look at the taped transcripts of the phone calls I made and see that there was no intent to screw up what was going on. I'm beginning to realize that the innocent don't always prevail. It's scary and I'm wondering how far this can go."

When Greg's squad members make no attempt to contact him the first week, he concludes that he's an outcast.

"I was afraid to call them in case what I was thinking was true. They've begun to call or stop by in the past few days and it's made a difference. They let me know that I had their support. I needed to hear that because I knew the rumor mill had started and that some people were saying, 'Strom's a dirty cop.'

"I'm beginning to think I could lose my job and my friends for something I didn't do. I don't like being in that position. I don't have a career backup. Law enforcement has gone from just a job to the only thing I want to do."

*   *

October 29. Greg is called back to Internal Affairs and asked if he wants to change anything in his previous statements. The question has a menacing cast to Greg, who feels that the meeting is more inquisition than interview. At one point, he says, a sergeant glared at him, asking, "Do you sell information? Do you sell protection?"

After nearly three hours, he's asked if he will take a polygraph test. He agrees and is driven 110 miles to Phoenix. Seated in the back of an unmarked police car, he feels like a criminal. The conversation with the officers in front is strictly small talk.

He leaves Phoenix believing he'll be vindicated by the polygraph. "I felt relieved, but I also thought that two of the key questions were worded in an ambiguous way."

In one of them, he was asked whether he had identified the undercover officers to anyone in the bar that evening. "I knew that I hadn't in words, but I thought I might have through my actions. It would have been more meaningful if I'd been asked if I verbally told anyone, for instance by saying, 'Hey, those two guys over there are cops.'"

The second troublesome question was whether he had divulged any police information that night. "We often talked about my job in general terms. If the words 'confidential information' had been included in the question it would have eliminated the ambiguity."

Internal Affairs disagrees, saying that any possible ambiguity was negated by the pre-test interview.

Greg is told the next day that the polygraph indicated untruthful answers to those two questions. Ten days later, he is fired, and his worst fear has now become reality.

His formal notice of termination advises him of his right to appeal to the Civil Service Commission. He knows it will be expensive both financially and emotionally, but a private attorney will at least guarantee that all of the evidence is examined.

"I don't feel that the punishment fits the circumstances," he says quietly, "and only getting back on the street will let me believe there's justice in all of this and that the system works the way it's supposed to work."

*   *

It's early February, 1988, and Greg and his attorney, Don Awerkamp, prepare for the appeal hearing. Greg takes a second polygraph test, believing it will clarify the interpretation of the earlier one.

He's now lost contact with all but a few of his officer friends, and this cuts deep. Greg realizes that some are avoiding him because of fear that they might be vulnerable by association, but he believes that "to most of them I've gone from buddy to asshole."

Since his divorce, Greg has lived in an apartment complex less than three blocks from the eastside substation where he started and ended each day's shift. Watching the comings and goings of police cars becomes too painful for him and he moves.

He keeps financially afloat by painting and detailing cars while he awaits his hearing, first set for March 30, 1988, and then postponed for three weeks when only two of the required three Commission members show up.

*   *

April 20. His hearing is convened just after 7 p.m. The process is similar to a trial in most ways. Both sides may call witnesses to testify and both attorneys have the right to cross-examine. Unlike a civil or criminal trial jury, the three Commission members may also question witnesses. There is no judge, but an attorney representing the Commission is there to rule on legal questions or challenges. The burden of proof is on the Tucson Police Department.

Greg is seated with his attorney at a U-shaped table less than six feet from the witnesses who are testifying against him. Directly across the table from Greg is Police Chief Ronstadt who had congratulated him and handed him his badge three years and one day ago.

184

Michael Wood, attorney for the Tucson Police Department, charges in his opening statement that Greg conducted an unauthorized off duty investigation, "tipped" the presence of undercover officers and then lied about his involvement.

"What went on was so egregious that TPD had no choice in firing him," he asserts.

Awerkamp counters by depicting Greg as an officer who had often been praised for his initiative and whose job performance was lauded by supervisors as "exceeding standards."

"If Greg Strom had recognized those officers and wanted to burn them, all he had to do was say, 'There's cops over there' and leave," Awerkamp contends. "Why would he have made telephone calls to the police identifying himself when he knew those calls were being recorded?

"He knew that he was in over his head and he panicked. He wasn't completely honest when he was confronted that night on the telephone, but you have to read it in the context that he was being (verbally) attacked by a sergeant. He became defensive, he didn't react properly, he didn't behave perfectly. That ought to get him disciplined, but it ought not end his career as a police officer."

The first of the two undercover officers testifies that he recognized Greg, but couldn't place him, thinking at first he might be someone he'd arrested or seen during the course of an investigation. Convinced that Greg was monitoring his movements, his partner phoned a friend to pick them up in her car so they wouldn't have to 'blow' the identity of their undercover vehicle. He testifies that he thought Greg was in some way connected to the business because of his access to the back office and that Greg appeared to know the suspected narcotics dealer.

The other officer testifies that both he and his partner believed they had "been burned real bad in the bar," causing the investigation to be abandoned. "If a narcotics suspect recognizes you, not only is the investigation in jeopardy, but your personal safety may be compromised," he says.

Smith tells the Commission that if an officer believes there's the possibility that he's chanced upon an undercover operation, "basic common sense should tell you to leave. If you've made observations you believe involve illegal activity and you're off duty and no one's life is in danger, you leave and you report that information."

Smith acknowledges that many off duty officers patronize topless clubs and that there is no policy against it. His issue is that he believes Greg "burned a narc and ruined an investigation."

185

The opening statements and testimony of the three witnesses have taken nearly five hours. The hearing is adjourned for the evening.

*   *

Thursday's session moves more quickly. A police lieutenant, a records supervisor and a police service operator relate the substance of their phone conversations with Greg on October 12. Those calls were recorded and there is no controversy over their contents.

Sergeant David Neri, who headed the Internal Affairs investigation, discusses discrepancies in Greg's initial statements. The department, he says, is more concerned with the result of the tipoff than whether it was intentional.

Ronstadt explains why the department decided to fire Strom.

"We had to consider the possibility that Mr. Strom was engaging in illegal activity and that perhaps his actions may have been motivated by his association with the target that the narcotics people had been working or with the manager of the bar. The other end of the spectrum was that Officer Strom was doing exactly what he ultimately told us he was doing, that he sincerely believed he had come in contact with some information about a possible narcotics target or suspect."

Ronstadt says that the investigation was not able to determine whether or not Greg had engaged in deliberate criminal activity.

"I tried to look at it in terms of common sense, in what experience he had as a police officer and in terms of rules and procedures. He was less than candid in some of his statements. We have terminated officers before for being untruthful, and unfortunately we will have to do it again. What Mr. Strom did showed incredibly poor judgment even in a best case scenario."

Gerald Settner, who administered the second polygraph test, testifies that he felt Greg's answers to the two troublesome questions were truthful when more precise wording was used. "I based my test on did he verbally or willfully tell anybody in that bar that these two people were police officers. I believe Greg was being truthful when he said that he had not done this."

Following a short break, Elash is called in. As Greg's sergeant, he has observed him closely for more than two years. "For his length of service, I thought he was an exceptional officer," he testifies, adding that "initiative was one of his strong points." Elash, the only officer to testify on Greg's behalf, says he'd be glad to have him back

186

in his squad.

Greg has sat calmly during two evenings of testimony, his arms resting on the table in front of him, fingers interlocked. Occasionally he has jotted notes on a yellow legal pad to share with his attorney. Now, at 10:43 p.m., Greg is the final witness. He walks five steps to the witness chair and faces the Commission.

He describes the road that led him to law enforcement, especially his desire to have a job with responsibility. He recalls how initiative and dedication were among the constant lessons at the Academy. "We were reminded by a screaming sergeant that we're law enforcement officers all the time and that we don't quit just because it's Friday."

Greg says that he knows he was over-zealous in his surveillance of a possible narcotics dealer, but that the information he had was vague and unsubstantiated. "My knowledge of what is observation and what is investigation has changed. I realize now that what I was doing was an investigation."

Wood cross-examines Greg in the most confrontive episode of the hearing.

"Do you lie?" he asks.

Greg reflects on the question for three seconds, then: "Not generally."

Half-shouting: "You did in this case, though, did you not?"

"I wasn't truthful."

"On several occasions."

"I wasn't truthful on a couple of occasions."

"Is your response in a panic situation to lie?"

"It's not my typical characteristic and in that situation I screwed up. I handled it wrong."

As closing statements begin just after midnight, Awerkamp pleads for Greg's career:

"People make mistakes every day. Police officers make mistakes every day. I would be willing to bet you that there's not a police officer who hasn't exercised poor judgment this past year. Greg exercised poor judgment that night. There's no question about that. The question is, how bad was it? Was it so bad that he ought to be disciplined? Was it so bad that he ought to be fired? You hear over and over again that there's no clear line, that it's a question of judgment. How bad does judgment have to be before a person gets fired?

"Maybe Greg should have received a letter of reprimand. Maybe he should have been suspended without pay for a week or a month or three months. He's been suspended now about seven months and I think it's time to put him back on the force."

Wood tells the Commission that "even in the best case, we don't know why he did what he did, and the worst case is there's something more afoot here that we're not able to establish. Don't get bogged down in trying to figure out how this came about or why he did what he did because I suggest to you you're not going to find an answer to that, but neither is it important to the decision.

"One of the things that officers have to have is good judgment and they're held responsible for the judgments they make. Maybe you get to do a lot of things with the kind of judgment Greg Strom exhibited that evening, but you don't get to be a police officer. He says he's learned, but I suggest that it's too late."

*   *

Unlike a courtroom trial where the jury discusses the evidence as it attempts to reach a verdict, the Civil Service decision is almost immediate.

Moments after Wood returns to his seat, one of the three Commission members taps her pen lightly on a note pad, looks up and says, "I move that we uphold the suspension and termination of Greg Strom."

Now it will take the vote of just one of the other two members to make the firing official.

Seconds later, the chairman calls for the question: "All those in favor signify by saying 'aye.'"

The decision is unanimous.

There is momentary silence, then adjournment. Commission members, attorneys and observers begin moving around the room. Greg remains seated for nearly a minute, showing no emotion. He and Awerkamp have a brief whispered conversation, then the two of them stand and step outside to the parking lot where Greg's parents have been waiting.

Greg walks slowly, wordlessly, toward them, and they know without being told.

7

The Smile of a Stranger

Les Beach is just a year away from his fiftieth birthday. The man who came out of the Police Academy convinced that his maturity would allow him to maintain an easy-going attitude is being worn down by trouble-makers and drunks. He started his mid-life career on the assumption that people were good unless they showed otherwise, but his 'default setting' is now often the reverse.

It doesn't help when the young man who injured him in the November 1986 confrontation, is sentenced to just six days in jail for the assault. Les lost three months of work to him; Brian's sentence is too little and too late.

As he heads across town after taking a prisoner to jail, Les observes a vehicle with two men in the front seat pull off of a dirt road and veer onto the street, tires screeching. The driver slows briefly, then makes a sudden U-turn and floors his gas pedal.

Les is in a strange neighborhood in the middle of the night. All he can do is announce the streets as he races through intersections at speeds which briefly exceed 100 miles an hour. The suspect pulls onto a desert road, leaving a trail of dust that even Les's high-power spotlight can't cut through.

He moves in cautiously, and when he sees the suspect's vehicle, eases out of his patrol car, gun drawn. The driver and his passenger have fled, leaving behind two loaded automatic weapons. "At that point, I was real happy they were gone," he says later. "I may wear cowboy boots, but I'm not John Wayne."

* *

It's 10:35 p.m. on the Friday before Christmas.

A loud party is reported at an apartment complex. There are

189

several young people there and although it's obvious that they've been drinking, the noise level appears reasonable. Les banters with them briefly and leaves.

Next, there's a fight brewing at a club featuring topless dancers. Ronald, an inebriated man in his late thirties, paid to watch a private strip-show and felt he was entitled to a 'hands-on' performance. Feeling the effects of too much liquid courage, he is trying to pick a fight with the bouncer who has told him to leave.

"Do you want him arrested or just removed from the property?" Les asks.

"We'd just like him out of here."

Les follows the straggly-bearded, pot-bellied man, who half-walks and half-staggers into the parking lot. Ronald is nearly six feet tall and weighs more than 200 pounds. The odor of alcohol on his breath cannot be missed.

"Let me tell you what's happening," Les says. "You came here to get a show and that's fine, but this is not a house of prostitution. They want you to leave the property and that's their prerogative. Are you driving a car, sir?"

Ronald nods.

"I can't allow you to drive, but I'll be glad to call a cab or have a friend come for you."

Ronald says he wants to file a complaint against the club, but when Les asks for his full name and address to document the charges, Ronald changes his mind and begins walking toward his car.

"Remember not to drive," Les calls after him.

Ronald sits in his car for about twenty seconds and then switches on the ignition. Les and officer Hank Masek sprint to him.

"Shut it off!" Les yells through the closed window.

Ronald ignores him and Les repeats the instruction. The door is locked, and as Ronald disengages the emergency brake, Les pulls out his nightstick.

"Shut it off or I'm going to break the window out!"

Ronald reaches for the gear shift.

"Shut it off and open the window or I'll break it!" Les screams, hitting it lightly as a warning.

Engine still running, Ronald opens the door with his left hand, but continues holding the gear shift with his right.

"Come on, get out of the car!"

"What's your problem?" Ronald asks.

"Don't ask me my problem. *You're* the problem; get out of the

190

car!"

When Ronald doesn't budge, Les and Masek reach under his arms and pull him out.

"What the hell are you doing?" he screams.

"Stop resisting!"

"I'm not resisting!"

"You are! Now put your hands behind your back!"

They force Ronald against the side of his car, stomach to metal, and hold him there so he can be cuffed.

"What the fuck's the matter with you guys?" he yells as he continues to kick and struggle.

Les slams his nightstick into Ronald's shoulders.

"Get your hands behind your back!"

Ronald is still fighting and Les strikes two more blows to the same area.

"I've got asthma. What's your problem? Please don't hurt me!"

"Then get your hands behind your back!"

"I got 'em!"

"You didn't! You ready now?"

"Okay, I'm ready!"

"Put 'em back, behind your back by your belt!"

Handcuffing Ronald is like trying to nail a bowl of Jello to the ceiling. He cooperates for a few seconds, then begins to struggle again when the officers momentarily loosen their grip to snap on the cuffs. They now use their nightsticks to hold his arms down.

"I've had heart surgery. Please don't do this to me! Please, God, don't!"

"You want to resist some more?"

"No, I won't, I won't."

Les, almost out of control: "I'll break your fucking arm right off! You dumb shit! You just don't pay attention!"

"I will. I swear to God I will."

The belligerence is gone and he begins to cry.

"Please release me. I can't breathe. I can't breathe. Please? Please?"

They stand him against the car and tell him not to move. Even now it takes several minutes of verbal jousting before Ronald agrees to identify himself.

As Masek prepares to take Ronald to jail, the bouncer walks over to Les. "Sorry you had to put up with that shit."

Les, unwinding now: "That's all right. It helps me get my coffee down."

Back on patrol, the disillusionment is clear.

"I've been on the street for less than two hours and I've already been involved in a scuffle. My adrenaline is pumped up and I don't feel like providing much in the way of community relations tonight. If I make a traffic stop right now, I'm not going to accept any excuses. If a guy says his mother is dying and he has two minutes to get there and see her, she's going to die without him because I'm going to write him a ticket. I'm going to unwind and feel more relaxed soon, but right now the way I feel is that anyone who breaks the law is going to pay for it."

*   *

Teenagers reported to be drinking in the parking lot of a convenience store are gone when Les pulls up.

Next is a house burglary. By the time Les arrives, there are three officers on the scene and a suspect sits handcuffed in the middle of the driveway.

Patrons of a bar have been parking in the private lot of a rival club which has fewer customers, but more parking spots. The owner of the less-patronized club has been retaliating by having the vehicles removed, and it's become a profitable late-evening business for the towing company which has been taking the cars several blocks away and charging $55 to have them returned.

Les responds tonight. Eight people are angrily milling around. Several of them talking at once, they head en masse for Les, who quickly extends the palm of his right hand, motioning them to stop. He explains that the vehicles were towed from private property, that the police have no legal jurisdiction and that his only function is to maintain order.

This does not please the complainants. They appear to be in their twenties and thirties, and all of them have been drinking. There's a lot of yelling about ripoffs and scams, and a few thinly-veiled threats.

Beth is particularly vocal, yelling alternately at Les and the tow truck driver. A short, sputtering fireball, she wants Les to make an arrest for auto theft, but Les explains again that the towing was legal because warning signs are posted at each entrance. When Beth says she won't pay, the tow truck operator says that her car won't be returned until she does and that there will be an additional $8 a day in storage charges. Beth screams a string of profanities.

"I'm going to take this sucker to court!" one of them yells.

"You have that right; that's what the courts are for," Les agrees.

His low-key acknowledgment doesn't help.

"Why aren't you out there catching murderers and rapists instead of hassling us?" another demands. It is probably the challenge cops hear more than any other.

Les reminds the man that he was asked to respond, but his logical reply is immediately lost in the emotional shuffle.

"If I ever get raped, I'll blow the son-of-a-bitch away with a .357," Beth retorts, apropos of nothing.

Although Les hasn't requested backup, two other officers pull up in case they're needed.

Getting no satisfaction from Les, Beth walks up to one of the other cops, puts her right hand on his upper arm and begins yelling.

"Don't put your hand on me! Don't even *think* about it!" he snaps, backing off two steps.

Beth glares at him, turns and walks away.

Another man demands for at least the third time that Les write a theft report, and Les explains for at least the third time that there's been no theft.

They continue to play variations of Catch-22 until the tow truck operator says he's going to leave if they don't pay. As he starts walking away, they reach for their wallets and purses.

Having clearly lost face, they direct their anger at the officers. Les and his partners are immediately caught up in it, now active and willing participants in a game of who can make the most biting or sarcastic comment.

When Beth's car is returned to the curb outside the lot, she insists that it be placed at the precise spot where she left it. Les says that's not necessary and Beth yells some more as she stomps off.

It's 1:32 a.m. when Les leaves. He's been there nearly ninety minutes and nothing has happened to improve his disposition.

As he's about to pull into a convenience store for coffee, he sees a well-dressed man tottering in an empty parking lot. He makes a U-turn and drives back to see if the man needs help.

Louis is about forty — a happy, mellow drunk who says he'd been partying with friends at a nearby bar, but was accidentally left behind. Home is across town, more than a dozen miles away. Les banters easily with him while they wait for a cab. For the first time this evening, Les has begun to relax.

Ten minutes later, a hospital security guard calls 911 to report a young couple in the parking lot arguing and shoving each other. The woman is gone when Les arrives. The man says they'd been drinking and that he'll probably go to a friend's apartment for what's

193

left of the night.

At Burger King, two men are reported to be intoxicated, belligerent and refusing to leave. Les pulls up, but they've already walked away.

At 2:53 a.m., he's dispatched to an assault victim waiting at a convenience store. A man is bleeding from the head, his shirt and slacks caked with blood. Kevin says he attended an office party with a female co-worker. After he drove her home, she invited him in for a nightcap. Soon, the woman's ex-boyfriend knocked at the door and Kevin hid in another room. When he heard them arguing, he feared for her safety and came out, sustaining his injuries in the ensuing confrontation during which he broke a large bottle over the former boyfriend's head.

Kevin's wounds are superficial and he goes home. The ex-boyfriend is driven to a hospital, intoxicated and in need of medical treatment for an open head wound and a possible concussion. Taking statements and completing the paperwork will consume the last two hours of the shift.

Les has responded to eight calls this evening and dealt with nearly twenty people. With only one exception, alcohol has been either the cause or the major contributing factor.

"It seems that almost everyone we run into at night has had a few drinks and either they don't want to pay attention or they're not able to listen to directions or advice," Les grouses as he sips a final cup of coffee. "There's a cumulative effect, and I think that's where the burnout comes from. You get so tired of talking to people who have been drinking. You might just as well be talking to a garbage can."

*   *

Three months later, Les is more his upbeat self.

"There are some valleys and peaks in this job. I had this period where I just wanted to tell people to go to hell, and if they wanted to get in my face and duke it out, that was fine with me, too. For a while, if someone even looked at me crossways, I was ready to knock them out. I went from being mellow to being so aggressive that I was getting citizen complaints on simple traffic stops. My attitude has been adjusted and I'm back to being a lot more laid back. I can joke with people again, even the ones who aren't very nice."

*   *

The Tucson Police Department has no quota system on motor vehicle citations, and the statistical average over a full year is about four per officer per week. Individual supervisors, however, may establish areas of emphasis based on safety issues, community needs and their own philosophy of law enforcement.

"When I first broke in, I was told that 'two citations a day keep the sergeant away,'" Les remembers. "While I was working for him, I made it a point to get them. The legitimate violations are out there so it wasn't usually difficult to do."

Here, too, there's been a shift in his philosophy.

"Often you don't really accomplish anything by giving a warning instead of a citation. To be blunt about it, the only way we can control people is to hit them in their pocketbooks. Then they might slow down because they can't afford to keep paying fines and accumulating points. I give a lot of motorists the benefit of any doubt, but if you really wanted to do the job properly, you'd cite everyone you stopped.

"Some officers follow this philosophy and I'm not sure that they're wrong. I try to let each person give me a clue. I rely on their attitude, their previous driving record, my perception of their sincerity and whether or not their license, registration and proof of insurance are in order. For the most part, *they* tell *me* whether they get a citation.

"Most people have fragile egos. Nobody likes to be caught and no one wants to be told he's done something wrong. Not only is the person embarrassed, but on top of that, he's probably going to get a citation from another human being who is no better a person except that the cop has a badge, a gun and a ticket book."

*　　*

Hazel Miller, accused of bludgeoning her husband to death on December 26, 1986, is convicted of manslaughter by a jury which deliberates for seven hours. Still claiming innocence, the seventy-three-year-old woman is sentenced to seven-and-a-half years in prison.

■

Derek Campbell is shot at twice in one week as his tour of duty with the DUI squad winds down.

It's about 1 a.m. on September 11, 1987, and Derek is preparing to administer an intoxilyzer test. There's a sudden flash of light, a loud report and the smell of gunpowder. It's over before he can even think of taking cover. Not hit, he whirls around in time to see an orange sedan speeding away. Derek jumps into his patrol car prepared to pursue, but realizes that his portable alcohol-testing machine is resting on top of the trunk. He radios a description of the vehicle, but a search is fruitless.

A week later, he's cruising just after 10 p.m., looking for impaired drivers. From a distance of about 150 feet, he notices an arm hanging from the driver's door of a car approaching him from the opposite side of the road. The arm extends outward as the vehicle nears his. Derek spots the gun and sees a flash in the same split second. He ducks instinctively and his patrol car swerves briefly to the right before he can straighten the wheel.

"Traffic 66, I've been shot at. Suspect vehicle westbound on Broadway from Indian House," he reports as he makes a U-turn and starts giving chase. It's happened so quickly that he can't provide a vehicle description. He loses the car, and again, several other units fan out in an unsuccessful search for a suspect.

Derek, who took the first incident in stride, is badly shaken this time and goes home early.

What is most frightening to Derek is that there was nothing he could do. He knows that the ounce or so of metal pinned chest-high on his uniform is a bulls-eye of sorts, a lethal target for someone who would like to kill a cop. His understanding is now on a new, deeper level, and although he minimizes the effect, a part of him will never be the same.

* *

Back on his eastside beat after eight months working DUIs, Derek is making another adjustment.

"I was spoiled big-time out there," he says of the relative freedom of that assignment. It was also financially profitable, with overtime pay when he was called for attorney interviews and court appearances. He worked six or seven days most weeks, quickly adjusting to little sleep. He'd get home at 3 or 4 a.m. and be back in court six hours later.

"I never got more than five hours at a time," he remembers, choosing to remain on the short sleeping cycle even on his rare days off to be with Sharon and her daughters. "I'm at the point now where it's nice to have the time off, but I still find myself staying up late and getting up early to take Nicole and Jessica to school."

Seven months after his below-standards performance review resulted in a temper tantrum and mandatory counseling, Derek gets an evaluation he's happy to hang his hat on.

"You work hard and steadily on assigned tasks and do extra work willingly," his sergeant writes. "You require very little direction or supervision and you can discriminate between relevant and irrelevant details to arrive at sound conclusions. You are exceptionally successful in dealing diplomatically with complaints and eliciting cooperation from others. You learn new things easily and make special efforts to improve your skills and knowledge."

His new rating shows him "exceeding full performance standards."

* *

The late-summer shots fired in Derek's direction have not been forgotten, especially when he's out of his patrol car during a traffic stop. Moreover, he knows that he's vulnerable even when weapons are not involved because his 'super cop' physical image makes him an attractive target.

Macho men seeking to earn status with their friends will seldom attack a female cop or a male of lesser physical stature. They have little to gain even if they get in a punch or two, but lose face if they're outfought. Taking on a cop of Derek's size is a no-lose situation for the same person. Not expected to prevail, he garners significant bragging rights if he gets the best of the brawl.

Aware of the physical damage he can cause, Derek holds back longer than most officers. To a man who threatens to "beat the shit" out of him: "You're welcome to try, but you'll probably end up in the hospital and I'll be home watching TV." The man backs down.

"Some people are going to be like that," Derck observes. "I won't instigate it and I'll do everything I can to avoid it, but if someone insists, I'm ready to accommodate. If it's going to be balls to the wall, I'm going to try to make sure it's *their* balls."

He already misses DUIs. "I'd go back in a heartbeat," he says, glancing upward as if to inspire divine intervention.

His next destination, unfortunately, will be the sidelines.

* *

It's April 3, 1988, Easter morning. Just after 2 a.m., an officer reports that an apparent drunk driver has jumped the median barrier and is going west in the eastbound lane. The late model Pontiac sideswipes another car and then picks up speed. By the time Derek approaches the scene less than a minute later, the suspect's car has blown two tires and the metal wheels are spewing cascades of sparks.

Derek looks on in amazement as the driver narrowly misses several other vehicles, then nearly T-bones his patrol car. The suspect drives over a curb, loses control and hits a trash dumpster and several parked cars in less than fifteen seconds. He jumps from his car, falls momentarily, but gets up and sprints to the rear of the parking lot. Derek brings him down with a flying tackle and the man lands face down in the dirt, Derek on top of him.

What Derek most wants now is to "drop kick that S.O.B.," but thinking better of it, he grits his teeth and, with the help of Ron Payette, begins walking the suspect back to the parking lot. After a dozen or so steps, Derek feels a sharp pain and falls to the ground, his right kneecap broken in three places.

Derek undergoes surgery three weeks later and then begins an almost daily regimen of physical therapy. It will probably be months before he can return to duty and he is not a happy patient.

"Every time I ask the doctor if I can go back to work, he laughs," Derek says without amusement. He's able to sit or stand for only about thirty minutes at a time, and with little to do except watch television and build scale model airplanes, he's eating more and gaining weight that he doesn't want or need.

■

A Board of Inquiry has ruled that Rene Gomez violated departmental rules and procedures during last June's lengthy car chase. The key to the Board's decision appears to be Rene's refusal to state with certainty that he looked both ways before entering the intersection.

His sergeant, Paul Thompson, writes the Board on Rene's behalf: "He stated he was sure he looked both ways prior to entering the intersection, but refused to state positively that he had done so. Knowing officer Gomez, I questioned him further in regard to this point. I found that his own integrity would not allow him to state that he was 100 percent positive and that some of the details had become cloudy due to the length of the chase and the duration of time since the chase occurred.

"I feel this is to be commended. As everyone knows, a high-speed pursuit requires (that) many things be done very quickly. It also often requires trained reaction rather than concentration on exactly what is happening. Standard defensive driving tactics require that you look both ways prior to entering an intersection as not everyone is going to stop. Add to this the fact that the light is red when you enter the intersection in a high-speed chase, it would only increase the caution.

"It is my judgment that officer Gomez did in fact use due caution in entering the intersection in accordance with the Code 3 policy. I recommend that no further action be taken against this officer and this matter be closed."

When he receives a written reprimand, the normally mild-mannered Rene is visibly agitated. "It's (the reprimand) pretty minor, but that's not the point. I don't feel I was wrong and now I'm being burned. I wouldn't change anything I did on that chase. I'm a good driver. This is the first accident in my life. If I know I'm wrong, I'm man enough to say so, but that's not what happened. It bothers me, but I don't want to make waves and be known as a cry-baby."

Police Chief Ronstadt, a street cop for the first twelve years of his career, understands the frustration, but wishes that his officers would worry less.

"Mistakes will happen and an officer must be prepared to take the consequences," he says. "Show me a cop without an occasional reprimand and I wonder how good a job he's doing. A reprimand used to be a badge of honor, and most of the best cops still have a blemish or two on their records."

Nonetheless, a month later, Rene is almost paranoid about his driving, mulling the consequences of an accident that *is* his fault. "I think what's happened has done more harm than good. It will really be on my mind the next time I get in a chase."

* *

It's mid-summer, and officers are investigating a hit and run accident. Lorraine Martinez spots the suspect's vehicle about a half-mile from a busy golf course. When she pursues, the car stops and two men sprint away. Cruising in the area, Rene sees two men matching their descriptions. They appear nervous and run as he approaches. One of them is quickly caught, but the other vaults a

199

fence, commandeers an electric golf cart and heads down the back fairway.

In a scene that could have been inspired by the Keystone Kops, officer John Kragnes jumps into the cart of a very surprised golfer and the two of them take off after the second suspect. As they move closer, Kragnes hops out and makes the arrest.

Rene expects his second reprimand as a result of a recent fight at a midtown bar. A man arrested by another officer and seated temporarily in the back of Rene's patrol car has stashed a packet of cocaine behind the seat. Procedure requires that an officer inspect his vehicle for evidence or contraband each time a prisoner has been in it. Rene's assumption that the arresting officer had made the search comes back to haunt him. "I should have checked and I'm going to take the burn for it," he says matter-of-factly.

* *

February 15, 1988. It's a slow Monday evening until a street dispute threatens to escalate. Members of one family charge that neighbors have burglarized their automobile. There are already two officers on the scene, but lacking anything better to do, Rene starts over.

The two suspects are Black, as is one of the cops. One, a trim six-footer, says only that his name is Rickie. The other is several inches shorter, but weighs at least 250 pounds. He, too, is unwilling to provide identification, saying he keeps it inside the house. Playing off of each other, they come across as thoroughly disagreeable as root canal without anesthesia.

"Why don't you get some ID and bring it out to us?" the Black officer asks.

"I didn't do anything," Rickie answers, the thrust of his jaw tilting his face upward.

"I didn't say that you did. Will you get me the ID?"

"No, I won't."

The car parked outside of their house is facing the wrong direction and the second officer radios in its license plate number. As the impasse continues, they decide to use this as leverage by saying they'll have it towed for illegal parking unless the owner identifies himself.

Rickie quickly says that it belongs to him. "I paid for it and I got plenty of tickets to prove it."

"All I'm asking you to do is get me something to show it. Is that anything hard to do?"

"No, it ain't hard to do, but I didn't do nothing and you're trying to railroad me."

The second officer steps in. "You're playing games with us and we can play games, too. The car's illegally parked and I'll just tow it."

Rickie's voice level, like the situation, is escalating. "You ain't going to tow it; I'll just get my God-damned keys!"

For the next few seconds, everyone's talking at once and the next word or movement could trigger a fight.

"I want you to come over here; you're making things worse," the Black officer tells the shorter man whose gut rolls in waves over the top of his elastic-belted coveralls. He leads him a dozen steps away.

The other cop, a veteran of nearly fifteen years, stands toe-to-toe with Rickie. "Let me explain something. We're asking you for identification. Now if you want to play hardball, I can tell you right now that I can play games that will just make your head spin. So if you want to get bad with me, I'll get bad with you. You want to treat me like a human being, I'll be nice to you. It's that simple. You got some ID, I want to see it."

Rickie's attitude changes abruptly. "Please don't tow my car; I don't have the money to get it out."

"Then cooperate. All we've been asking (for) is some identification and then we're going to walk away from here. Fair enough?"

Rickie turns, goes into the house and is back with identification in less than two minutes.

There's no indication that either Rickie or his friend had tampered with the neighbor's car. The officers could cite Rickie for illegal parking. It would demonstrate their power and offer some degree of satisfaction, but they opt not to.

Discussing the call later, the White officer explains what it took to resolve the situation: "All I had to do was threaten the guy with his car and look what happened: 'Oh, well, I be gettin' whatever you be wantin' from me.'"

The mimicry would seem demeaning and prejudiced, except that the retelling is done in the presence of the Black cop. He makes no effort to hide his feelings about the second man who had been working hard to turn the situation more volatile. "Now, the fat boy, I'd like to take him down. I'd like him to come at me so I can beat his ass."

Cops sometimes utilize a 'good guy, bad guy' strategy in which one of them is demanding and the other conciliatory. Properly used, it can reduce tensions and lead to a 'win-win' situation.

Rene has found that a second officer can sometimes offer a face-saving scenario and accomplish what the first one can't. "It's often just a matter of the personalities involved. If I see that someone doesn't like me, but responds to someone else, I'll step back. If giving the citizen that bit of choice or control helps defuse a situation, I'm all for it."

Tonight he has remained on the fringe of the confrontation, ready to move in if needed.

Rene's attitude toward the job and the public doesn't appear to have changed much in three years. He is still very much the jokester until he slides behind the wheel of his patrol car.

"I like what I do," he says. "The only thing that's changed is my patience with people who are trying to hurt me or jerk me around. If I'm gonna have to dance, I'll use my nightstick to protect myself."

He is a homeowner for the first time. "It's nice knowing I can go back to my own place. I've worked hard all my married life for this moment, and there's a lot of satisfaction in having something to show for it."

The extra space will soon be needed. After two miscarriages, Sylvia is four months pregnant and Rene is ecstatic with anticipation.

■

Although it's months after the fatal shooting of Michelle Tindall, Pat Horbarenko still feels emotional after-shocks. As an emergency room nurse in the early 1980s, she often worked with George Eppley as they battled against time to save lives. "It must have been a terrifying role reversal for him to have had to take a life," she laments.

There have been police-related shootings to the east, west and south of her in the past year, and Pat wonders why her area of the city has been spared. "It's a feeling of impending doom. I almost wish it would happen to me so I can get it over with," she says, fully aware that there's little logic in her observation.

A month later, it almost does. A psychiatrist from a mental health center requests a welfare check on an agitated and possibly suicidal patient who has phoned to say he smashed his fist through his living room window. When Pat and two other officers arrive and identify themselves, Tony yells, "Get the hell out of here! I don't want no fucking cops around!"

Looking through the window, Pat sees that he's bleeding. As she negotiates with him to come outside, he takes off down the hallway and slams a door behind him.

Lorraine Martinez goes through the broken window and opens the front door.

"I've got a gun. Leave me alone or I'll shoot you!" Tony screams at them through the closed bathroom door.

Jim Grade kicks it open. As it bounces off the wall jamb, Pat jumps to safety, but she catches a quick glimpse of the distraught man as he kicks the door shut again. He's holding a gun and it's aimed at the spot Pat has just vacated.

Cops are taught to assume the worst — that the gun is real, that it's loaded and that the suspect is prepared to use it.

The SWAT team and a police psychologist are called. After nearly two hours of tense negotiations, Tony agrees to put the weapon down — it turns out to be a toy gun — and surrender for medical treatment and a psychological evaluation.

Pat was the only officer who saw a weapon. "Having one pointed at me was scary enough, and there was the added pressure knowing that all of this manpower was there because of what I saw in a split-second glimpse."

*   *

While some routine calls have moments of high drama, others contain elements of humor or the bizarre.

Pat recalls the first time a suspect ignored her order to halt. "I was eastbound on Speedway with a motorcycle in front of me. It looked like it had expired plates, but I couldn't see real well. I turned on my overhead lights and he pulled over. As soon as I started getting out of my car, he jumped back on his cycle and took off. When I started after him, he stopped again, put the bike down and ran. I lost him for a few seconds and then picked him up again. I yelled 'Police! Don't move!' and pointed my gun at him. He looked at me, mumbled something and sprinted off.

"I knew that I couldn't shoot him, so I took off after him again, radioing his description and the direction of the chase and trying to snap my gun back in its holster at the same time. I was moving pretty fast, but he was really rabbiting. Tim Vesely intercepted him a block or two away. When I got there, the biker was covered with blood and I was thinking, 'I know I didn't shoot him and I know Vesely didn't either, because I would have heard the shot.'

"It turned out he had just come from selling blood plasma and popped his cork during the chase. When I asked him why he ran, he said it was because he didn't have a driver's license, but I found out later that the bike was stolen. Meanwhile, I felt like a real ass because he should have stood there and put his hands up when I told him to in the first place."

Later, Pat notices what appears to be an abandoned car in front of a residence. It has no plates and is missing two tires. As she red-tags it, giving notice that it can be legally towed after forty-eight hours, a tiny woman in her sixties walks outside, smiles and thanks her. She is carelessly dressed and Pat senses that something is not quite right, but, seconds later, she's dispatched to the scene of a traffic accident.

Pat returns later, and when she knocks, the woman partially opens the door, but seems to be intentionally blocking Pat's view inside.

"Do you live alone?" Pat asks.

The woman responds with another wide smile, then nods agreement. Pat asks permission to come in for a few minutes, and as she waits for what would normally be an automatic invitation, a shrill voice calls out, "Help me! Help me!"

"I thought you said you lived alone."

"Yes, I do."

Again, the voice:

"Help me! Help me!"

"Who's in there with you?"

"No one, no one's in here."

Pat tries to walk past her.

"You can't come in!"

Like hell I can't, Pat tells herself, wondering what she'll find when she crosses the threshold. She gently pushes her way inside, supporting the woman with her arm as she goes by.

The floor and furniture are covered with newspapers, rags, animal feces and an assortment of trash which Pat must sidestep as she walks. Almost lost in the clutter is a bird cage standing precariously in the corner of the room.

"Help me! Help me!" a parrot says, looking up momentarily, then tapping at its reflection in the mirror.

Pat suppresses a laugh, aware now that she's dealing with a

204

woman a few bubbles off plumb. Adult Protective Services will evaluate her ability to care for herself.

*　　*

A barefoot, long-bearded, amply-tattooed man is ambling along a midtown street, carrying a four-foot spear. The extent of his clothing is a feathered headband and a towel around his waist. He might not have attracted attention a few hundred years ago, but on this chilly late-winter afternoon, he's as out of place as Lawrence Welk conducting a heavy metal band.

"Hi, how are you today?" Pat greets him.

He's amiable, and asked his name, responds, "William Tell." He says that he's come to Earth from another planet to save mankind and that his tattoos represent a cosmic language. He's committed no crime and continues on his way, minus the illegal spear portion of the stick.

*　　*

A woman is screaming in the courtyard outside of an apartment complex. Pat pulls up to find three people scuffling. Two of them — a young married couple — are arguing with Jim, the woman's former boyfriend. They run to Pat, taking shelter behind her.

Jim starts toward them, and Pat raises her nightstick, motioning him to stop. He gets within a half-dozen steps of her and suddenly topples to the ground, making no attempt to break his fall. With no backup officer to help, Pat's first instinct is to be grateful for an unexpected break. She sits on Jim's butt and snaps on the cuffs — "Easy pickings," as she later describes it.

But that quickly changes. When Jim doesn't move or respond to her questions, she radios for medics. She reaches underneath and turns him on his side. His face is dirty from the fall, a trickle of blood is coming from his mouth and the odor of alcohol almost overwhelms her. Jim makes gurgling sounds and is again silent.

As an emergency room nurse, Pat has watched patients take this route into heart failure. She prepares to administer emergency CPR, but medics pull up and sprint to the disheveled man who has now begun breathing on his own.

Relieved, Pat sighs and starts walking toward the witnesses who have been standing about twenty-five feet away. Before she reaches them, one of the medics calls out, "Oh, shit! He's coding!"

In less than thirty seconds, they rip off Jim's shirt, slap on electrodes to try and jump-start his heart, begin CPR and place an oxygen mask over his nose and mouth. They attempt to insert an intravenous line, but can't locate a vein. There is still no indication of what is wrong with him.

With all of this going on, Pat attempts to remove the handcuffs, but Jim's arms are between his back and the ground, and she needs to work around the five medics who are thumping on his chest, pumping oxygen to his brain, and sending a series of 350-joule electrical currents to his heart in a frantic effort to get him to breathe. When he doesn't respond, they scoop-and-run, half carrying and half pushing him into an ambulance.

Officer Manny Ochoa arrives, takes in the scene, turns to Pat and asks in bewilderment, "What did you do, Horbarenko, cuff a dead guy?"

Jim is hospitalized in critical condition.

*   *

Pat is again talking about leaving Steve, still frustrated that there's almost no affection in the marriage and perceiving him as unable to change. She remembers the getting-to-know-you days of their courtship when they'd sit talking, holding hands and feeling close.

"He's so supportive when it has to do with me as a cop, but it doesn't carry over to my need to be appreciated as a woman. We're not killing each other, we're not yelling or throwing things. Steve is a wonderful guy, one of the most gentle men I've ever known, but something important is missing. When I talk about it in group (counseling), it's tossed back to me that I have to decide if the rest of the relationship is good enough. They ask me why I'm still with him and all I can say is, 'I love him.'"

A new problem is that Steve has accepted a position at the Academy, where he will be responsible for helping establish and monitor training standards.

Pat has not forgiven ALETA for expelling her in 1985.

"I want to say that I'm so proud of him for winning the promotion, but I can't because of that damned ALETA," she says, viewing Steve almost as a traitor for accepting the position.

Some of the Academy's methods and policies have been softened, and the assignment will enable him to work for more change, Steve has told her, but the issue with Pat is emotional, not intellectual.

Indeed, Steve recently asked her to visit ALETA with him. After first resisting, she agreed to go, but began hyperventilating and they turned back.

Steve volunteers to decline the career-enhancing promotion, but Pat realizes it would cause resentment. Knowing that she can't stand in his way, however, has added to her stress.

"I realize I'm taking what happened to me at the Academy too hard and I'm just going to have to work it out."

■

Robert Garcia has been on the street less than fifteen minutes on August 21, 1987 when the emergency tone sounds. There's a fight brewing outside a nearby apartment building and one of the participants is reported to have a gun. Robert, about two miles away, advises that he's en route. The ground is wet from a monsoon that quickly swept in and out of the city, so he must be doubly aware of the potential for a collision as he switches on his overhead lights and siren.

"It will be in the parking lot on the south side of the complex," the dispatcher reports. "Complainant called from number 813. He heard someone say, 'Go ahead and shoot him.'"

Robert pulls into the driveway in less than three minutes. There are about a dozen people spread out in several small clusters. A few of them are talking loudly among themselves and one is crying, but a quick glance suggests that there is no gun and no one injured.

A short, stocky man walks toward Robert. His hands are cupped at his waist and Robert calls out, "Back up! Back up! Put your hands apart for a second."

The man stops and shows his empty palms. Two more officers arrive and others are approaching. With no information on what provoked the incident, nearly everyone has something to say and they're all trying to say it at once.

Robert takes control, assigning one officer to each group to gather information and keep the disputants apart.

Soon, the basic pieces fall into place. A resident started the chain of events by telling a towing company to remove a vehicle parked in his assigned space. The truck operator 'hooked' the offending car, but was challenged by its owner and several of her friends as he prepared to drive away with it. As they walked toward him, he drew a .357 Magnum with a six-inch barrel.

Although everyone appears to agree on these basic facts, there are substantially different interpretations. The car owner is Liz, a tall, somewhat inebriated twenty-eight-year-old wearing black and white leotard tights and a halter top revealing a butterfly tattoo over her right breast. She says that she only wanted to be allowed to rescue her car from being towed, but that the gun was pointed at her head.

The tow truck operator tells Robert that Liz and several of her friends cursed and threatened him. He says he drew the gun when one of them attempted to corner him, shouting "We'll kick your ass!" He claims he never pointed it except toward the sky.

Even with five officers there, Liz and her friends are hostile and argumentative. After taking a statement from a witness, Robert concludes that the tow truck operator legitimately feared for his safety when he drew his gun.

This decision doesn't please Liz and one of her friends places both arms around her shoulders in a failed effort to calm and restrain her.

"That fucker put a gun to my head and you're not going to do anything about it?" she yells.

Robert attempts to explain, but she's not buying it. The tow truck driver agrees to unhook her car and waive the service charge. This placates most of her friends, but Liz is still not satisfied.

"It's my car; keep the fuck out of it!" she yells at them.

As she backs it out a few minutes later, Liz turns the wheel too sharply and dents the rear panel of another car.

"I had bad vibes about today," she sighs, lighting a cigarette.

*   *

Tammy's first ridealong with her husband provides an interesting twist. A woman Robert is ticketing walks over and says, "Hi, officer, how would you like to go out with me?" Tammy glares at her and says dryly, "I don't think he's gonna want to be going out with you." Robert spends the rest of the shift swearing that it's the first time he's been propositioned. Tammy doesn't appear convinced.

*   *

Robert makes three unusual arrests in a four-month period. He books the son of a Sheriff's Department deputy for auto theft, and the son of a police lieutenant on a burglary charge.

In mid-October, he charges a young man with breaking into an automobile and stealing the stereo system. The teenager tells Robert that his father had been a captain with the Tucson Police Department. Robert doesn't recognize the name until the following morning when he joins several officers gathered around a television set watching the rescue of Jessica McClure, the toddler trapped in a Midland, Texas well. A lieutenant points to an image of the police chief who is coordinating the operation.

"That's the father of the kid you arrested," he says.

Robert is only briefly nonplused. "I did my job. I don't care who it is. We're not exempt from the law and neither are our kids. If they want me to not do my job, just tell me in writing, 'Please don't arrest officers' kids.'"

There is no pressure, no repercussions. Several weeks later, fellow officers give him a T-shirt emblazoned with the words, "Attention: Cops' Kids Arrested Here."

*   *

Late in 1987, Robert gets a three-month assignment as a junior detective. Most of his time is spent investigating assaults, larcenies and shoplifting cases. Like most successful investigators, he has a built-in polygraph that helps him sense when a suspect is lying or withholding information. Robert is also enough of a realist to have learned that the criminal justice system is not always just and that the handcuffs often appear to be taken off the wrists of the defendant and placed on the wrists of the police.

Nonetheless, it's a challenge he relishes. "You do the investigation, see the complaint, get the warrant and help make the arrest. When you take the case to the County Attorney, you have to be a salesman. You have to sell the complaint like a product because if they're not pleased with your product, they're not going to prosecute. Then you have to keep in touch and keep them excited about it and hope they'll decide that it's court-appealing. If you can't get it to court, you at least want to plea bargain it."

One of those he arrested was a childhood friend. "Ronald was surprised to see me after nearly ten years. He didn't know I had become a cop and I didn't know he had become a crook."

*   *

March 8, 1988. A woman is shot to death and her live-in boyfriend is injured in an explosion of gun fire north of Tucson. The

209

suspect is Kimberly, an eighteen-year-old exotic dancer believed to have biker connections, and Robert is assigned to join three other officers with a warrant to arrest her.

Robert isn't wearing his bullet-resistant vest, but returns to his locker to put it on. He reaches for a shotgun and drops four shells into the barrel before meeting the other officers several blocks from the home where Kimberly is reported to be staying.

The sergeant in charge of the operation assigns Robert to position himself in the alley behind the target house in case the suspect leaves from the back door. He doesn't explain the plan of action for making contact with the woman or what steps are being taken to minimize the risk to officers.

"Let's see what happens when we get there," he says.

"All right," Robert responds, but his reaction as he begins driving is "Oh, God." He drives east along the alley, looking for house numbers through a cluster of fences, brick walls and desert brush. The sergeant comes on the radio to identify the house as having a windmill on the roof.

"I see it now," Robert responds, stopping his patrol car about 175 feet away. He steps out, reaches back for the shotgun and jacks the first round into the firing chamber. Crouching for cover, he walks slowly toward the house, but before he can establish position, a voice on the radio reports that the situation is under control.

Robert, surprised that officers apparently entered the residence before he was in place, asks if the arrest has been made, and is told that it has. He returns to his car, unloads the gun and drives to the front of the house in time to see officers leading the tearful suspect out.

"Can you believe that?" he grouses as he drives away. "Can you believe that someone would risk lives like that by not letting us know what's going on? It's amazing." The operation has gone smoothly, but there was a potential for disaster. He blames himself on one count. "I went along without asking questions instead of expressing my concerns. We take too many risks when we just rush in."

He feels complacency is especially dangerous in undercover operations, and is still incredulous as he recalls a recent one.

"I was working on a surveillance involving the purchase of more than two kilos of cocaine. My job was to move in and provide backup as undercover officers arrested the suspects, but no one told me who would be where. As I came running in, there was a guy pointing a gun at the back of the suspect's house. I put my gun on him and told him to freeze. When he said that he was a cop, I told him

210

that he was going to have to prove it. He said that his badge was in his trousers, so I told him to put his gun down, turn around slowly and show it to me.

"They usually know they're going to do these busts enough in advance to take the time to have everyone meet and understand what's going on."

Robert could have discussed his concerns with the officers involved, but decides not to.

"One thing I've found about this department is that you can't offer suggestions without someone getting mad at you," he complains. "There are too many egos involved. If you want your career to advance, you don't want to step on the wrong toes. I think that too many people are missing the point, which is to improve our chances to not be hurt. If another officer is seeing something in the way I work that might jeopardize his safety or mine, I want to know about it. I at least want to take a look at it and see if I need to change.

"What I hear, though, are comments like 'I've been doing it this way for fifteen years and I haven't been killed yet.' They don't realize that things have changed, that there are more hard drugs and a lot more violent people who would like to kill a cop."

■

Anita Sueme's semi-annual evaluations document the consistent progress she has made since completing the Field Training Program in which she patrolled with more experienced officers while honing her street skills.

Late in the summer of 1987, she is selected to help train cops just out of the Academy. Anita is both surprised and flattered.

Her first rookie is a disappointment. "Fred appeared bored and distracted. There was just no response or enthusiasm from him a lot of the time, and this was really surprising to me because he'd been a cop in another state."

Fred says he burned out in his former job, but thought it would be different in Tucson. He resigns the second week and says he'll find another profession. Anita's squad immediately brands her "the rookie killer."

*   *

It's September 18, 1987, and two twelve-year-old boys with more curiosity than common sense run a metal wire from an industrial grade battery to a machine gun cartridge. The bullet

211

explodes and Gabriel is rushed to a hospital minus two fingers on his right hand and with metal fragments in his shoulder. Ernesto, at whose home the incident occurred, is frightened, but not hurt.

As Anita leaves the hospital, she's dispatched to a shopping center parking lot where kids are reported to be congregating. Although it's nearly 11 p.m. — past curfew for most of them — at least 150 youngsters are milling about. Anita walks from group to group, telling them that it's time to call it a night. A few ask why they have to leave, but most are good-natured. They begin rounding up their friends, and within fifteen minutes, there are only a couple dozen stragglers. Anita walks back to her car and resumes patrol.

Just after midnight, she's dispatched to a street fight between two men. The complainant says that one of them might be hurt. As Anita and another officer walk up, the older of the two greets them with a derisive "Bullshit!"

Rochelle, a slim woman with a high forehead and striking blue eyes, is positioned precariously between them, attempting to keep them apart. No one appears to be hurt. What is taking place is a lot of yelling and posturing over Rochelle's romantic allegiance.

Randy, the louder of the two, stalks around, waving a partially-filled beer cup. Anita asks him for identification. He says he hasn't any, although there's a wallet-sized bulge in the back pocket of his jeans.

"Why don't you turn around so I can check to make sure you have no weapons," Anita asks.

He shakes his head, spewing an arc of tobacco juice from his mouth.

"It's standard procedure. Turn around, please."

Randy doesn't move.

"You won't turn around? I'll walk around you."

There are no apparent weapons, but definitely a wallet in his pocket. If he were in a vehicle, he'd be subject to arrest for refusing to show identification, but here on public property Anita doesn't have legal cause to search without his permission.

She asks him his name. He shows a big smile, but doesn't answer.

"You have a wallet on you and you don't have any ID," Anita says, shaking her head. It's more statement than question. A pause of a few seconds, then she asks again, "What's your name?"

"Uh, Smith."

Rochelle has told the other officer that she's the man's ex-girlfriend and wants him to leave.

"No one's in any trouble," Anita tries to assure. "We just want to make sure nobody's hurt and then we're going to leave. It's as simple as that. What are you being so defensive about?"

Randy, pointing: "This guy's been sleeping with my girlfriend."

"That's not our concern. All I'm asking for is some ID."

"I don't have an ID. My name is Smith."

Anita, still calmly, but beginning to show frustration: "You're lying through your teeth, aren't you?"

Randy: "You asked me for a name."

"I asked you for *your* name."

There's no reply, and Anita abandons the name game and attempts a different line of questioning.

"You guys been living together?"

"What? Breathing, eating, talk. . ."

Anita, interrupting and spacing her words for emphasis: "Have you two been living together? Are you both on a lease together? I would like a straight answer."

"How do you define living?"

Anita backs off a few steps to make sure she doesn't lose her cool.

The second officer, who has been standing nearby with Rochelle, turns to Randy. "She doesn't want you here tonight. She'll talk to you in the morning when you cool down. She's not mad, she's not upset and she doesn't want anyone to go to jail."

Anita: "Just go home, get some sleep and stay away from her. You don't want to go to jail tonight; it's not worth it."

"That's cool. I understand."

Rochelle has given the other officer Randy's last name and date of birth.

"As soon as I check the computer to make sure that you're not a homicide suspect from Sing Sing, we're going to get out of your face," he tells him. "Just remember, Randy, when your emotions are involved and you've had a couple of drinks, things can get out of hand."

A computer check shows no outstanding warrants. Randy begins to walk away, but seconds later, starts back toward the other suitor.

"He definitely assaulted me. I could press charges."

The men are yelling at each other now, but stop when told that one or both are about to be arrested for disturbing the peace.

Randy drives off, but is back twenty minutes later, knocking on Rochelle's door. She's not there and her nervous teenage son phones

911.

Anita, back on the scene, attempts to reason with Randy, but he continues his verbal game-playing.

"You've been warned twice now," she tells him.

Where Randy is concerned, memory serves its own master. "No, no! When have I been warned?"

"I warned you to stay away before I left and I'm warning you now."

"No, you didn't tell me before!"

"I did, and you're being warned now. Go to your apartment."

"Okay, well that's one warning then."

"You show up at this front doorstep again and. . ."

"I'm not showing up at a front doorstep."

"I know you're not because you're going to go home and to bed."

"You can't tell me to go to bed!"

"Just go; now!"

"Yes, but you can't tell me. . ."

"Don't argue; just go. I've got more important things to do than argue with you."

"Then go do them. I'm not hurting anyone."

"Randy, just go. Goodnight. I don't want to come back here."

"I do need my cigarettes, though."

"You have cigarettes on you."

"Yeah, but I need others. They're the ones I lost on the ground."

"You're just using that as an excuse to hang around here. Get by with what you've got in your pocket."

She finally walks him away from Rochelle's apartment and watches as he strides back into the night.

"I'm a real patient person, but my patience is running out fast," she says as she resumes patrol. Three blocks later, a car in front of her at a traffic light makes no effort to move although the signal has been green for several seconds.

"Okay, get moving, asshole," Anita says in frustration.

"There's a lot of them out there," she observes, chuckling now, "but I try to reserve that attitude for the real assholes."

Tonight, Randy has clearly earned a prime spot as one of the real assholes.

*   *

It's the first week of January, 1988, and Anita receives a temporary assignment to work undercover with the Major Of-

214

fenders Unit. The group's primary focus is to identify residential burglars and monitor their activities after they are released from jail.

On her first day with the detail, she's driving a 1979 Monte Carlo, a clunker without seat belts or even such minor amenities as a heater or car radio. Working with a veteran undercover officer, they 'sit' on a stolen car, hoping the thief returns for it. He doesn't, and when they spot Matt, a known burglar, they begin to tail him.

Matt, with two male passengers aboard, appears to be randomly cruising a midtown neighborhood which has been hit with nearly fifty burglaries in less than a month. Matt stops at a residence with an empty carport and one of the young men walks to the door and knocks. There's no answer. They drive away, but return a few minutes later. This time, both passengers walk casually to the back of the house. Anita and her partner are parked nearly a block away, while another undercover officer positions himself close enough to the house to hear the sound of a door being kicked in.

Three minutes later, the men return to their car and drive down the alley where the stolen items have been left on the ground. They jump out and have everything inside their car in less than twenty seconds.

Anita and her partner have wrapped fluorescent orange police jackets over their civilian clothing. They position themselves about a block south of the burglars' vehicle and advise other units, including uniformed officers, of their direction of travel.

Although few burglars carry weapons, officers must have a sense of tactical awareness, even when making low-risk arrests. They follow the suspects' car for nearly a mile before there are enough officers in place to make the stop.

One cop sprints to the driver's door, while Anita, gun drawn, runs to the passenger side and orders the young man out. He sits there, eyes wide in either fear or amazement, but doesn't move. As Anita repeats the instruction, a uniformed officer opens the door, pulls him out and pushes him to the ground in one continuous movement.

It's been a productive start on what is often a dull assignment.

"After that first day, I found out how incredibly boring the job can be," she says. "Most of the time, you wait for your target to go somewhere or do something, but he seems to be taking the day off. You sit in the same spot four, five or six hours waiting for something to happen. The work is tedious and it can be difficult to concentrate after a while. You do whatever it takes to stay awake." Anita does a lot of bird-watching.

Answering one of nature's urgent calls is another problem. "The guys have a big advantage when they need a potty break," she concedes, chuckling. "There were days I had to go so bad that I was in pain. They just kidded me, 'Go in the bushes like we do or carry a cup.'"

Finally, there's the basic need to remain out of the line of sight of the suspects being watched. "It's not as easy as it sounds, and if you're not careful, you end up stumbling into them and blowing the whole thing. A high priority when arresting a career burglar is not letting him get a good look at you since you'll probably be tailing him again if he's released on bond. You learn to throw a windbreaker or T-shirt over his face as soon as you can."

Anita's two months as an undercover officer also introduce her to the world of 'boosters' — thieves who go into supermarkets or stores carrying a large purse or backpack camouflaged under loose-fitting clothing. They stash meat, cigarettes, Levis and other hard-to-trace, easily-marketed items. Most are drug addicts who must steal hundreds of dollars in merchandise every day to support their habit.

A woman tells Anita, "Getting a fix is the first thing I think of when I wake up every morning. I ask myself, 'What am I going to have to steal today to get it?'" This afternoon, Anita has caught her with cuts of ham worth more than $100 stashed in a Jordache tote bag. The woman, twenty-six, says she's been addicted to heroin for nine years.

"Some of them are so hooked and so desperate that they beg you to let them take a quick fix before going to jail," Anita says.

She returns to her squad with a new understanding of how pervasive the burglary problem is and with the frustration of knowing that most of those she arrests will be back on the street within twenty-four hours.

To Anita, burglars have a seemingly endless supply of 'Get Out of Jail Free' cards. "All you can do is just keep putting them in jail until the system finally decides to keep them," she says.

*   *

After a dry spell of nearly five years, Anita has a man in her life. Johnathan, a physically imposing but gentle, soft-spoken man with six years of law enforcement experience with another agency, is assigned to her squad, and the attraction between them is almost

216

instant.

At the end of their shift one evening, they park their cars side by side in the police parking lot and talk for three hours.

Pat Horbarenko remembers Anita's excitement at the start of the relationship:

"He's gorgeous," Anita tells her.

"I just know that you're going to keep it strictly professional," Pat responds, nearly managing to keep a straight face.

"I know, I know, but look at him. What a hunk!"

Johnathan is Black, and as the after-work chats between them become an almost daily ritual, Anita fears negative reactions from some of the officers she works with.

"They're good friends and great to work with, but some male cops are real conservative," she says. Her apprehension appears unfounded and there's no outward antagonism as word of their relationship spreads. The newer members of her squad continue to come to her for professional advice and feedback.

"I see no resistance at all, and it makes me feel good. I keep things mellow and I don't act like I'm a know-it-all. They know I'm not going to give them the macho super-cop routine and I think they appreciate that."

Despite her size and mild demeanor, she's still not had a one-on-one knockdown, drag-out confrontation with a male suspect. There have been a few wrestling matches with drunks and mental patients, but a second officer has generally been on the scene to help. One of the advantages of being female, Anita believes, is that a macho image isn't necessary.

"I don't need to prove how much balls I have since I don't have any to begin with," she says, laughing. "I can usually talk myself out of fight situations, and that's just being smart."

■

It's mid-evening, and Jeff Moore is following a van without tail lights. He uses his rooftop speaker to instruct the driver to pull into an adjacent apartment complex. Jeff asks the husky man for his license, registration and proof of insurance. In halting English, he says he lives in the complex and has the papers inside.

He appears nervous and anxious to leave, and Jeff, suspicious now, asks him his name and date of birth. He mumbles something

217

unintelligible and sprints south through the parking lot, tossing away an electronic pager and a small package.

Jeff inadvertently drops his nightstick as he takes off after the man. "One running westbound," he advises, and the dispatcher activates the emergency tone. Two units start up and Air One makes a skyward U-turn halfway across the city.

Jeff catches up as the suspect reaches a five-foot high brick wall and attempts to pull himself over. Jeff dives at him and their impact causes the top half of the wall to crumble. They roll on the ground just clear of the rubble until Jeff grabs him by the shirt with one hand, brandishing his flashlight over him with the other. The suspect looks up at Jeff and surrenders.

The dispatcher has been trying to raise Jeff on the radio, and when he doesn't answer, she sends two officers to check on him.

Jeff, meanwhile, has begun the long walk back to his patrol car. Approaching the parking lot, he sees nearly a dozen men headed in his direction. He reaches for his radio and realizes that it's on the wrong frequency. He resets it, advises that he has one subject under arrest, but that he needs additional units immediately. His words are breathless and fragmented, and the dispatcher assures him that help is already on the way.

As the men move to within 100 feet of him, Jeff holds his cuffed prisoner in front of him as a makeshift shield. He's prepared to reach for his gun if they advance much closer, but now the sounds of approaching sirens begin to cut through the night and the men back off and scatter.

After the suspect is placed in a police car, Jeff locates the jettisoned pager and a package of cocaine. A search of the van turns up two automatic weapons, including a loaded 9mm machine gun, and Jeff realizes that the outcome could have been deadly.

"If he had gotten out with the machine gun, there's no way I could have drawn on him. It would have been all over."

As he prepares to leave the complex, a tousle-haired youngster walks up to him. "Officer, you dropped this," he says, handing over the forgotten nightstick.

*   *

The widely publicized California Freeway shootings which began during the summer of 1987 have inspired copy-cat shootings in Tucson. There have been at least five separate incidents and one serious injury. Today, an eighteen-year-old cruising in his pickup truck points a handgun at several passing vehicles. He doesn't fire.

He can't, because the gun is a replica, but the frightened motorists don't know this.

The pickup is soon spotted in a shopping center parking lot, the weapon visible on the floor mat. While Jeff secures the realistic-looking gun to protect the chain of evidence, other officers walk into an adjacent restaurant and charge the man with threats and intimidation.

A brief late-summer monsoon has left many roads flooded, and Jeff helps several motorists whose cars have stalled. It's a generally quiet Saturday until less than a half-hour before the end of his shift when a thirty-one-year-old man who has been arguing with his wife most of the day threatens to shoot her and their three children. She flees to a nearby store with two of them, but their youngest child, ten years old, stays behind, hiding in his bedroom.

Jeff is the second officer at the house. He opens the front gate and heads for a sheltered position between two windows. To get there, he must bypass a snarling German Shepherd which, although chained, stands between him and his destination. He extends his nightstick and the dog retreats.

With officer Joe Webster positioned at the front, Jeff now pulls himself over a metal fence and stations himself in the rear where a brown-and-white Chihuahua begins yelping. Two other officers arrive, as does the man's wife, who provides a key to the house.

The suspect ignores the knocks from the officers, and after more than ten minutes, there has been no contact with him. The Shepherd remains disinterested as long as no one enters the yard.

Officers receive a break when one of them looks through a window and spots the boy alone in what appears to be his bedroom. Two cops unlock the front door and enter, guns extended. Less than a minute later, the youngster, crying, but safe, is led outside and into the arms of his mother who waits for him in a car about 200 feet away.

Other officers join the first two in the house and the man gives up without a struggle. As he's led out a few minutes later, he turns to the Shepherd and says sharply, "Sic 'em!" The dog growls, but doesn't move.

The episode has taken nearly a half-hour, during which time the Chihuahua has yelped almost without pause.

*   *

Thanksgiving week. Jeff and his wife have been back together for several months.

219

"It's sometimes rough, but getting better," he offers. "We're pulling together and working on the relationship. I try and look at it like the partly-filled glass. I see it half full, not half empty. I like to think there's something good in everything, that positive thoughts and positive deeds make a difference. I'm putting all of my energy into my marriage and feeling a lot more secure with myself."

A silent alarm is reported at a recently built office building. A large broken window greets Jeff. He uses the wall for cover as he listens for sounds of activity inside. There are none, and soon he and Fred Erdman step over the shards of glass to begin a room-by-room search.

It's a building of seemingly endless corridors. There are nearly 100 rooms to check, most of them small and still vacant. There's an almost ballet-like rhythm to the search. Jeff and Erdman position themselves, guns drawn and aimed. They alternate turning the knob and lightly kicking each door open. That room is searched, then it's on to the next. No one is found.

It's difficult to maintain a peak level of intensity after you've followed the same ritual several dozen times, but someone with a gun could just as well be waiting behind the last door as the first.

"The frame of mind must be the same at every one," Jeff emphasizes. "You need to keep asking yourself, 'Where's the bad guy? Is he in this room? Will he be in the next one?' I've found burglars during searches. So far, no one has had a gun, but the next one might."

■

July 29, 1987. A sixty-year-old man lies dead on the floor next to his bed, nine empty beer cans nearby. His daughter has found the body after spending the night at her boyfriend's, and she's feeling guilty.

"I should have been here last night," Patti laments. Her boyfriend strokes her back and shoulders as she tells Bernie Harrigan that her dad suffered from respiratory problems, but wouldn't see a doctor.

She phones family members, working hard to hold her emotions in check. "He loved you a lot," she tells one. To another, "I love you. Will you be alright?" Patti appears to be the glue that holds this family together. She asks to spend a few private minutes with her father before two men from the Medical Examiner's Office zipper him into a plastic bag, strap him onto a gurney and wheel him out.

It has been a busy week. Two days ago, Bernie had his first experience with an AIDS victim. William, a husky thirty-year-old six-footer, had attempted suicide by swallowing most of a bottle of sleeping pills. His stomach is pumped, and now he has walked away from the hospital wearing only an off-white gown.

Bernie and two other officers go to the home he shares with both his wife and his male lover. The woman ushers them in, saying that William is in the bedroom closet. Asked if there are any guns in the house, she shakes her head.

Bernie stands to the side and opens the closet door. William is sitting on the floor. Looking up, he spots the protective plastic gloves Bernie is wearing.

"Get those fucking gloves off! I can *spit* and infect you!" he says angrily.

Bernie nods and peels them off. "This is what we've been taught. If we need to be taught differently, let me know."

William turns calmer now, but insists that he won't go back to the hospital.

"Let's talk about it," Bernie responds.

"There's nothing to talk about. I'm not going."

Bernie persuades him to come out of the closet and sit with him at the kitchen table. He could easily grab William now, but he'd rather encourage him to talk.

Speaking softly, William says that his AIDS is terminal and that he should be allowed a dignified death of his own choosing. A friend arrives and asks to speak with him. She holds him gently while he sobs out his anger, fears and frustration.

Bernie telephones the hospital and is told that a psychiatric evaluation has been ordered. William again insists that he won't go, but soon realizes he has no choice. He asks that his wife accompany him and that he not be handcuffed. Bernie mulls the requests for a moment before nodding agreement.

The encounter has had a sobering effect on Bernie. "I felt badly seeing him cry, and I understood his anger over the plastic gloves. We're advised to wear them, but it *is* insulting."

*   *

Three Hispanic men who have been drinking in a neighborhood bar strike up an argument with a young couple. The men follow them into the parking lot and when the couple walks away, the men jump into a truck and run down the man, killing him. In their haste to get away, the driver loses control, leaves the roadway and crashes into a concrete wall.

One of the passengers is taken to a hospital with minor injuries, and Bernie is dispatched to question him. Bernie, who once patrolled the streets of New York City's Spanish Harlem, still retains some knowledge of the language. His suspect, however, is intoxicated, and with the added distraction of doctors and nurses walking in and out, it's taking Bernie a long time to get the information he needs. The problem is further compounded when the replies to his questions come back at a speed approaching fast-forward.

Eventually, a Spanish-speaking intern offers to interpret. He speaks with the injured man for about a half-minute, then turns to Bernie: "He says he wants you out of his face so bad that he'll confess to anything."

*   *

Bernie's romantic life remains in disarray. Dorothy has decided that they should have a trial separation, telling him, "I love you, but I'm not in love with you." Bernie's translation: "I don't have the hots for you, but I love you like a brother."

He'll visit Anne in Connecticut during the Christmas holiday, although he's troubled by seeming to resume an old relationship before the current one has ended.

The trip ends in disappointment as he quickly realizes that the years have changed his feelings. Perhaps he was groping for someone to love in the fallout of his breakup with Dorothy, he concedes, but in any event, he knew by the second day that going had been a mistake.

Adding to the trauma is a visit with Timmy, his brain-damaged son who lives in a New York nursing home. "He's just wasted now; they can't do any more for him," Bernie laments.

His only consolation is the time spent with Robert, the love child he hadn't seen in twenty years. "He looks a lot like I think Timmy would have looked if he hadn't suffered through all of those physical ailments," he says, shaking his head

Frightened and lonely, Bernie returns to Tucson, struggling to hold his tenuous emotional world together. Now Dorothy becomes more important to him, but that relationship is very much in limbo.

"I want us to be together, but there's not much I can do about it and I'm not going to give up and die if she doesn't want me," Bernie says weeks later. "I'm not unattractive and I have a good income. The waiting and uncertainty are the worst part."

On the street, the former New York cop appears to retain his enthusiasm, but questions whether policing is what he wants to be doing. "I'm not always up for the job, and the rush-rush-rush sometimes gets to me," he says. Asked what shift he cycles to next, he replies, "Midnights." He pauses, then adds, "If I'm still here."

Moments later, he's dispatched to the home of a rape victim and there will be no more time for discussion tonight.

*   *

Officer Tommy Knickerbocker, an ALETA Class 102 graduate and Bernie's racquetball partner, is now a member of the DUI squad. Knickerbocker's next goal is an assignment with the coveted motorcycle detail. He owns a late-model Kawasaki 1000 Ninja, a powerful machine which he rides regularly.

It's late Sunday evening on June 19, 1988, and Knickerbocker has the next two days off. He mounts the cycle, twists open the throttle and heads away from the city's oppressive heat.

Shortly after midnight, a sheriff's deputy sees a small brush fire in the desert just south of the city. Checking the area on foot, she spots a twisted cycle with a ruptured, still-burning gas tank. Knickerbocker, age twenty-eight, lies dead in a drainage ditch nearly 400 feet from the spot where his bike hit a curb and became airborne. His head has literally exploded within the confines of the helmet he was mindful to strap on.

Bernie learns of Knickerbocker's death at the Pima County Jail where he is booking a prisoner. Stunned, he soon offers to go to the Medical Examiner's Office to identify the body.

The darkness and empty streets give Bernie an eerie feeling as he drives there alone just before 4:30 a.m., and he wonders silently what possessed him to volunteer for the awful task. An attendant unlocks the door and motions him inside. Knickerbocker lies on a metal table in a ten-by-twenty-foot refrigerated room. Four other bodies, including an unidentified John Doe, share the room.

The attendant unzips the plastic pouch which covers Knickerbocker. An orange identification tag wrapped around his left ankle bears the number 88643, signifying that 642 men, women and children have preceded him there in death since the start of 1988.

Bernie looks at the face inside the helmet, but can't say with

223

certainty that it's Knickerbocker. He gazes intently at his friend from several angles, shakes his head slowly and says, "I don't recognize you, Tommy. How can that be?"

A few more seconds pass, then Bernie turns and walks outside.

The accident report shows that the Kawasaki's throttle was wide open on impact. Skid marks on the roadway indicate speed in excess of 110 miles an hour, and an autopsy shows a blood-alcohol level of 0.22 percent, more than twice the legal threshold of intoxication.

Bernie derives a measure of comfort by serving as a pallbearer at the funeral. Later, he expresses both sadness and anger as he begins to come to terms with the death of a friend who lost the last big gamble of his life.

"Tommy liked speed. He worked hard, he played hard. . ."

A pause to reflect, then, "And he died hard, too."

8

Rites of Passage

Tucson — less than seventy miles from the Mexican border — has become a city with a serious drug problem. South American cartels are using both dirt roads and the interstate highways to send tens of millions of dollars worth of cocaine and other narcotics northward each month. The movement has been heightened by intensified law enforcement pressure in southern Florida, and Arizona now rivals Florida as the nation's major smuggling corridor and distribution center. While most of the cartel shipments move quickly through Tucson on their way to other destinations, some of the drugs remain in the city to meet local demand.

The situation has become more volatile as members of the Crips and Bloods gangs branch out from the increasingly competitive and saturated Los Angeles market to set up shop in Tucson.

Cocaine sells on the street for upwards of $500 per ounce, and with so much money at stake there is considerable potential for violence. From the street-level peddler on up to the multi-million-dollar smuggler, sellers are protecting their merchandise, and for the most part they are protecting it with heavy firepower. The use of semiautomatic weapons is commonplace, and even automatic assault rifles are not unusual. Most dealers are more afraid of losing a load than they are of law enforcement, and a 'runner' who fails to complete his assignment may pay with his life.

On March 27, 1989, five men are discovered bound and shot execution-style in a shed behind a rented house. It is the worst mass slaying in Tucson history.

A few days later, the bodies of twelve men and women — most of them tortured and mutilated — are found on an abandoned Mexican ranch about 125 miles south of Tucson.

225

Following an investigation by both local and Federal law enforcement agencies, U. S. Senator Dennis DeConcini reports that the two incidents were connected and drug-related.

Although the number of these homicides has risen dramatically in the past two years, no Tucson officer has been killed. The message, however, is clear: A cop is just another obstacle, and killing one might simply be part of the cost of doing business.

Jeff Moore approaches even routine traffic stops with the awareness that a nervous drug dealer might be inside the vehicle. He knows that someone could be waiting to kill him.

"There used to be the premise that if you're nice, we're nice," he says, "but now we need to be more alert and more assertive, especially after dark when it's difficult to see inside a vehicle."

*　　*

It's mid-summer, and a truck believed to have been involved in a recent drug shooting is spotted by a detective cruising in an unmarked car. There are two men inside the truck and one of them matches the description of the suspect. The detective follows the vehicle to a southside motel and watches as a third man approaches, hands over several small packages and then gets into the truck with them. The detective radios for uniformed officers to assist as the three men drive across the parking lot, enter a motel room and close the door behind them.

Jeff is one of the first to pull up, and within ten minutes, more than a dozen other cops have set up positions out of view, simultaneously blocking the only exit to the street. Other officers station themselves to prevent motel guests from inadvertently walking into a possible shootout. A single unmarked vehicle observes the suspects' room.

"They're mobile," he reports nine minutes later as the three men get back into the truck. As they turn the corner, they are greeted by two rows of squad cars and a dozen officers drawing down on them. The suspects are pulled out of the truck and handcuffed almost before they can digest the movie-like drama in which they are suddenly playing starring roles.

A sergeant pulls up as the arrests are completed, scans the scene and maintaining a straight face, remarks, "This is really impressive, isn't it?" A search of the suspects, their truck and the motel room yields no drugs, but uncovers $132,000 in cash and a kit used to test the purity of cocaine.

Shortly after noon six weeks later, Jeff responds to a report that a woman has been found dead in her home. The studio apartment has been trashed. Tables, chairs and lamps are strewn everywhere and Jeff uses his feet to clear a path through the debris.

A thirty-eight-year-old woman with more than a dozen stab wounds to her face, chest and pelvic area is dead on the bathroom floor. Several broken blood-covered knives lie nearby and a curling iron is still plugged into a wall outlet, the end of it forced up her vagina.

Jeff is shaken by the degree of the violence. "It was obvious that the person who did it intended not only to kill her, but to degrade her, too."

Although nearly 10,000 people live in his beat, Jeff is dismayed when something bad happens while he's on duty.

"I take that personally. If it's a slow day, it tells me I could have been doing a better job, that there was something going on that maybe I should have been aware of. These are my people, even though I don't live in their neighborhood. Sometimes I know that I've made a difference in someone's life. Most of the time I don't, but the important part is to try. It would be terrible to do nothing simply because you know that you can't do everything."

There are no suspects in the homicide, and today Jeff is both angry and frustrated.

■

After more than three years on the street, Anita Sueme has her first knock-down, drag-out fight. It's 1:30 a.m., and two men are reported to be scuffling in the street two blocks from where Anita and her trainee Rolf Averill are cruising. When the officers pull up less than thirty seconds later, the men run into an adjacent apartment complex, then veer off in separate directions. Averill corners David under a stairwell and attempts to handcuff him. When Anita runs over to assist, Frank — the other combatant — follows her, and all four are soon on the cement in a free-for-all.

Anita breathlessly orders them to stop fighting and begin talking. Her words are either lost or ignored in the escalating scuffle as both men simultaneously attack Averill.

227

Anita pulls David off of her partner and attempts to calm him. For a moment or two it seems to be working, but a few seconds later, she's flat on the ground. David is sitting on her chest, alternately shaking her shoulders and pushing her head in the dirt while screaming that he has a black belt in karate and could break her neck if he wanted to.

Averill, barely holding his own against Frank, manages to key his radio and call for help. His words come across the air fragmented, but with a clear sense of urgency.

"We have two (unintelligible), and we need a 10-84, 10-18." Anita, overpowered and aware that she could be seriously injured or even killed, hears Averill's transmission and thinks to herself, "10-84, 10-18, hell! Make that a 10-99."

Officers listening to the commotion in the background 'cover' each other as they advise that they're en route. Concerned that they might be preventing vital transmissions from Anita and Averill, the dispatcher instructs them to remain 10-3. A half-dozen squad cars race toward the scene, two of them ignoring the request for radio silence.

Anita, although still pinned down, knows that help is on the way. Attempting a diversion, she flails at David with one hand while trying to unholster her gun with the other. "I was looking for a chance to pull it out, but even more important, I knew I had to keep *him* from getting to it."

As Anita tries to gain control, David, perhaps hearing the wail of approaching sirens, suddenly pushes away from her and stands up. Anita shakes off the dirt and runs back to help Averill, who is still trying to subdue Frank. She drives her nightstick into Frank's ribs three or four times, but he doesn't seem fazed.

Just one minute and thirty-nine seconds after Averill's call for help, the first backup officer screeches to a halt and begins looking for them.

"I don't see them in here anywhere," he reports.

Dispatch: "3-Tom-51, 10-20?" There's no response, and the dispatcher repeats their last known location as other units pull up.

"He just went right by us!" Anita hollers as an officer passes about seventy-five feet west of them in the darkness.

Officer Gary Freeman arrives with his dog, Boris, and sees Frank rolling on the ground with Averill. He shouts a release command in German, and Boris leaps into the fight, biting Frank on the leg as he pulls him away. Looking up now at a growling 100-pound dog less than three feet from his head, Frank immediately

228

surrenders. David, standing passively nearby, is also arrested and handcuffed.

Officers are occasionally bitten, especially when several combatants are entangled, Freeman says. "In a fight situation, police dogs can't really be trained to recognize the good guys from the bad guys. Most of them pick up the distinction after they've been on the street for a while, but we don't know how they do it.

"Training the dogs to rely on a uniform would not be effective because many officers work in plain clothes and some suspects wear uniforms. Police dogs have a pretty good sense of what's happening and what needs to be done. The dog focuses where there's the most movement, so I generally won't send Boris in when the officer seems to have gained control or has a suspect pinned down."

Anita has a chest contusion, knee bruises and minor injuries to two fingers. But more than that, it's the first time she has felt that her life might have been in danger. "I was mentally prepared to stick the gun in his stomach and pull the trigger," she says. Safe now, her fear gives way to anger.

"They were friends, and the whole thing was totally unnecessary. All they had to do was calm down and talk to us. What I learned is that I don't think I'm cut out for a one-on-one fight, especially with a karate expert."

*   *

It's just before dawn a week later when Anita and Jim Christian respond to a family disturbance. There are red welts on the side of Ethel's face and her left eye has already begun to swell. Christian talks to Vince, the live-in boyfriend, while Anita walks Ethel into another room.

"What started the fight?" she asks.

Ethel, a plump Black woman in her thirties, vents her frustrations. "He wanted me to fuck him. I work ten hours a day trying to support him and my three kids. I come home to a messed up house most every day, and by the time I clean it up and get to bed, it's past midnight. Can you believe he woke me up at five o'clock this morning because he wanted to fuck. I told him I was too damned tired for that, and anyway I had to wake the kids, get them off to school and get me to work."

Vince goes to jail and Anita — pausing to drink a soda and catch up on paperwork, observes, "You could tell how hard she was working to keep her home and family together, and how irritating it

229

was to deal with this man when all he could think about was fucking, and how she had more important things to do at five in the morning."

"I loved it, it was great," she says, admiration for Ethel in her voice. "I know it's stereotyping, but can you imagine a White woman explaining that to a cop?"

*   *

October 1, 1988. Just after 9:30 this evening, Anita spots a boy straddling a bicycle and staring at an overhead street sign. He appears lost or confused.

"Hi, are you alright?" she asks.

A cute Hispanic youngster barely five feet tall with intense, but sad eyes looks at her. "I was talking to a girl I met at the shopping center and she walked away with another guy."

"That can really be upsetting, I know. How old are you?"

Tony is thirteen.

"Don't worry too much about it. You've got plenty of time for girls."

"I know, but she was pretty and I love her a lot."

"Tony, don't worry about it. You're still young. When I was twenty-five, I asked guys out to dinner and I got turned down."

"What's it going to be like when I grow up?"

"Well, you're a cute kid and you're going to have lots of girls running after you in a few years. Why don't you just go home now and talk to your family or watch some TV? I'd say go home and have a beer, but you can't do that."

Smiling for the first time: "I could have some root beer."

"You're going home now?"

"Yeah, but I'm going home sad."

"Well, don't be sad too long. Tomorrow's another day."

"I'll try."

Tony mounts his bike, goes around the corner and pedals out of sight.

*   *

April, 1989. The past few months have been stressful. Her relationship with Johnathan has ended and Anita is still coping with feelings of sadness, anger and abandonment. "Looking back, I can see he was giving me indirect messages that he wanted out, but they were too subtle. Sometimes I need to be literally hit over the head."

230

The death of Cleo, her sixteen-year-old Shepherd/Labrador mix, has also taken an emotional toll. "Cleo was always such a loyal and loving dog, happy just to have me around. In her last days, she couldn't even stand up. She just lay there, scared and shaking and barely able to eat."

Anita took her to a veterinarian knowing that she needed to make the decision to end Cleo's suffering.

"She was in a walk-in cage and I just sat there and held her for more than an hour until I found the emotional strength to let her go."

Anita lifted Cleo onto a blanket, then carried her to the examination table. With tears running down her face, she watched as the vet wrapped a tourniquet just above Cleo's elbow and injected a fifteen c.c. dose of Beuthanasia/D into a vein. Cleo's quivering stopped almost immediately and a painless death came in seconds. Anita had Cleo cremated, keeping the ashes as a bitter-sweet reminder of years of mutual loyalty.

■

Labor Day, 1988. Derek Campbell has returned to work after losing nearly five months as the result of the knee injury sustained in April.

He acclimated to the easy life once his knee started to heel. "I could have stayed out another couple of months," he says, laughing. He's wearing his vest again, an acknowledgement of having been shot at twice a year ago. His level of vigilance remains high, but he says he doesn't reach for his gun more quickly than he did a year ago. "If I feel something's not right, I'll keep my hand on it."

Evicting a romantically inclined young couple from a park several hours after curfew, he doesn't write a citation. "As long as they leave and don't hassle me, I'm not going to hit them in the pocketbook. I had the same hormone imbalance when I was a kid."

*   *

As Derek begins his shift five months later, a seven-year old girl is reported missing from an elementary school. It's several miles from Derek's beat and closer units respond. He has had five separate missing children calls in less than three weeks, and although all of the youngsters turned up quickly, the circumstance troubles him.

231

"You can't do much more than circulate in the neighborhood to look for them."

Twenty minutes later, dispatch reports yet another missing child. Millie, an eleven-year-old, is described as having shoulder-length black hair and being dressed in a white and turquoise outfit with tennis shoes. "She walked out of her class and might be trying to get back to a former neighborhood," the dispatcher advises.

An assistant principal tells Derek that Millie recently moved to the neighborhood, misses her old friends and has had problems adjusting to her new environment.

Millie's teacher is called to the office. "We were grading spelling papers and I asked the students to exchange theirs with a friend," she tells Derek. "Millie wouldn't do it, and when one of the other girls said something to her about not cooperating, she started grabbing things from her desk and throwing them on the floor. I tried to calm her, but she just got up and ran out of the room. I've never had a child run away before," she says, nearly in tears now.

Derek asks another officer to check the girl's home, less than a half-mile away, but a knock on the door goes unanswered. A puppy is seen inside, but there is no other sign of activity. Other officers check a nearby park and shopping center. Derek briefs his sergeant, adding, "My gut instinct — and I have a big gut — is that she's gotten on a bus and is trying to get back to her old neighborhood."

A city-wide attempt-to-locate is issued, and southside officers are dispatched to check her former school. Just after the ATL is broadcast, Millie's mother phones from her office to say that Millie has just called her and is hiding at home.

Derek drives back and knocks. "Millie, open the door, sweetheart. It's the police department."

A pretty, sad-eyed girl lets him in. Alternately dabbing her eyes and stroking the puppy, she laments that she misses her old friends and that she doesn't think anyone in her class likes her.

While they wait for her mother to arrive, Derek softly assures her that he knows how difficult it is to move, especially in the middle of a school year.

"It's not easy being eleven years old, but I know that your teacher and classmates like you and they're really worried about you," he says.

Millie says she's embarrassed to go back. "People tell me that I'm too hard on myself," she says, "but that's the way I usually am." Derek again tells her that she'll feel better now that her feelings are in the open.

The missing seven-year-old arrives at school two hours late, telling an officer that she lost her way while following "a pretty cat with a long, puffy tail."

* *

Dozens of law enforcement agencies have begun authorizing the on-duty use of 9mm semiautomatic handguns which hold up to nineteen bullets and fire one round each time the trigger is pulled. Tucson officers who wish to use them must purchase their own at a cost of more than $300 and then take sixteen hours of certification training. Although Tucson cops receive an annual $250 allowance which can be used to purchase safety equipment, many who would like the extra firepower are holding off in the hope that these weapons will soon become standard issue.

Derek received his at Christmas. "There were only two presents for me under the tree. When I opened the large box, there were about 100 little pieces of paper inside. On each one, Sharon and the kids had written, 'Bang! Bang!' When I got down to the bottom, there was a note saying that the gun was waiting for me at the Academy.

"I had no idea that she was planning to buy it. She'd just quietly been putting money aside for months. It was an incredible surprise and it just makes me appreciate her that much more. Sharon has been the best, the most stabilizing person in my life."

Derek has taken an examination which he hopes will lead to an assignment with the motorcycle unit. He narrowly misses the cutoff score and cannot reapply for two years. Instead, he'll ask for a return assignment with the DUI squad.

* *

June, 1989, and Derek is in what he calls his semi-annual cynical stage. "I just get temporarily disillusioned with the job." He doesn't know why, but says it passes quickly. "It lasts about a week, and when I'm this way, my motto is 'lay low and take it slow.' I'm in day number four now."

Tonight he chats amicably with a homeless man said to be acting suspiciously in the parking lot outside a convenience store. He asks the man his name, then: "Do you have any guns, knives or nuclear bombs in your pocket?" The thin man smiles momentarily, shakes his head and mumbles something unintelligible. There are no warrants against him and Derek tells him he'll have to move on.

Derek is extremely protective of Sharon's two daughters, now ages eight and nine. He wonders aloud for a few seconds if he's overly cautious, but quickly decides that he's "just being sensible."

They're out of school for the summer and with Sharon at work, he picks them up from day care in the early afternoon and chauffeurs them to dance lessons, the roller skating rink and art classes. It makes for a short night's sleep, since he ends his shift at 7 a.m. and doesn't get to bed until nearly 8. Some days he's able to nap for an hour or two in the late afternoon or early evening.

Halfway through the summer, Derek is told that he's being reassigned to the DUI squad. He's ready now, but he'll have to wait until mid-September to start.

■

Robert Garcia is another officer hoping for a new assignment — an investigator with the Burglary Task Force. He is nearing completion of an Associates in Criminal Justice degree from Pima Community College and feels that this will help his chances.

He enjoys the life of a street cop, but is always mindful of its dangers.

"Tammy doesn't like to talk about it, and I understand that. I make sure we spend a lot of time together as a family. The boys (Bobby, now ten, and David, seven) are more verbal about their fears, and once in a while I remind them that this is the job I chose and that I love doing it. I want them to know that in case something happens to me.

"Bobby still makes sure I'm wearing my (bullet-resistant) vest before I leave for work. Sometimes he'll say, 'Watch out' or 'I hope you're okay' when he kisses me goodbye. I can see the concern in his eyes and that troubles me. But everything's fine when I come home. They just want to hear stories of what happened, and they break out in big smiles when I tell them I arrested one of the bad guys.

"I know that something could happen and I might never see them again, but I certainly don't dwell on it. We're trained to recognize danger and respond to it, but cops make mistakes, too."

*   *

It's mid-summer, 1988, and there's a report of a brawl involving several dozen people in an eastside bar.

234

"By the time I arrived, there were five or six units already there, but they hadn't been able to do much to contain the fighting," Robert recounts a few days later. "I looked through the large plate glass window and my first reaction was, 'Oh, shit!' It was kind of like the cowboys against the Arabs, with people duking it out all over the place.

"I put on my helmet, grabbed my nightstick, muttered 'Charge!' and sprinted toward the front door just as a body came flying out of the window. It was a big dude, at least 200 pounds, and all I remember thinking was 'I'm going to die now because if someone can toss this guy through the window, what are they going to do to me?'

"Officers were trying to separate the fighters. Some were yelling at them to stop; others were using their fists, arms and nightsticks. I'd been inside less than ten seconds when a burly man with straggly hair headed for me, both fists raised. I mulled my next move for about a fifth of a second, long enough to realize that it was baton time.

"I pulled that sucker out faster than I thought it could be done. I whacked the guy on the forearm as he came within a step of me and then stepped out of his path. He backed off, and about that time, most of the others started to wind down either from exhaustion or the effects of alcohol. We had the situation under control, but the bar was a wreck, with chairs, tables and shattered glass strewn everywhere. I've never experienced anything like it. It was the kind of destruction you see in the movies."

*   *

A few minutes after 2 a.m. a week later, an eleven-year-old girl is awakened by her mother's screams. She dials 911 and within seconds is patched through to a service aide.

"Tucson Police. Can I help you?"

"My mom's gettin' beat up. Please come over and save her." The youngster's voice is surprisingly calm.

"Okay, just stay on the phone with me while we get some officers on the way over there."

Robert is one of four who start toward the apartment complex.

The girl is sobbing now and the service aide asks her name.

"Kimberly."

"Okay, Kimberly. Is your mother okay?"

The service aide can hear screams in the background.

"Does she need an ambulance over there?"

There's no response.

"Kimberly?"

"Uh huh."

"Is your mother okay?"

"I don't think so."

"Who is she fighting with?"

"I don't know who he is."

"Okay. Do you have any weapons, Kimberly?"

"Uhm, yes, we have a gun, but it's a rifle."

"Where is your mother at?"

"Uhm, he's still over here. He told (my sister) to shut the door. I think he's gonna do some (inaudible)."

"Okay. Let's get a description of this person who's fighting with your mother, okay?"

"He's Black and he's got like braids in his hair."

"Black male. About how old is he?"

"Uhm, about twenty-five."

"What color shirt and pants does he wear?"

"I don't know. He's picking my mom up by the hair and throwing her."

"Is it somebody your mother knows?"

"I don't know. This is the first time I . . ."

"But you don't know if he's a boyfriend of your mother's?"

Kimberly is crying hysterically now.

"We have police on the way over there, okay?"

Kimberly doesn't answer and more screams are heard in the background.

"Okay, Kimberly, just stay on the phone with me."

"He's got real long hair."

"We have officers on the way over there. If you can give me a better description of him. . ."

"I'm not sure, but it's a red or blue shirt, 'cause I know he has something, uh, and he's got brown eyes. Didn't see any tattoos or anything."

"Okay, just stay on the phone with me until we get somebody there. Do you think your mother needs an ambulance to check her out?"

"Yeah, please."

"Okay. Do you know where he's at right now, Kimberly?"

Her response is inaudible.

"Can you lock the door where you're at?"

236

A pause, then, "I locked it."

"Is your sister with you?"

"No, she's (inaudible)."

"The officers will be there in just a minute."

"Uh, huh."

"You don't know why they were fighting?"

"No, I just woke up to her screaming, 'No, no, don't do that.' And I was just sort of standing there watching 'em."

"Okay, just stay on the phone with me and I'll let you know when the officers are there."

"Uh, huh."

About ten seconds pass, then, "We do have four officers there, okay?"

"They're here?"

"Yes."

Suddenly calm: "Okay."

"Now I want you just to stay in the room there until someone comes in and lets you know everything's okay out there, okay?"

"Uh huh. Well, bye."

The service aide doesn't want her to hang up.

"I'm gonna just keep you on the phone."

"Hope they come in."

A few seconds, then Kimberly whispers something, but the service aide can't hear it.

"What is that?"

"He's trying to unlock the door."

The service aide's mind races: Is it a cop or the assailant attempting to open the door?

Kimberly needs her full attention now.

"I'm so scared. I want my mom really bad."

"Can you look out your window?"

"Well, we've got a back yard."

"Yeah, go ahead and look out the window. The officers want you to look out."

"Okay, hold on." About ten seconds pass, then, "I see a helicopter."

"Okay, I want you to stay on the phone with me until they tell me everything's okay. Alright?"

"Sounds like he's trying to break out the back window."

"Who sounds like that?"

"The guy, 'cause I just heard him go in the bathroom."

"You just heard him go in the bathroom?"

237

"Uh huh."

"Does it sound like he's trying to get out the window there?"

"Beating on it like crazy."

"Okay, what are you hearing now?"

"The door's getting knocked on. Yeah."

"Your door?"

"Uh uh, but he's beatin' on the window like crazy."

"Okay, but who's knocking on your door right now?"

"I bet it's the police. I'm not sure." Sounding frustrated now: "My mom's not being helped. (Inaudible) held in the bathroom with her. Tell 'em to beat on the door if they have to!"

"He's holding your mother in the bathroom?"

"I guess, or something, but she's yelling (that) nothing's happening."

Officers don't want to force their way inside and possibly escalate what might already be a hostage situation. The best course is to get the children out.

Kimberly's younger sister has remained in her own bedroom, frightened and afraid to do anything. Robert, on the west side of the apartment, hears the girl's cries, moves toward the sound and sees her through the curtained window.

She comes to the window and tries to open it, but the thumb-lock stops the movement after just an inch or two. She alternately cries and screams as Robert and officer Nick Aussems force it open and pull her out.

Robert advises other officers on the scene that they have the younger girl and that Aussems is going to break the window and climb inside.

Kimberly can now hear police radios nearby. She turns away from the phone and screams, "Come in, come in! Open the door! Oh God, mommy!"

"Just stay on the phone with me, Kimberly," the service aide says again.

"They're breaking our window!"

"Kimberly, the officers are trying to get in right now."

About fifteen seconds, then: "They're getting (her) out! Oh, they're taking my mom. They got my mommy!"

She hangs up, leaving the service aide — not certain who "they" are — with a disconcerting dial tone in her ear.

The suspect runs out the front door and is immediately wrestled to the ground by two officers. Kicking and screaming obscenities, Thomas is pinned face down on the concrete and handcuffed.

The younger girl, still crying, wants her mother. She wraps both arms over Robert's shoulders as he carries her inside where her mother now sits on the livingroom couch. Kimberly is already there and in seconds all three of them are huddled together, sobbing softly.

Robert is assigned to drive Thomas to the police station where he will be read his rights and questioned. Since he hasn't yet been 'Mirandized,' Robert is not permitted to ask questions, but he can *listen.* Thomas volunteers that he is the woman's ex-boyfriend and tells Robert, "the mother-fucking bitch likes my dick."

He's booked — and later convicted — on rape and kidnapping charges.

*　　*

Robert has honed his interrogation techniques.

"When I interview a suspect, part of my style is what I call attack and retreat. I throw a series of questions: Where were you? What time was it? Who was with you? What did you do? What happened next? Then what? It's just boom, boom, boom. I pay attention to the details, and then go back and ask the same questions again, looking for discrepancies."

He has also learned that as he moves physically closer to a suspect it increases the level of anxiety.

"As soon as I begin to get conflicting answers and the suspect realizes that he's screwed up, I back off for a few seconds to let him digest the situation. I know now that he's lying to me and he knows that I know. I'll talk softly to him then and say, 'When you're ready to tell me, I'm ready to listen.' He may confess at this point, but if he doesn't head in that direction, I'll begin to pick up the tempo again, using whatever opening he gives me.

"He might say, 'Well, I was in the back yard.'

'What were you doing in the back yard?' I'll ask.

'I was just standing there.'

'What did you see while you were standing there? Were there toys, a bicycle, lounge chairs?'

'Yeah, I saw them.'

'I was there right after the burglary and I didn't see those things. How could you have seen them? Obviously you were doing a little bit more. Why don't you just tell me about it.'

'Well, yeah, I was standing outside the patio door.'

'You were standing outside the door, but you never went inside the house?'

239

'Well, I opened the door and looked in a little bit, but I never went inside.'

'Okay, what did you do?'

'I just looked around.'

'I know that you were inside the house. What did you see while you were there?'

'Well, yeah, I guess I was inside for a minute, but I didn't take anything. I just looked around and left.'

"You just go piece by piece, inch by inch," Robert explains. "They almost always tell you and that's all there is to it. If they still deny any involvement, their body movements will usually give them away. They'll look down or away from you to avoid eye contact. They'll fiddle with their fingers, pick their nose, play with their ears, rub their hair.

"I'll look directly at the suspect and say, 'Your mouth is lying to me, but your body is telling me the truth.' Then I'll start the questioning again. All I need to do is place the suspect in the house. As soon as I've done that, they've admitted to breaking the law. If two or more burglars are working together, it's even easier. You just separate them and wait for them to incriminate each other."

He especially likes the challenge of working a cold trail.

"They fascinate me," he says. "You just look for similarities with other burglaries and try to build your case with what you have and with your knowledge of the neighborhood. The more complex it is, the better I like it. There's not much challenge when you go to a shoplifting and the complainant says, 'Yes, he did it, here's what he took and here's the videotape of him taking it.'"

*   *

June 8, 1989. It's been an emotional week for Robert. Yesterday, he responded to St. Joseph's Hospital where a middle-aged woman was being treated after a suicide attempt. She tells Robert that she swallowed most of a bottle of sleeping pills. "I'm just tired of living," she says.

As a social worker enters the emergency room and starts a conversation with the woman, Robert walks to his patrol car. A few seconds later, there's a report that an unconscious three-year-old boy has just been pulled from a swimming pool. When Robert hears the address, he stiffens. It's the home where Robert's oldest son attends Cub Scout meetings. Their friends' youngest child is three

240

and Robert wants to be there to provide emotional support while other officers begin the investigation. He's about seven miles away and begins moving around traffic to speed his response.

Two minutes later, officers are advised that the young boy is being transported to St. Joseph's Hospital in a family member's car. Robert makes a U-turn. If he had a description of the vehicle, he might be able to intercept it and expedite its way. Instead, he heads back toward the hospital and waits outside the emergency room.

The youngster is sputtering, but breathing fitfully on his own. The woman who overdosed lies less than fifteen feet away in the same trauma room.

The moment is bizarre and incongruous to Robert.

"Doctors are trying to save the life of a child, and two beds away is a woman who doesn't want to live." He pauses and shakes his head. "Two beds apart," he repeats in disbelief.

Today, there's another dose of frustration when he's dispatched to a home where a fourteen-year-old girl lies dead in a widening pool of blood. This was the first week of summer vacation for Lisa, an honor student.

Her father explains tearfully that he had scolded her for failing to follow through on her house-cleaning chores. She went into his bedroom, raised his gun to her head and in a final act of desperation or anger, fired a single bullet through her right temple while two younger sisters watched television in the next room.

This incident is even more disturbing to Robert than yesterday's.

"Lisa's father already blames himself and he's going to be living with it for the rest of his life, but how can you say it was his fault? He says he's overly strict and maybe too much of a perfectionist, but he's a single parent trying to raise his kids the best way he knows. What gets to me is how something we perceive as being minor can be so overwhelming to someone that the only way they see out of it is to end their life."

When Robert goes home today, he'll not only remove the bullets from his gun, but dismantle the weapon as well.

"You think you know your family, but sometimes you find that you really didn't. Anyone who decides to shoot himself in this house is going to have to learn how to assemble a gun first."

"The kids know that it's okay to be angry or sad, but that it's important to talk things out," he says. "They may hear Tammy and me disagreeing or arguing, but they also see us kiss and make up. They know that we have problems like everyone else, but we tell them that nothing is going to separate us. Tammy is an angel. She

241

loves the heck out of me and the kids, and I just appreciate her more and more."

*   *

May, 1989. Robert doesn't make the test cutoff which might have led to an assignment with the Burglary Task Force, and he's both disappointed and angry. He estimates that he's caught at least twenty burglars during the past two years and that his investigations have resulted in the arrest of at least fifteen others with a combined total of at least 200 burglaries.

His reputation for persistence has continued to grow.

"A few months ago, a kid actually turned himself in to me," he says with pride. "He phoned the station and left a message for me to call him back. When I did, he said, 'My friends have been saying that Garcia is looking for you and he's going to find you, so you may as well just give up.' He came to the station with his mother and confessed to a burglary and also to stealing an automobile.

"His mom could hardly believe what she was hearing. She looked at me, shook her head in bewilderment and said, 'I haven't gotten a confession out of him for anything since he was a child.'"

"I feel strongly about pushing burglars out of the neighborhoods, and it's something I want to do full-time."

For now, he'll have to wage his battle against burglars without the title.

■

There is much frustration in the criminal justice system and real-life cops often lose their man even before they have him in custody.

As Rene Gomez completes his lunch break just after 2 p.m. on October 13, 1988, he observes a man in his mid-twenties wearing a torn T-shirt and cutoffs and carrying a suitcase. Instinct tells Rene that something is out of place, but suspicion alone doesn't give him the right to conduct a search. He's allowed, though, to ask if the man is willing to *show* him what's inside.

Jacinto nods his head, unsnaps the hinges and raises the lid, revealing a guitar, a tape recorder and the remote control unit for a video cassette recorder. He says he bought the suitcase and its contents from a second-hand store earlier in the day. Jacinto has no receipt and doesn't remember the name of the store. All Rene can do is give dispatch a description of the items. There's no record of them having being stolen and Rene tells the Jacinto that he appreciates his cooperation, then watches him board a cross-city bus.

Less than an hour later, a woman returning from a doctor's appointment finds her home burglarized. Among the missing items are a tape recorder, the remote control for her VCR and her daughter's $200 guitar.

"Damn," grouses a frustrated Rene, whose only consolations are that his instinct was correct and that he now has a good physical description of the young man to pass on to other officers.

*   *

Rene, who is generally the fun-loving comedian of his squad, can also be moody, especially when he thinks about getting old. Although not yet thirty-three, he occasionally convinces himself that he's already on the downside of life with not much to do but "sit back and count the years."

He's mellow this evening, though, and nothing happens during the shift to diminish the peaceful space he's in. He provides chauffeur service twice within an hour.

The first to benefit is a young couple who, with their infant son, are stranded outside of a food market when a friend fails to pick them up. The other is an inebriated man sleeping in his car in a parking lot at 1 a.m. Rene could cite him for DUI even though the engine is not running, but it would not serve any useful purpose, so Rene drives him home. He feels that "doing this is an appropriate use of my time when there's not much going on."

Later, there's a report of a woman screaming in a nearby apartment. Pausing at the door, Rene listens for any sound of conflict, then knocks. There are two men and a woman inside. It's clear from the smell of alcohol that there's been a lot of partying going on, but there are no signs of violence. Rene, turning to leave: "I just wanted to make sure you were all okay. I'm not going to hassle anyone; you all look pretty happy."

His daughter, Cori Daniele Gomez has reached her first birthday. "I thought I was going to live my whole life for my boy (Rene, Jr., now five years old.) Now I have Cori and it's double the fun," says the man who grew up in a home without a father.

"Sometimes thinking about them distracts me from my job, but I love them with all my heart and I just can't wait to be with them.

243

If something bad happened to me, the reason I would fight to live would be Sylvia and the kids."

■

It's July 24, 1988, and two men doing construction work in a vacant house detect an odor that seems to be coming from the cooling system of the home next door. A week later, the sickly sweet odor is even more pervasive — "too strong to ignore," one of them tells police.

Officers work their way around more than a half-dozen abandoned vehicles, old sinks, assorted debris and heavy brush surrounding the property. The windows are boarded up, but peering through a small opening, they see what appears to be a brown blanket over a chair.

Gaining entry through a side door, officers walk a narrow pathway through magazines, newspapers and garbage stacked about five feet high until they reach the brown blanket — in reality the badly decomposed body of an elderly man. A calendar on the desk is opened to October, 1986.

The dead man had been reclusive for more than twenty years, according to one neighbor, and most of those who live nearby say they had never seen him. An autopsy indicates that he died of natural causes and that he and at least four cats have lain there for nearly two years.

The house is in Pat Horbarenko's beat and she has patrolled that street hundreds of times. There had been no reason for her to go on the property to check, but now she wishes that she had. "It made me sad that the old man was dead for so long and no one missed him or wondered about him. Now when I see houses with no sign of activity, I'm going to get out and poke around."

A week later, Pat is dispatched to the office of a dentist reported to be suicidal. "He had injected himself with novocaine and then used a scalpel to slice open his chest and throat. There was blood all over the place, but he was alive and conscious and we were able to stabilize the bleeding.

"I asked him why he tried to kill himself, but he didn't answer.
'Do you have problems at home?'
'No, I have a wonderful wife and family.'
'Is your business not doing well?'

'It's doing real well; I have all the money I want.'

'Then why did you do this?'

'Because I don't like myself.'"

At the hospital, he tells a nurse that he has AIDS, then denies it, saying he just wanted to "blow everyone's mind."

Pat and four other officers and medics who had been splattered with his blood are tested for the HIV virus and she is frightened.

"Dr. (Robert) Levitin drew blood to establish a base line and said there would be periodic followups. He told us that we could be at high risk if the man had AIDS. The message I was hearing was that we could expect to die if we tested positive."

A court order is obtained, directing that the dentist be tested for AIDS, and a few days later, Pat and the others are told that he does not have the virus.

*   *

December 16, 1988. A woman phones 911 and says that her husband assaulted her with a partially-cooked chicken pot pie before fleeing to his father's house. Susan is barely five feet tall, weighs about 180 pounds and is wearing red Bermuda shorts and a too-tight striped T-shirt without a bra. Pieces of diced carrots and potatoes hang from her hair, and Pat needs to concentrate to avoid giggling while she gathers information.

Although Susan's injuries are minor, Pat and officer Dave Silva go to arrest Rick. A long-haired, amply tattooed man with no front teeth, he doesn't challenge Susan's story. When Pat explains that he's under arrest, he steps backward into the kitchen, the most dangerous place for a confrontation.

There's a large knife on the drain board, but Rick has his back to it. He shakes his head, tells Pat that he's "on neutral territory" and won't go to jail. As he clenches his fists, his facial muscles tighten. Silva quietly radios for more units while Pat buys time making small-talk.

Two other officers arrive and it takes all four of them to wrestle Rick to the floor and restrain him. His anger played out, he turns calm and walks quietly to Pat's patrol car.

"Why did you hit her with the pie?" she asks him as they begin the drive to jail.

"I came home from work and asked what we were having for supper," Rick recounts. "When she showed it to me, I said, 'You know I hate chicken pot pie! What's more, you had it in the

245

microwave, and look at this shitty crust. You want it, you eat it!' I guess her head got in the way when I tried to give it to her."

Halfway to jail, he turns angry again, telling Pat that he's a fifth-degree black belt and that it took nine cops to subdue him the last time he was arrested. While she's digesting this, he announces, "I get claustrophobia in cars. I'm gonna go crazy and when I do, I'm not responsible for my actions."

Pat requests that a guard meet her at the jail entrance, but Rick becomes lamb-like once more and the booking process is completed without incident. As Pat prepares to leave, he motions her toward him. "I'm sorry for what I did. Usually I hate cops, but you treated me real fair."

Another man in the process of being booked turns toward Rick. "I wish the cop who arrested me looked like that," he says, pointing to Pat as she walks away.

Later in the evening, screams are heard at an apartment complex. A neighbor points to a door near the center courtyard, but there are no visible lights inside and no sound.

Pat knocks, steps aside and waits for a response. There is none, and she knocks again, louder this time. Still no answer. Now she raps the door with her nightstick six or seven times. Approaching footsteps are heard and the door is flung open. On the other side is a very large, very muscular man in his mid-twenties, wearing a pair of boxer shorts and an ugly scowl.

Pat explains why she's there, then asks, "Are you by yourself?"

"Yes," Tony responds.

"Can we come in and look?"

"No!"

"Well, we need to check inside."

Planting his feet firmly just beyond the doorway, Tony yells, "Do you have a God-damned search warrant? Get out of my face!"

Officer Kim Kircher tries to calm him. "We have a report that there was a fight here. We need to check the place and then we'll be gone."

"You woke me up! I have to get up at five o'clock in the morning and go to work!"

Pat, softly: "I apologize for that. Just let us make sure everything's okay."

Tony steps aside, still yelling: "Then come on and look! Just come on and look!"

Pat leads the way, edging cautiously around Tony and prepared to react if he makes any move in her direction. He doesn't. They walk through the bedroom and check the bathroom. No one is there and there's no indication of a struggle. The brief search has taken less time than the verbal confrontation which preceded it, and they turn to leave.

Pat: "Thank you, sir. Goodnight."

"Just get the fuck out of my house!"

Tony kicks the door shut, but it bounces off the threshold, popping open momentarily before he slams it again, still cursing.

This is an instance where the presence of a female officer may have helped stabilize a potentially volatile situation. Kircher has remained a couple of steps behind Pat and opted to let her do most of the talking.

Pat realizes that Tony probably disliked cops even before tonight's encounter, and wonders how many well-meaning parents prejudice their children against officers. "I hear them say, 'The cops are going to get you' or they'll tell their kids, 'You better be good or I'm going to tell the officer to arrest you.'

"A few weeks ago, I had to chase a man who assaulted his wife and then ran off carrying his four-year-old boy. When I caught up with him, he put the child down and threw himself over the hood of a car and screamed, 'Look at what the cop's doing to your father! Tighter, tighter! Make those cuffs as tight as you can! Go and cut off my circulation!' If this youngster gets lost or frightened tomorrow, do you think he's going to ask a cop for help? Can you imagine what he'll think about cops when he grows up? It's really sad."

*　　*

It's March 24, 1989, and Pat is completing three months on the midnight shift, the worst of all possible worlds to most officers. While the first couple of hours are often fast-paced, there is a sharp letdown by 3 a.m. when most of the drunks, batterers and robbers have called it a night. Other than the sound of the patrol car's engine as it cruises residential streets and empty shopping centers, a city cop's world is virtually silent now.

Officers may park their vehicles and sit for a few minutes, but catnaps are not permitted. Except for a thirty-minute meal break and brief stops to complete paperwork, they must continue to 'work' their beats.

By about 4 a.m., the lack of activity takes its toll. The sound of the patrol car can now become hypnotic, possibly even deadly. When the eyelids begin to droop and the head follows them south,

247

a cup of coffee often provides the best jump-start.

"You get so tired it's almost like being mesmerized," Pat says. "There have been times when I was jolted with the realization that I was about to hit a curb or a parked vehicle. It really scared me, and I've learned to get out of my car and do foot patrol until I'm fully awake."

Pat worked midnight shifts as a nurse, but it was easier then because she could go home and sleep after work. As a cop, she must often spend part of the day meeting with attorneys or testifying in court. When this happens, her sleep time is fragmented, making the following shift still more difficult. Occasionally, she has two court appearances the same day, but several hours apart. She keeps a sleeping bag and pillow in her locker at the police station and sometimes naps on the floor rather than make the ninety-minute round trip to and from her suburban Tucson home.

*   *

As she begins her 4 p.m. to midnight shift eight weeks later, Pat drives by a neighborhood convenience store which had been robbed at gunpoint earlier in the week. She tells the worried clerk that detectives are still working on that case as well as on the armed robbery of a nearby gasoline service station in which the suspect description and method of operation were similar.

An hour later, she's dispatched to the gas station where Betty, a frightened woman in her early twenties, says she thinks the robber is Leroy, an acquaintance of her boyfriend's, who has been living with them for the last two weeks. Betty says Leroy told them that he no longer had a financial problem and would be leaving soon. Meanwhile, he hasn't been out of the apartment for several days and appears nervous, she adds.

Leroy's physical description closely matches that of the suspect in the robberies and Pat asks for additional officers to set up positions in the area. Betty has now been gone nearly an hour after telling Leroy that she would be back in ten or fifteen minutes.

Not willing to risk a possible hostage situation, Pat asks Betty to stay away from the apartment until Leroy has been detained for questioning. As Betty points out the apartment from about a half-block away, Leroy walks outside, crosses the street and moves quickly into an alley between rows of homes and disappears.

Pat, frustrated that she was within a minute or two of nabbing him, can now only use her portable radio to relay his description to

248

the five officers who have fanned out looking for him.

While Pat stands outside the apartment, a neighbor says that he recently saw a man matching Leroy's description toss a multi-colored shirt into the trash dumpster. Pat is excited again because the suspect in both robberies was wearing a Hawaiian shirt.

She puts on plastic gloves and begins to climb into the dumpster, but as she grasps the top and starts to pull herself over the grease-coated lip, she slides backward. There's neither sufficient height nor time for a feet-first landing. Pat's buttocks land first, snapping the antenna off of the police radio clipped to her waist. Her head hits the ground and she lies there a few seconds before getting up.

As she 'walks off' the fall, Sergeant Max Davis, about seven blocks away, reports that he has Leroy under arrest. Another officer makes it safely into the dumpster where a brief search yields the Hawaiian shirt.

Although Pat's worst injury seems to be to her dignity, she's driven to a hospital for precautionary X-rays. They are negative, but she's told to expect to be in pain for several days and that she probably won't be permitted to work for at least a week.

Pat has filed for divorce for the second time and says that she'll go through with it this time.

■

"Most people don't like seeing cops," Bernie Harrigan muses midway through a late-summer shift. "It's usually a reminder that something in their life has gone wrong. I mean, how often does someone call us because something *good* happened?"

He views the breakup of the family as the biggest problem facing both society and law enforcement. "You go out to family fights and it seems that nearly everyone has a different last name. The kids may have been shuffled from family to family, a lot of them have been abused, there are alcohol and drug problems and not enough access to community services."

He continues to rely on humor to make his job easier. After helping a man and woman in their early twenties exchange insurance information following a minor accident: "There you are, everything you ever wanted to know about each other, but were afraid to ask."

Another young woman can't start her car. There's a service

station a block away and Bernie offers to have a mechanic respond: "They'll come over and jump you."

"I hope not," she counters, a brief expression of shock across her face.

Sometimes the humor is self-deprecating, as when an elderly woman complains that a neighbor has been verbally harassing her.

"Was he young or old?" Bernie asks.

"About forty-five or fifty."

"Oh, he's old, huh?" deadpans Bernie, now less than eighteen months from his fiftieth birthday.

Nonetheless, he generally avoids being overly friendly because "someone you're throwing smiles at now might be the person you have to arrest five minutes later."

Bernie says he's still not always comfortable with his skills as a street cop. "In many ways I'm more relaxed than I was in New York, but I have the impression that you can get burned more as a cop in Tucson. There's a certain amount of apprehension when you come home, turn on your answering machine and hear a message to call Internal Affairs.

"You know that you can always be second-guessed and some situations are going to backfire on you no matter how good a job you do. You don't usually get recognized for the good things, but on the call that could go either way, you're probably going to hear about it."

Bernie has been on both sides. In New York, he served a year in Internal Affairs.

"I could send shudders through an entire precinct just by walking into their building," he reminisces.

From a safety standpoint, he sees more potential danger in Tucson. "First, we're vulnerable as a result of the drug trade and the fact that many dealers protect their investment by carrying semi-automatic and automatic weapons. Then, too, this is a small city by comparison with New York. It would be a lot easier for someone wanting revenge to find me here."

*   *

June 1989. Bernie and Dorothy have been back together for six months.

"I bought her a lot of flowers and candy, and sent a lot of letters. I courted her like hell," he says, adding that he feels he is more committed to the relationship than she is and that she may not remain a part of his life.

250

Dorothy is in New York where her mother is scheduled for eye surgery and Bernie has just returned from Seattle where he interviewed for a police department job. He loves that city, but wonders whether Dorothy would go with him if he's offered a position. In any event, he says that he's prepared to move if the relationship doesn't work out. He has heard favorable things about both the city and its police department.

"You know me — have gun, will travel," he says with a smile.

■

For the second time in two years, Les Beach is going through a period of turmoil on the job. His style is to hold his feelings inside, and although Sharon is concerned, she knows that Les is more likely to open up when he doesn't feel pressured.

Two weeks later he tells her of "the little things going wrong on calls" that have left him questioning his effectiveness as a cop. But he realizes now, he says, that he sometimes has unrealistically high expectations of himself.

One of his continuing frustrations is the generally poor interaction between officers and teenagers. As drivers, teens receive a disproportionate share of traffic citations. Worse, there seem to be few places for them to socialize without drawing complaints.

In Tucson, as in thousands of other cities, parking lots of shopping centers and fast-food restaurants are favorite hangouts for kids in pickup trucks and low-riders, as well as for those who congregate when they don't have the 'right' vehicle or gasoline money for cruising.

Les recalls how he kiddingly told a sergeant that it was time to go and harass the kids. "The sergeant laughed, looked at me and asked, 'Yes, but where are you going to tell them to go?'"

It's a question without a satisfactory answer. All Les can do is tell them that they're on private property, that there have been complaints from store owners and that they can't stay.

"I'll say, 'I know you have no place to hang out and I know it's frustrating for you and you feel hassled. We don't like having to tell you to move on, but that's what we've been told to do.'

"Unfortunately, we're not giving them any guidance. We're telling them what they can't do, but we're not giving them an alternative. It's shitty public relations and a no-win situation for us

251

and the kids. Sometimes they're understanding about it, but usually there arc too many guys trying to show their girlfriends how macho they are," he says, adding that officers often contribute to the problem by the negative way they relate to young people.

Macho guys and nasty drunks notwithstanding, Les is mindful of the job's built-in perks. "You have a lot of power at your fingertips. You can clear a fast path through traffic by turning on your overhead lights and siren. You can order any vehicle to pull over, you can question any citizen, and you can shut down an entire street or intersection at an accident or crime scene.

"That can be pretty heady stuff, and you learn quickly that it must be held in check when its use is not appropriate. Sometimes I find myself going faster than the speed limit, both on the job and in my own car, and I have to remind myself to slow down. In reality, though, I know I'm not likely to get a citation for a moving violation while I'm off-duty. I'm going to 'badge' the officer who stops me and use it to my favor."

*   *

October 31, 1988. A man holding a rifle is reported to be standing on the roof of a house. As Les and two other officers start up Code 3, dispatch advises that the man with the weapon is kneeling behind the cooling unit.

Les knows that the immediate priorities will be to cordon off the area, call out the SWAT team and begin evacuating people.

Layton Dickerson, the first officer on the scene, parks a half-block away and advances cautiously on foot. A long minute later, he keys his microphone and reports, "Code 4, it's a mannequin with a BB gun." Relieved officers knock on the owner's door to compliment him on his creativity and suggest that he consider a less realistic Halloween display.

Later, Les responds to an accident in which one of the vehicles has struck the major traffic signal in the intersection, bending it to the point where there is a danger of it snapping off. The other signals are shut down and cones and flares are spotted every ten to fifteen feet. Les and two other officers direct traffic, wearing bright orange vests and waving high-power flashlights for emphasis.

The makeshift system is working well until a determined woman flattens several cones and proceeds through the flares in an attempt to enter the closed left turn lane, nearly striking a patrol car as she proceeds. An officer sprints over and tells her that she can't turn left, but must drive through the intersection.

The woman is about five-foot-nothing, weighs perhaps ninety pounds and can barely see over the steering wheel of the Pontiac Bonneville. She nods, but as soon as he turns away, she heads again for the left turn lane, driving directly toward Les who is frantically waving his flashlight to get her attention.

She's traveling less than ten miles an hour, giving Les just enough time to jump to the side. He tattoos the hood of her car with his flashlight as he pushes safely away, yelling, "Stop your car!" as he falls. She does, then looks around, a puzzled expression on her face.

"Where are you going?" Les asks in somewhat less than his his most polite tone of voice.

"I'm going home."

"Don't you realize you can't turn here?"

"I always turn here. This is the way I go home."

Les wants nothing more to do with her. He writes a citation for failure to obey a police officer, and hands it to Ron Payette, telling him, "Give it to her, have her sign it, and then drive her at least 200 feet down the road before you let her go. I don't want her behind the wheel anywhere near me because she'll probably run over me for spite."

Payette, returning a few minutes later: "Tsk, tsk, Officer Beach, she's mad at you."

*　　*

April 29, 1989. Les turned fifty three days ago, and Sharon has invited family, friends and fellow officers to celebrate the occasion. It's an evening of toasts and roasts, complete with an R-rated skit in which several female friends review and parody his sexual fantasies. No one seems to enjoy it more than Les's parents, both in their late seventies.

Les's father has ridden patrol with him twice, being reminded each time, "Don't get out of the patrol car no matter what happens." Both shifts were uneventful.

Sharon, herself nearing fifty and long past the school-girl crush stage, speaks of Les as "my sweetie and the love of my life."

Payette — barely half Les's age — recalls how he was initially concerned that Les might not be able to take care of himself in tough situations.

"I decided that I'd do most of the fighting and let Les stand aside until it was time to put the handcuffs on," Payette says to a round of laughter. "I quickly learned that Les was more than capable of handling any situation and I've seen him keep going when I was winded and ready to call it a day. Besides teaching me about being a good police officer, he's taught me many things in life that have nothing to do with law enforcement."

As the evening is about to end, the man who waited more than twenty-five years for the chance to be a cop, has something to say. The words come slowly, gently:

"You're my dear friends, and even though I don't drink any more, I still get emotional about these things. You have made me very happy. I've met some very good friends and very good cops, both male and female.

"I'm health-conscious and I work out a lot because I'm fifty years old and these 'Adam-Henrys' we meet out on the street are young and a hell of a lot stronger and quicker than I am. I stay as fit as I can, not (just) for myself, but for the other guys I work with, and I do whatever I can to make sure that you don't get hurt and I don't get hurt.

"The last person I want to thank is Sharon. She's the best thing that ever happened to me."

A pause, a deep breath, then softly, not quite holding his growing emotion in check, "You all know that I dearly love this job, but if she asked me to give it up tomorrow, I would."

Sharon is sitting across the room.

"I know that he would, and I'd never ask him to," she says, turning misty-eyed for a moment.

9

Being There

Fate or coincidence occasionally finds people in the middle of unexpected situations. Some are in the right place at the right time, but not able to do much more than pick up the pieces. Others become heroes by being in the right place at the *wrong* time, perhaps a bit too close for comfort when the line between life and death can be measured in inches or seconds.

It's August 7, 1989, and Anita Sueme is working early days. She arises at 4:15, lets her dogs outside, then scatters food for the rabbits and birds that share the desert around her home. She's going back to work after a rare three-day weekend, and doesn't feel at all inspired to return to the streets — not an unusual feeling given her low level of energy at this hour.

She spoons down her morning oatmeal and sips a cup of herbal tea before pushing herself away from the table. She showers, slips on a pair of shorts and a tank top and slides behind the wheel of her Nissan Pulsar just before 5:15. The temperature has already climbed into the high seventies and the first hazy light of morning is visible in her rear view mirror as she approaches the midtown police station after an almost-trafficless twenty-minute drive.

By the time she begins patrol at 6:25, the flow of vehicles headed downtown has picked up, although the commuter peak is still nearly an hour away. She cruises randomly, lowering her visor each time she heads east into the already-blinding sun. She's dispatched to the scene of a minor traffic accident and then to a Circle K to mediate a boyfriend-girlfriend dispute.

Back in service, Anita is driving south on Alvernon Way at 8:51 when she observes a gray 1971 Ford pickup truck ease into the roadway from a side street and pull in front of her. The driver seems "a little bit in a hurry," and when he turns west into an alley instead of continuing to the intersection, Anita follows.

The driver parks his truck outside of an automobile paint and body shop, jumps out and sprints around the corner of the building. Anita pulls up as he disappears, thinking that he was probably late for work or in a hurry to pick something up.

She has no valid reason to go in after him, but drives onto Speedway and stops in front of the business. "I don't know why, but something just didn't feel right," she says later.

As she brakes to a stop, Anita looks through the window from about forty feet away and sees him standing inside, arm extended, holding a gun and cranking off rounds. She's listening to the sound of pop-pop-pop, and thinking, "Oh, fuck, he's actually shooting someone!" The initial shock is like a slap in the face.

Stunned and almost in disbelief, her training and instinct take over.

She grasps her radio: "3-Adam-51, I have a shooting." Her words are clear, but the pitch of her voice sounds at least a half-octave higher than normal.

Dispatch: "10-4. What's . . . do you need . . . (3-Adam)-51, where are you?"

"Speedway and Alvernon."

The dispatcher activates the emergency tone, repeats Anita's location and calls for backup units. Her request is just a formality because, within seconds, virtually every officer within a four-mile radius is headed in Anita's direction. Two of them announce that they're en route; the others just push through traffic to get there.

Anita uses the steering wheel to push herself out of her patrol car. She lifts her gun from its holster and runs along the east side of the L-shaped building. She can no longer see the man in the window and thinks he might have run outside.

Dispatch: "(3-Adam)-51, give me some information as soon as you can."

Anita's radio is clipped onto her belt. She wants both hands on her gun in case she needs to shoot, and she's thinking, "Please leave me alone, I don't know what's going on here yet."

Sergeant Jill Vogel, fortuitously just a few blocks away, reports that she's already approaching the scene.

Nineteen seconds have elapsed since Anita announced the shooting. She's looking for a way into the building, but can't find one. "We're talking a super case of tunnel-vision now. I'm looking and not seeing an open door."

256

What she *does* see are about six people standing outside of an adjoining building. No one appears to be moving or talking. They might be in shock, she thinks as she runs toward them, yelling for them to take cover.

She keys her radio microphone now: "Come in on foot. I'm at the automotive place. It's the northwest quad."

Vogel asks if more information is available, but Anita doesn't have any yet.

Officers Paul Hawks and Martin Espinoza pull up and begin walking toward the building's front entrance.

Another officer calls Anita's designator, but she doesn't hear it above the noise of the workers who are beginning to give her information.

Dispatch, repeating: "3-Adam-51?"

Anita responds this time, some of her words lost amid the confusion: "He's in the shop. (Unintelligible) baseball cap."

Dispatch: "I copy he's got a baseball cap?"

Anita's reply is garbled, and the dispatcher asks her to repeat it. "He's in the . . . He's in the corner."

Dispatch: "I copy he's in the corner."

Sergeant Bob Torres asks for an ambulance. It's 8:55 a.m., and there are now six officers on the scene, most of them 'covering' each other as they attempt to ask questions or relay information.

The suspect runs out of the building, dropping a black revolver on the ground as he leaves. Espinoza turns the corner and confronts him there.

"Put your hands above your head!" he orders.

Ignoring Espinoza, he kneels and grabs his gun.

"Drop the gun! Drop the gun!" Espinoza screams.

The suspect raises his weapon, his index finger on the trigger.

Espinoza fires seven shots, and Hawks, moving up from behind, squeezes off four — all in less than two seconds. The suspect is pushed backward by the impact of the bullets. He staggers momentarily, drops his gun, then slowly slumps to the ground.

The sound of the automatic weapons rings in Anita's ears as she approaches the corner leading to the east side of the building.

"We have shots being fired," Sergeant Max Davis reports.

"Suspect is down," Hawks advises as several officers attempt to transmit simultaneously.

Dispatch: "Radios breaking. Suspect down. 10-9 anything else."

There is no response.

Anita can hear Espinoza yelling, "Leave the gun alone!" She

257

runs toward the sound of his voice, kneels low on the concrete and peers around the corner. The man is lying on his side, bleeding, but still reaching for his weapon. Anita is about twenty feet away, and draws down on him as she moves in.

"Put your arm behind your back!" she yells. He does, and Espinoza kicks the gun toward her. Anita picks it up, starts to remove the remaining bullets, and then thinks, 'Wait a second, somebody might be dead here, and I'm going to have to mark where the bullets are in the chamber.'

Torres: "I need Sueme to come on the air."

Dispatch: "3-Adam-51?"

"We've got the subject on the east side," she says. "He's been shot."

Espinoza: "Where's Meds?"

Dispatch: "Meds are en route."

Torres: "We have one subject on the ground. I need to know if he is a victim or the bad guy."

Anita responds, "There's one bad guy, he's been shot, we've got him and it's Code 4."

Anita places his gun in the trunk of her car, then she and Vogel enter the building where they find fifty-six-year-old Eugene Dietz lying motionless on his back, a trickle of blood beginning to dampen his dark blue sports shirt. Anita places her index finger on the victim's neck and wrists, but can't find a pulse.

Torres kneels by the victim and turns to Anita: "He's gone."

Anita uses a stick of white chalk to outline the position of the body, then walks outside.

Davis: "The owner here indicates there's only one bandit. If we have him in custody, I think it's Code 4."

He repeats the earlier request for an ambulance.

Dispatch: "I copy the scene's secure and the 10-59 can move in?"

There's no immediate reply. The dispatcher waits several seconds, then asks again: "Any unit at the scene that can advise me? The 10-59 can move in, 10-4?"

Vogel: "10-4."

Anita, realizing that she has blood and chalk on her hands, re-enters the building in search of a washroom or sink. She walks into the back room and gasps as she sees the body of a young woman on the floor, her mouth and eyes still open in death.

"My God, we have another one!" she says silently. The woman's shirt has been pulled above her chest, and from marks on the floor,

258

it looks like she had been dragged several feet before being shot through the heart at point-blank range.

In the last seconds of her life, twenty-nine-year-old Debra Ann Dietz made a desperate call to 911, but was apparently yanked away from the phone before she could ask for help. The telephone is off the hook, its headset on the floor where it had fallen.

It's 8:58 a.m., and it's been less than six minutes since Joseph Wood, the suspect, closed the door of his truck and entered the building. Conscious although shot nine times in the chest, thighs, arm, wrist and hand, he's rushed to a nearby trauma center.

Officer Mark Napier is assigned to follow the ambulance to the hospital, and instructed not to let Wood out of his sight. The intent, of course, is to make certain that he doesn't attempt to escape while being treated, but Napier — taking his instructions literally — dutifully scrubs down, puts surgical clothing over his uniform and spends more than three hours in the operating room while Wood lies sedated on an operating table.

For the next two weeks, until he is well enough to be taken to jail, the Tucson Police Department will station an officer in the room with Wood twenty-four hours a day.

*   *

Anita returns to the midtown station. After she dictates a taped statement to Detective Karen Wright, Sergeant Glenn Hendricks of the Behavioral Sciences Unit asks how she's feeling. Anita, not even aware of the sweat running down her face, keeps telling Hendricks that she's fine. After about five minutes, he looks directly at her and says, "No, you're not fine; you're bouncing off the walls." She's debriefed and told to take a few days off.

As she starts home around 1:30 p.m., Anita is suddenly aware that she's hungry. She stops at Jack in the Box for a sandwich and a diet Coke, then goes home where the first thing she does is to give her ninety-pound Shepherd as big a hug as she can muster. Later, she drives five miles to her parents' house for dinner.

"My mom's reaction was, 'Oh, my God, you could have gotten shot!' I told her that, yes, I could have, but I wasn't."

Home again after a brief visit, Anita turns on her telephone answering machine and drifts off almost immediately.

"I told myself that I was going to sleep and not think about it. I did sleep pretty well and got up in time to watch the sunrise. I had a pretty quiet morning, but spent part of the time replaying the shooting. I know that I was mentally prepared to shoot him, and there was no doubt in my mind that I was going to pull the trigger if I had to. Knowing now what he did to two innocent people, I think what upset me the most was that I didn't have a chance to shoot the asshole."

Realizing that she couldn't have prevented the tragedy, she has no guilt feelings. "I had no reason to stop his truck, and even if I had, he was already in the building before I pulled up."

Three days later, much of the episode has become dream-like. "All I have are fleeting images of the things I did. No matter how hard you try not to, you do get tunnel-vision. When I was trying to get the bystanders and witnesses to a safer place, I don't remember anything but thinking, 'Why are they standing out there? I've got to get them out of the way.' I found out later that one man climbed out of a window to escape, but I have no recollection of that even though I saw him do it."

*   *

Anita has a setback two weeks later when an elderly woman overdoses on sleeping pills. Anita had met Emma a year ago when Emma was punched several times by a neighbor. Anita returned to chat a few times, but then lost touch, and now Emma lies dead on the couch of her second-floor apartment, a suicide note and a Hemlock Society pamphlet near her body.

"I wanted to stop back to check up on her, but I never found the time to do it. I thought of her a lot, but I just kept putting it off," she says, sadness and perhaps guilt in her voice.

The following weeks continue to be stressful as Anita deals with the remnants of a difficult summer during which her Rhodesian Ridgeback puppy needed expensive surgery and her Shepherd killed her ten-year-old cat.

She still harbors unresolved anger over the end of her relationship with Johnathan. Particularly galling is the oak television cabinet she gave him just before the breakup. "I didn't buy him that to have it sit in some other woman's apartment," she says with clear resentment.

Her younger sister has given birth to a girl, but even this happy news has a dark side. "It was always important to me that I have the first grandbaby." Nonetheless, she's happy to be an aunt and has spent $700 for baby furniture for her niece.

Anita has been told by friends that White cops won't ask her out because she dated a Black officer. "He's a fine cop, and the people he works with like him and think he's a great guy, but there's still that unspoken prejudice," she says.

She soon hears that Johnathan is planning to marry his new girlfriend, and this is even more hurtful and galling.

"He told me he could never marry me because I would be unacceptable to his family. When I asked him to clarify how a woman with a college degree, her own home, a nice car, a yearly income of $33,000, a relatively nice person and not too bad looking could be unacceptable, I was told that the fact that I'm White made me unacceptable."

Johnathan doesn't agree with some of Anita's recollections, but feels "it would serve no good purpose to debate them."

Weekly counseling sessions have helped as she struggles to accept the end of the relationship, but after several months they have become a financial drain. She has used up most of her vacation time, but has accumulated sixty-eight sick days "for future maternity leave."

Anita has discovered another effective, but less-expensive therapy.

"When I heard that he was going to be married, I was livid," she recalls. "I wanted to torch his car, but I thought better of it and blew off steam by going out in the heat and digging wells for five shade trees."

She dug and planted two more on Johnathan's wedding day.

Now, she says, "the guys in the squad sometimes tease me by asking, 'Sueme, did you plant any trees this week?' I tell them, 'No, I'm not angry at anyone this week.'"

Six months after the murders of Eugene Dietz and his daughter, Anita has still not listened to the police tape of those first dramatic minutes, and she doesn't know if she ever will.

Despite verbal support from her peers and a statement from the Board of Inquiry that she handled herself well in a stressful situation, Anita is still uneasy.

She has occasional disconcerting dreams, but says that they don't seem to directly relate to the horror of looking through a window and watching a man fire shots at another human being.

She's quick to agree that the year has been a learning experience and a test of character.

"And I don't ever want to go through another one like it," she adds.

Hollywood, California, July 18, 1989: Actress Rebecca Schaeffer, who appeared in Woody Allen's *Radio Days* and co-starred in the television series, *My Sister Sam,* is shot and killed on the doorstep of her home. Tucsonan Robert John Bardo quickly becomes a suspect when Los Angeles detectives learn that Bardo was obsessed with Schaeffer and was seen near her West Hollywood apartment around the time of the shooting.

Tucson, Arizona, one day later: Just after 9 a.m., a pedestrian tells officer John Norton that a disoriented man on foot is darting in and out of traffic on the downtown exit ramp of Interstate 10 and has nearly been struck several times. Norton spots the man from a distance of several hundred feet and begins moving toward him. He could be drunk, suicidal or disoriented, and the first priority is to get him away from the remnants of morning rush hour.

The man appears to be about twenty. He has long hair and is dressed in jeans, a dirty white T-shirt and sandals. He doesn't see Norton approach because his attention is focused on a Department of Public Safety officer who is also headed in his direction. Norton reaches him first and together they walk to an empty lot near the bottom of the ramp.

Norton tells the young man that he's concerned about him, then asks, "What are you doing?"

"Trying to kill myself," he replies.

When Norton asks why, the man lowers his head in silence.

Tucson has a Mobile Acute Crisis Team, a county-affiliated mental health service with the authority to order psychiatric evaluation of any person believed to pose an imminent physical danger to himself or others. Norton asks that members of the team be called out, but they aren't immediately available.

Norton again turns his attention to the obviously troubled man and asks him his name.

"Robert Bardo," he replies.

Norton has not heard the news of Schaeffer's murder. He has not, in fact, even heard of her.

Bardo says that his parents live in Tucson and gives Norton their phone number. Norton asks the dispatcher to contact them.

The dispatcher soon reports that Bardo's father feels his son might have been involved in a California homicide.

"Any idea how they know that?" Norton asks. "Does anyone

want him for questioning?"

"Stand by," she replies, then comes back on the air two minutes later to advise that Bardo's father believes he was in the Los Angeles area.

Norton asks if there is probable cause to arrest Bardo. The dispatcher says that she'll check and advise. She asks for another officer to assist Norton, and when no one is immediately available, Police Chief Ronstadt, approaching his downtown office, advises that he's in the area and will respond.

Ronstadt arrives, wearing his service revolver under civilian clothes. Bardo speaks calmly, but the words come hesitantly and fragmented. His nose is running and Ronstadt wipes it with a tissue, then pats his head and tells him to try and relax.

Part of what Bardo is saying has to do with a homicide in California, but he's not being specific.

"Who are you talking about?" Norton asks.

"Look at the cover of *People Magazine*," he says.

Ronstadt is aware that Schaeffer had been featured in a recent cover story. "That's when the penny fell for me," he says later. "I'd heard about the shooting on the radio, and I'm thinking, 'Oh shit, we have him.'"

Less than fifteen minutes later, a detective with the Los Angeles Police Department telephones Tucson police to advise that Bardo is a suspect in the homicide and to request help in locating him.

When the call is received, Bardo is already being interviewed at police headquarters, and is soon booked into Pima County Jail on bond of $1 million while he awaits extradition to California.

■

October 9, 1989. It's about 7 a.m., a typically quiet Sunday morning, and Jeff Moore is sitting in his patrol car enjoying the luxury of a cup of coffee when Marc Mardocco reports that he's in pursuit of a bronze Oldsmobile Cutlass which has passed him at high speed. As Mardocco comes within about 125 feet of the vehicle, its driver suddenly slams on the brakes.

Mardocco tries to stop, but there is too little time and he skids into the back of the Olds. The driver leans out of the window, fires a flurry of gun shots toward Mardocco, hitting the front of his patrol car several times. The suspects speed away as Mardocco reports excitedly that he's being fired on now by both the driver and the passenger, and that they are using automatic weapons.

Mardocco doesn't shoot back because there are other vehicles in the area. Instead, he backs off a bit, but keeps 'eyeball' on the fleeing car. Less than two minutes later, the driver swerves and hits a curb, blowing out the car's front right tire. The two point their weapons at Mardocco as he pulls up, then run into a residential neighborhood and disappear.

Although patrol staffing is light because it's early on a weekend morning, a half-dozen officers are quickly en route, including U. S. Border Patrol agents working a nearby marijuana-trafficking investigation. A tracking dog is requested and officers begin a search of the area within five minutes.

Jeff is soon waved down by an elderly woman who is half walking, half running to a friend's home to call 911. She breathlessly tells him that she saw two men break a window of her daughter Elma's home and go inside. Officers surround the house, then enter and search it. The suspects are gone, but they've left behind two rifles and a .357 Magnum. Elma and her car also are missing.

Elma's mother is not sure whether or not her daughter was home when the men broke in, so it must be assumed that they have her car and might also be holding her hostage.

Elma returns home a few minutes later, tearfully telling officers that the men huddled on the floor of her car while forcing her to drive them to an apartment complex several miles away. She is terrified, but uninjured.

Although an extensive search fails to find the suspects, a search of the stolen car they were driving when Mardocco spotted them turns up a loaded Uzi submarine gun and about 200 pounds of marijuana.

Twenty-four hours after the chase, a man taking an early-morning walk in the desert, discovers two men lying across cactus plants, their bodies partially covered by a red blanket. They match the descriptions of the drug suspects and detectives speculate that they might have been killed as punishment for abandoning a load worth more than $200,000.

*   *

As Jeff sped to Mardocco's aid, his thoughts were racing at an even more dizzying pace: "You're thinking family, you're thinking survival," he recalls later. "What are you going to do when you get

264

there, how will you react if you're under fire, and what kind of fool are you for being in this business in the first place? You're scared shitless, and all the time you're pushing down harder on the accelerator rushing to get there, you know that desperate people are firing automatic weapons and you might just be rushing to get killed."

■

His relationship with Dorothy still unsettled, Bernie Harrigan has applied for a position with the Seattle Police Department. He flies there for a written test and is ranked second out of more than 250 candidates.

Three months later, he's invited back for five days of extensive testing, including an oral board, a polygraph examination and a session with a psychologist.

When the psychologist asks him what he needs most in life, Bernie's response is "love and understanding." His best-kept secret: "I started using Lady Clairol to remove some of the gray from my hair and no one has noticed."

The testing has detected some repressed anger, he's told, but he's made the cut and moves on to a lengthy medical examination where his only difficulty is that he's not hearing high-frequency sounds.

"I was in a sound-proof booth with earphones on," he says later. "They gave me a buzzer to press every time I heard a sound. I'm holding it and I'm waiting and waiting, but I'm not hearing shit. Finally in frustration I just started pressing it like I was hearing something. After a minute or two, the technician walked into the booth, looked at me, smiled and said, 'Your hearing's not that great, is it?' It was more a statement than a question and there wasn't much I could do but nod."

Bernie fears that this will ruin his chances, but he regains his optimism later in the day when the lead physician says that his hearing problem should not be a problem because it appears to involve only the high register sounds. He's now optimistic that he'll be offered a position and is fairly certain that he'll accept, even with the realization that Dorothy is not likely to follow him there.

*　　*

As he awaits word from Seattle in the autumn of 1989, Bernie's romantic adventures take another turn. He meets Penny, a receptionist for an optometrist, while being fitted for glasses, and senses an immediate connection between them.

A few minutes of small talk quickly lead to what Bernie describes as "kind of dancing around each other. We were both putting out feelers, but not saying anything specific." By the time he leaves a half-hour later, Bernie has decided that "this girl is the marrying kind, not just someone I'd like to fool around with."

He can't get Penny out of his mind, and five weeks later he invites her out for breakfast.

"You'll never meet anyone like me," she tells him, and he is smitten. By Thanksgiving, they're talking about getting married. The Seattle Police Department phones a few days later to say that Bernie has been accepted and that his academy class will begin the first week of January. Bernie and Penny set a wedding date of December 28, less than three weeks away.

His final working shift is December 15, 1989. Three days later, he flies to New York City where his twenty-five-year-old son Tim — born with brain damage — is still confined to bed in a nursing home, his health continuing to deteriorate. His body is twisted and contorted, reminding Bernie of pictures of Jews dying in German concentration camps. Tim's weight has dropped to about eighty-five pounds, and he must be fed through a tube inserted in his nose.

Bernie visits Tim every day, sitting by his bed and talking to him.

"You don't really know what to say. I ask him how he's doing, but I know there won't be an answer because he can no longer talk. I tell him that I love him, but I don't know if he understands. Sometimes I tell him to blink if he understands what I'm saying. I think at times he responds, but maybe I'm just believing what I want to believe. I don't even know if he knows who I am. It's just sad."

December 27, 1989. Penny picks him up at the Tucson airport after midnight and Bernie has less than four hours of sleep before beginning his final day with the department. An exit interview takes less than ten minutes. Most of the day is spent filling out forms and turning in uniforms and equipment. He hands over his badge at two minutes past noon. The only item he can't account for is the pair of ceremonial white gloves he wore just once, the day he helped carry Tommy Knickerbocker's casket to its final resting place.

Bernie appears hyper, fragmented and forgetful as he drives from place to place. He cleans out his locker with no apparent emotion, dropping almost all of the accumulated notes of thanks and mementos into a trash can. Just after 2 p.m., he returns for the last time to the midtown station where his squad has just started its daily

266

briefing. He's no longer a Tucson cop, and without a key to the building, he has to be let in. Officers shake his hand or hug him as they wish him well.

"I guess I don't like long goodbyes," he observes after he has left the station. "You talk about keeping in touch or getting together, but you know that they're promises not likely to be kept."

He's well aware of his many failed relationships with women.

"I wanted things to work out with Dorothy, but she couldn't forgive me for not being honest about parts of my personal life, and I guess I don't blame her. It will be different from now on. Penny is a wonderfully loving and caring person and I feel very lucky to have someone like her. There's a hard side of me and I don't want to have that with Penny. I want to be vulnerable. I've made a lot of mistakes, but I also believe I've learned from my failures. This time I won't do anything to mess it up."

He has a ready answer when asked to sum up his five years in Tucson: "I had a good time here and that's all one can ask, isn't it?" The words are matter-of-fact and without emotion.

10

The Adrenaline Express

To most cops, a bad day is when nothing is happening. There hasn't been a decent call in two hours and the dispatcher needs to raise them on the radio to see if they're still breathing. A good shift is a foot chase, capturing an armed robber, a messy homicide and perhaps rescuing a busload of children about to be wiped out by a runaway train.

The cumulative effect of the 'good' and the 'bad' days is a gradual undermining of both the mind and the body. Cops start their careers excited and challenged by the high expectations of what they'll contribute to the community, but the process of disillusionment soon begins.

They witness more human tragedy and suffering in their first year on the job than most people see in a lifetime. Many of them believe they must play a Super Hero role. On the job, they should be invincible and without fear. They have both the law and a gun on their side, after all. Then, at shift's end they're supposed to shut down the cop role and go home to their families, calm, happy and unaffected by their work.

They would really like to do that, but most of them cannot. They've seen too much and they don't know what to do with big chunks of it. Tossed back and forth between euphoric highs and crashing lows, the erosion process begins and they are in trouble.

"That image and way of life can kill cops, and it does," says Dr. Kevin M. Gilmartin, a Tucson psychologist who supervises the Behavioral Sciences departments of three southern Arizona police agencies.

"It's easy for the officer to construct mental images of death during a bank robbery shootout, but in truth, most of them don't realize that their off-duty risks are far more serious than anything that is likely to happen to them on the streets.

"They are perpetual heat-seekers at work, but off-duty they are often withdrawn, isolated, negative, impatient, angry or depressed. They're on a biological roller-coaster. The 'up' portion is great, but when you hit the bottom of the adrenaline curve it feels like someone has injected you with lead."

Quoting a national study, Gilmartin says that for each officer killed in the line of duty, three others commit suicide, dozens develop heart disease or peptic ulcers, and three of every four of their marriages end in divorce.

"These are frightening statistics," he says, adding that "for cops to admit that they might have a problem is equal in their minds to admitting that they can't handle the job."

Most officers start out believing they can make the world a better place, Gilmartin says, "but this changes as they become frustrated, not only with the people they are supposed to be protecting, but with the police administration and the criminal justice system.

"An emotional shutdown starts within a few years and most of them begin to divide the world into two groups — the cops and the assholes. You'll hear them say, 'I used to like people before I became a cop, but now I just want them to stay out of my way and leave me alone.'"

The new belief system is that people are bad; just give them a chance and they'll prove it to you, Gilmartin says, emphasizing that this attitude is not limited to cops. "It's also true of many human service providers who are asked to give more and more of themselves until they have to stop and ask if there is anything left for *them*. When you are asked to give too much too often, the emotional battery wears out, and the burned out professional is in serious jeopardy of losing his family."

Gilmartin believes that young male officers are especially vulnerable. "They live for the job and they dread coming home. The wife wants some attention, but he just wants to vegetate on the sofa in a semi-hypnotic state.

"She tries to talk, and he grouses, 'Can't you see I'm watching TV?'

"'I know,' she says, 'but you're watching a dog food commercial.'"

Gilmartin maintains that cops who want to survive as human beings need to control what he calls "The Adrenaline Express" and make time for family and for friends who are not involved in law

269

enforcement.

"Successful and happy officers have off-the-job roles that are family and hobby-oriented," he says. "They can break the cycle by making specific plans in advance and then following through.

He tells of the wife of a police officer who said, "Let's go out to dinner and a movie on your next day off."

"We don't need to make plans; I'd rather be spontaneous," her husband replied.

"You haven't been spontaneous in five years."

Gilmartin says that the planned event can be as simple as a picnic, a bike ride, a walk after work or a quiet evening sharing conversation and a couple of beers.

"This sounds simplistic, but it works," he says. "The flip side is that an officer is headed for serious trouble if his only other role in life is Off-Duty Cop."

*   *

At the Police Academy, where job and survival skills take priority, there is little time to prepare cops for the stress they'll carry home at the end of the work day, and even those who hear the messenger disbelieve the message.

"I know that it happens, but it's not going to happen to me," is heard frequently.

When relationship problems begin, there is often a reluctance to acknowledge the situation or to admit to outsiders that a problem even exists. Police psychologists are available, but they are seldom contacted until there's a major crisis, and support groups are poorly attended considering the number of troubled marriages within the department.

Virtually every officer brings the job home, and if there is one common denominator, it is that they all need to talk. What they also require is an implicit understanding that they alone decide when to talk, when not to talk, and how much to say. The excitement and frustration of the day may begin spilling out almost as soon as the threshold is crossed, but more likely will be tabled for another time.

*   *

The spouses are very much aware of this.

Rene Gomez's wife Sylvia is six months pregnant with their third child. She works in the radiology department of a Tucson

270

hospital as a processing clerk, but after fifteen years, functions more as an office manager.

Sylvia remembers the difficulties adjusting to life with a cop and how it almost ended their marriage.

"We had a lot of problems the first two years. When he was in the Academy, our son was an infant and it was hard for Rene to study. After he went on patrol, he spent a lot of time going out drinking with his squad. When he did come home I thought it was because he felt he had to, not because he wanted to. He was under a lot of stress and we almost split up a couple of times."

"We communicate so much better now," she says. "He doesn't go out with the guys more than once or twice a month. When I tell him it's okay to go, he says he'd rather be with us, but I still think sometimes that he might be feeling tied down."

Sylvia understands now Rene's need for space after a stressful shift.

"He'll usually come home and tell me how it went. When he doesn't say anything, I know he's probably had a bad night and that something is really bothering him, especially when a child has died. He'll hug the kids and rub my stomach. I think he's remembering my miscarriages and feeling that hurt again. I tell him I'm ready to listen whenever he's ready to talk, and eventually he'll open up. When he's ready, I try and shut out everything else to listen to him and we've gotten closer because of that."

*   *

Les Beach also has a tendency to withdraw at times, his wife Sharon says.

"He's had to learn to share feelings. I'll ask, 'How do you feel about that situation?' or 'What was going through your head at the time?' I think that I've been able to cut through the occasional moodiness and bring out what he's thinking," says Sharon, a legal assistant who works for a Tucson attorney. That strategy usually works, but she remembers one particularly troublesome time.

"There was a period of a week or two when he was really withdrawn. I'd ask him if there was anything wrong and get nothing. I took it inward and started wondering if there was something wrong with our relationship. When I asked him, he assured me that it had nothing to do with us.

"I let it drop, but when he was still that way after a few more days, I thought there might be something going on at work that I

271

should know about, and I called one of his buddies."

The friend told Sharon about an incident involving a small child whose parents had been drinking and arguing. Unable to locate another family member, Les decided that Child Protective Services should take temporary custody of the boy. The three-year-old was crying hysterically as he was led away, and Les couldn't stop second-guessing his decision.

Sharon decided to wait for Les to work it out himself.

"A few days later, we were sitting in our jacuzzi and he said that he'd really been a shithead for the last couple of weeks. I asked again if it had anything to do with me. He said, 'No, it's about work. I just don't know whether I'm doing the best possible job.'

"He really cares about people and I think he started in law enforcement with an idealistic and somewhat unrealistic feeling of what he could accomplish. I've seen the cynicism that begins to creep in. He realizes that he can't help everybody and I think he's having difficulty dealing with that. What he's learning now is to do the best he can eight hours a day and then come home and forget about it."

Les and Sharon socialize with their law enforcement friends, but for the most part seem content being with each other. They hunt and cycle together, and even have matching cobras tattooed on their right shoulders.

"We're best friends and truly like doing things together," she says. "I never think, 'Oh, I have to put in another day with him.' We disagree sometimes, but we don't fight or yell. We're just very confident in our relationship."

*   *

When two police officers marry, each knows the baggage that goes with the job, and it might seem a shortcut to stability. The statistics say that the opposite is true, and Pat and Steve Horbarenko — now divorced — are a good example of what can go wrong.

"It's awful hard to have time together being a two-member police family," according to Steve. "It takes a lot of understanding, a lot of caring and an ability to back off and not get too involved with one's job. I know it was a life-long ambition for Pat. When she went to work, I was always thinking about how she was doing, whether she was safe. I tried to guide her and help her make her own decisions, and I think that was one of my failings. I became too critical and tried to make it easier for her instead of letting her

272

develop her own skills and her own way of doing things. A lot of times I created friction.

"The commitment to the relationship must come before the commitment to the job. You see your partners and your squad members a lot more than you see your family. You have to really limit the amount of talk about police work. I became much more career-oriented than she did and didn't pay enough attention to having a stable home life and fulfill her needs there. Before we knew it, we weren't talking for days at a time and when we did, it seems that we were at each other's throats.

"The one positive thing that came out of the divorce is that I think we're closer now. We understand each other, we can talk to each other a lot better, the pressures aren't there. I still worry about her, though."

Steve says that one of his reasons for accepting the ALETA job of Training Supervisor in 1988 was "to try and do something about the wrongs and injustices there. ALETA had progressed a lot in the way they treated cadets, and when I went there I know it kind of tore Pat apart because I was working for the people who gave her all that grief. She was terrified about even going there to visit, and I created problems by trying to force it on her. Things have changed and a lot of it is a result of what she and others went through."

He pauses and reflects on the end of their marriage. "Maybe I wasn't strong enough to hang in there and give Pat the support she needed from me as her husband. I kick myself in the rear end and ask why I gave up a lifetime for just a career.

"Looking back at it, work is not worth giving up your family for."

*   *

Jeff and Nancy Moore's marriage has survived the trauma of her brief 1986 relationship with another man.

Nancy, a contract administrator for a construction company, closes her eyes for a few seconds, and remembers how it was.

"I had quit my job and moved down to Tucson where I knew nobody. I was stagnant with a four-week-old baby plus a son ready to start in a new school. Jeff had family here, he had finally reached a goal in his life and he was so involved and enthusiastic in his new job. I thought, 'How dare you!' I wanted to bring him down with me. I needed someone to fill that void in my life."

She felt uprooted and alone. "I grew up insecure, not very sure of myself, and with Jeff I finally had a best friend, someone who was

273

everything to me. When I felt left out and alone, I needed to have someone I could turn to, someone who said he understood."

Her recounting is that of explanation, not an attempt at justification.

In the aftermath of the affair, Nancy went into therapy. "There was a lot of guilt. I left Jeff with the kids, the bills and the house to worry about."

Counseling paved the way for a reconciliation, but the first months back home were difficult. "There were a lot of angry things said and a lot of holes in the wall," she says.

Some anger still remains, but Nancy says that they're both moving toward forgiveness. "I've loved and learned from Jeff for eleven years, and slowly we're getting there," she believes.

"I think what bothers me the most is that there are so many law enforcement couples blaming their problems on the fact that one of them is a cop. I think that's wrong. Very few of our problems were caused by his being a police officer.

"Our problems would have occurred no matter what job he was in. The counselor focused so much on 'Well, it's because he's a cop.' I think a lot of couples use that as an excuse for not facing up to the real personality problems. I think it's just an easy out."

Nancy perceives Jeff as often stressed by the job.

"I think he really believes that he can suppress it, but I know there are times when his calls bother him," she says. "Sometimes he's pretty good about sharing his feelings and sometimes I really have to pump him.

"One of the most difficult things for me to do is put aside my anger when I hear of courtroom injustice. I've also learned to cry in silence when I know a child doesn't stand a chance in this world."

Nancy often watches as Jeff prepares to leave for work, pulling together his equipment, including the gun, nightstick and handcuffs that she wishes he didn't need.

"The police officer stands alone in his job," she feels. "He is asked to do the dirty work that we turn our backs to. He is overworked and underpaid and rarely appreciated."

Her personal wish list is short: "I'd just like us to have more time to go places together."

*   *

Derek and Sharon Campbell also moved to Tucson just before Derek applied for a job in law enforcement.

"Five years ago, everything was new," remembers Sharon, who

is the computer systems manager and drafting supervisor for a civil engineering firm. "We were on our own without family and friends, we'd just gone into new careers, and we were dealing with all of it at once. We've gotten a lot more settled, a lot more mature."

Sharon feels that the most important thing they learned from their failed first marriages was that you can't take a relationship for granted.

"I don't think you have to work all that hard to keep your marriage strong," she says. "It doesn't really take that much effort if you've learned how to communicate. I think you have to work to ruin a marriage."

Sharon glows when she speaks about Derek and wishes that everyone could see him as the "big, tender teddy-bear" she knows. His relationship with her daughters is a bonus.

"He takes them on what he calls Daddy-Daughter Days," Sharon says with a broad smile. "They go out to eat, roller skating or to a park or the movies. He'll spend most of the day with them and it's something special they look forward to."

Derek has begun the process of formally adopting eight-year-old Jessica and nine-year-old Nicole.

"It just seemed time to do it," Sharon observes. "He's the only father they've had for six years and I know that if something happened between us tomorrow or ten years from now, he'd still be there for them."

Despite the gun shots fired toward Derek in 1987, Sharon rarely worries about his safety. "Everyone runs a risk," she says. "We take a chance just leaving our house or crossing the street."

What troubles her is the potential for a car accident. "Once in a while I get overwhelmed. I see him running Code 3, flying through the city and someone turns in front of him and that's going to be it. That's my big fear."

She believes that Derek has been able to handle the job stress.

"Although he's become more cynical and more opinionated, most of the changes are for the better. He's gotten a lot more honest with himself about what he can accomplish as an officer. I think the illusions are gone. He sees things as they are, not necessarily the way he'd like them to be."

*   *

Robert Garcia has changed, too, after five years on the street. Tammy sees him as "more moody now, and sometimes short-tempered. We don't have fight-fights; they're more like disagreements

275

or arguments. He usually realizes when he's that way and we're able to talk about it. We try not to ever say anything that we're going to regret later. We've always been able to talk, even if it needs to be at three o'clock in the morning. We've stuck it out and we don't run to our parents every time we get into a little fight. I don't know if the moodiness is because of the job or the frequent change of shifts. It's hard sometimes to adjust to an officer's schedule, but I think it's easier for me because I don't work outside of the house."

Almost all of their friends are the families of other cops. Tammy talks frequently with the wives of officers in Robert's squad, occasionally visiting back and forth or going shopping or out to lunch.

She has developed more independence, partially because of Robert's irregular hours. "We used to do almost everything together, even the laundry and the grocery shopping. He was very jealous when we first married, but he's changed. I think it's because he's secure in the love we have for each other. I'm really proud of him."

Tammy knows that he could be hurt or killed, but tries not to think about it. "If I sat here and worried about what could happen I'd be a nervous wreck." She draws comfort hearing his voice on their police scanner, especially when he's working the evening or night shift and the children are in bed. She listens especially closely when his assignment involves someone with a weapon.

Five-year-old Melissa has announced that she wants to be a policeman, "just like my daddy."

"No, you don't," Tammy tells her.

*   *

Like Tammy, Sylvia Gomez misses old friends.

"We don't keep in touch anymore. We've moved from our old neighborhood, but it's more than that. I don't think they're comfortable now that he's a policeman. It's the same with our friends from high school. Our new friends are mostly neighbors and they respect Rene's need to not talk a lot about police work. They wait for him to bring it up."

Also like Tammy, she worries about her husband's safety, knowing how vulnerable Rene would be should he find himself in the way of a drug dealer.

Sylvia makes certain that Rene is relaxed when he leaves for work. "I make sure that everything is calm before he goes, that the kids are behaving and that we don't have an argument. I want to be sure that he leaves with a clear head."

She walks him to his car every time he leaves for work, even if it's late at night and even if she has to get out of bed and walk outside in her pajamas. It has become a ritual, but its meaning goes far deeper.

"I have to. Maybe I'm afraid that . . . I don't like to feel that if I didn't, and . . ."

She knows the words, but she can't bring herself to say them yet. She lowers her head as tears begin to well in her eyes. "It's so hard to watch him go." Silence for a few seconds, then almost inaudibly, "I'm afraid I might not have that chance again."

She doesn't talk to Rene about her fears. "I don't want him to know that I worry and that I sometimes have bad dreams. When the phone rings late at night, my heart just starts pounding, but then I tell myself that if anything happened to him, I wouldn't just get a phone call, someone would come to the house."

Cori toddles into the room and Sylvia reaches out. Cheeks still wet with tears, she draws her twenty-three-month-old close and hugs her.

11

Full Circle

January 7, 1990. The morning is warm and cloudless as forty-eight new cadets report to the Arizona Law Enforcement Training Academy. Several of the original group of 1985 cadets have come to mark the fifth anniversary of their own arrival at the Academy. Pat Batelli, still angry at the way she was treated there, is not among the curious.

The newcomers carry their belongings to their dormitories, then walk to the cafeteria to be photographed and have their blood pressure checked.

Rene Gomez — his own blood pressure rising with anticipation — sits at a table with Derek Campbell, Robert Garcia and Les Beach. Although the new cadets have been on Academy grounds for more than two hours, they haven't heard a discouraging word. There has been no confrontation, no raised voice.

Sergeant Kevin Loeffler walks to the front of the room, his measured steps echoing lightly off of the tiled concrete floor. He pauses briefly, pivots, then screams: "Up! Get up! On your feet! Get on your feet!"

About half of the cadets jump to attention, but it takes five seconds for the rest to follow. Loeffler strides up to one of the stragglers.

"You want to get with the program? When I give you an order, you're gonna do it NOW! Do you understand?"

"Yes, sir."

Loeffler steps back, addressing the entire group now:

"When you're given an order, you're going to follow it immediately. Is *that* understood?"

A fragmented response.

"How about 'Sir, yes, sir!'"

They respond in unison this time.

"From now on, the first word and the last word out of your mouth is 'Sir.' Is that understood?"

"Sir, yes, sir!"

"I'll be your class supervisor for the next thirteen weeks, and it's going to be a long thirteen weeks from looking at you people. It never fails that the first class of the year I get all the rejects that nobody else wanted from last year."

A few seconds for this to be absorbed, then:

"Where's Chip?"

"Sir, here, sir."

"I hear you're very proficient at presenting arms. Is that correct?"

"I don't believe. . . "

"I believe you *do*. Why don't you give us a 'present arms' with your left hand?"

A terrified look, but no response from Chip.

"DO IT!"

"Sir, I don't know how, sir."

Turning away: "You people make me sick already!"

The confrontation is over as quickly as it began, and Loeffler sends them to their dorms to change into physical training clothing.

Fifteen minutes later they assemble on the slab — a concrete patio area where they begin learning military commands and formations. Each movement is explained, then demonstrated, then practiced. The cadets are not doing much better or worse than their counterparts did five years before, but the instructors are patient almost to the point of stoicism. There are occasional mild rebukes, but no yelling.

*　　*

Department of Public Safety Captain Terry Tometich has been at the Academy for about two years, first as Training Director and currently as Commander of the facility. Although he believes that stress is still a necessary part of basic training, he feels that it's more focused now that it's not necessary to "break them down before you build them up."

There have been changes in the physical training routine since 1985. Cadets now run only three days a week instead of five, using the extra time for survival training and exercises in officer safety and defensive tactics.

"We decided that the physical training was being viewed as physical punishment," Tometich says. "When something you do is perceived that way, it becomes a negative, so we keep exercise separated from punishment.

"I don't want to make it appear that what was done in the past was wrong. It was probably right for its time, but as philosophies change, programs should change, too. There's still a weeding-out process, but we don't count our success by the number of failures we have."

Perhaps the biggest change is a strict limitation on the use of profanity by instructors. "We don't allow swearing and vulgar language from the cadets and we don't allow it from staff members," Tometich emphasizes, saying that pitting cop against cop delivers the wrong message.

Training Director Lieutenant Danny Sharp of the Tucson Police Department agrees. "If I call them names, what am I teaching them? We demand discipline, but we're not into public humiliation. We're here to turn out good cops, not to see who can take the most abuse."

Profanity is still used during training exercises where instructors play-act scenarios so that officers will be prepared for the verbal abuse they'll receive on the street.

*　　*

Derek, Robert, Les and Rene had heard that ALETA no longer espouses the level of screaming that can be measured on the Richter scale, but they're surprised by the virtual absence of confrontation.

"Loeffler could have yelled a lot louder than that," Robert observes as they join Pat Batelli and Anita Sueme for dinner at a downtown restaurant.

Derek: "It was bullshit!"

"It's bullshit compared to what we went through," Les concurs, "but if they're finding that this is the way to do it, then maybe it makes sense."

Rene: "There were a couple of times I thought, well here it comes, but it never came."

Les corrects him: "Well, they got about a minute of it."

Robert: "He didn't even blow off the tuning towers."

Les: "You're right. The tiles didn't even move. If that had been (Richard) Pettitt, even the other instructors would have been afraid."

Derek: "I think they still felt the same kind of fear we did."

Robert: "You could see the expressions on their faces. They were pretty nervous."

Les: "To us it's a very drastic change because we didn't have that type of first day. Personally, I think they've gone too far the other way. It's nice to be their friend and say, 'This is the way you're supposed to do it,' but I think they were way too lenient."

Rene agrees: "When one of us screwed up the way *they* did, we were all slam-dunked, and I feel cheated that they don't have to go through what we went through."

Derek: "The fear factor has its place. Why was it the way to do it when we were going through it?"

Les: "Because you were tough, Derek."

*   *

Two officers are missing from the dinner table. One of them is only a few hours away from ending his law enforcement career, while the other still dreams of returning to the streets.

Bernie Harrigan has completed his first day as a forty-nine-year-old rookie at the Seattle Police Academy where most of the cadets are barely half his age.

It's been overcast and rainy for three days, and Bernie — spoiled by Tucson's predictable sunshine — wonders if he'll ever again see a blue sky.

"There was this spit-and-polish captain who looked like he'd just stepped out of West Point," Bernie recalls a few weeks later, "and I'm doing drills in the rain, thinking, 'Left face, right face, about face.' I asked myself, 'What am I doing here?'

"Even with all my experience, I never felt that much confidence as a street cop in Tucson. I know that I appeared confident and did my job adequately, but I often felt insecure and that gnawed at me. I also started doubting my physical abilities.

"I'd think that if the shit ever hit the fan, I might not come through. There were just a lot of misgivings."

One of the misgivings is the prospect of being away from Penny, his bride of less than two weeks. She's with him now in Seattle, but will have to return to Tucson and her children while she sells her home.

Bernie resigns and drives back with her.

"I'm not looking for a whole lot of challenge," he says, smiling. "A wife and three kids is challenge enough."

He'll soon find a job outside of law enforcement, but mean-

281

while, he has no fixed schedule for the first time in nearly thirty years.

* *

More than two years after being dismissed by the Tucson Police Department, Greg Strom has picked up the pieces of his shattered life and moved on.

He has remarried, and credits his new wife for helping to pull him through.

"Julie stuck with me through it all, even paying the bills while I was out of work," he says. "You don't find people like that every day."

His daughter lives with his ex-wife in a nearby town, and Greg sees five-year-old Jennifer regularly.

He works as a pattern-maker for a manufacturer of decorative architectural products. The job is a showcase for his woodworking and artistic skills and he enjoys it, but he can't forget his aborted career as a cop.

"I still have a bad taste in my mouth," he says. "It's just like (it happened) yesterday, and it makes me wonder whether or not I want to go into it again when things like that can happen."

"It's scary," he admits. "It's almost like I'd rather not try. If you try, they might say 'no,' but if you don't try, you'll never know. I'm balancing out whether it's going to bother me more to not try, or to try and maybe not be accepted."

Yet, a large part of Greg *does* yearn to wear that blue uniform with a badge neatly in place over the left breast pocket, and he's torn.

"I feel inside that police work is what I was meant to do and that I did it well. I don't think I've forgotten very much of what I learned and did for three years."

He pauses to reflect for several seconds, then:

"I still think about it every time I see a patrol car go by."

* *

The sun has slipped behind the Tucson Mountains west of the Academy, and a nearly full moon is almost directly overhead. The new cadets have the rest of the evening to unpack, shine their boots, polish their brass and perhaps review the first week's reading material. Most of them appear apprehensive or restless.

They converse in small groups, quietly for the most part,

perhaps fearful that any sign of levity will set off another cafeteria-style outburst from a sergeant who might be lurking nearby. Radios and television sets are not permitted in the dorms, and one cadet wonders out loud who won the National Football League playoff game between the Los Angeles Rams and the New York Giants. No one responds and his question is left hanging.

Several cadets, including some who are living away from home for the first time, queue up at a pay phone to tell family members that they've survived the first day. One rookie has already resigned, saying that he "just wasn't ready" for Academy life.

* *

As they finish dinner, the five-year veterans have stopped debating the pros and cons of the 'new' ALETA. The topic now is the frustration they feel as cops. Surprisingly, it isn't how they believe they're perceived by the public that bothers them the most, but rather what they term unnecessary supervision by police administrators.

They realize that the para-military structure of a police organization expects their passive obedience, but feel they are trapped in a system that penalizes error more often than it rewards initiative. They view most superiors as generally unappreciative of their efforts and largely disinterested in their personal and professional concerns.

They've been told that the department dispenses far more commendations than reprimands, but they are still skeptical.

All of them feel they have been unfairly reprimanded for minor infractions not involving citizen complaints: A patrol car one quart low on oil; a dirty utility shovel in the trunk; seven extra minutes taken for a meal after going without lunch twice in that same week because of a heavy call load.

"Whatever happened to the brotherhood of police officers?" Robert asks. "Now you leave your dome light on and someone's probably going to write you up."

Pat remembers being told when she started the job that "it's often your own people who will screw you over, and that's just what I've found."

"You're right," Les says, "and I think that a lot of times they feel forced into it because if they don't do it to you, someone will do it to them."

Anita feels that the department has simply gotten too big. "We used to be a small, close-knit group. You knew almost everybody else and there was time to be friendly. Now I go to court and a lot of the cops don't say shit to me. If you're a beat cop, it sometimes seems that everyone is checking up on you."

Les agrees. "There are too many 'you shalls' and 'you shall nots.' I think we need more gray area to operate from."

"That's why I like DUIs," Derek says. "You're either drunk or you're not, and if you are, you're gone. You get them off the street for the night, send them to court and bang them in the pocketbook where it hurts."

Robert knows that Arizona's tough drunk driving laws have had a positive impact, but he doesn't see much progress in other areas, especially when it comes to prosecuting burglars and sending them to prison.

"Most of the ones I arrest are back on the street in a day or two," complains the man whose favorite childhood pastime was playing cops and robbers — as long as he was the cop. "The court process is really frustrating. The way I look at it now is that the entire system is a big game and we're just some of the players."

Robert, like the others, perceives the job disillusionment. "We can try and change things on the street a little bit at a time, but if you try and push it upward in the department, you just hit walls, so why bother? There should be a standard way of evaluating officers, but too much of it is at the discretion of a sergeant's personal priorities."

Most of them feel that departmental politics is the problem. "You often get lousy positions if you don't have connections," Anita says.

Derek nods in agreement. "If I could get another job with the same pay and the same benefits, I'd quit in a heartbeat."

"How about Animal Control?" Pat asks.

Derek ignores the good-natured barb, knowing that his friends will never let him forget the morning he shot the pit bull terrier that was lunging for his throat.

Rene shakes his head. He remembers being "scared as shit when I started on my own, not wanting to get hurt and not wanting to screw up."

"I have no regrets at all," he says. "It's a fun job, a good job. Being a cop is what you make of it. I love it and I wouldn't quit even if I won the lottery."

"I love this job, too," Robert says. "It's just that the department takes away so much of the joy. I'm not as gung-ho any more. I've learned that the only satisfaction you can count on is self-satisfaction.

If I left, it would be to be a cop somewhere else."

Derek: "You have to understand that you work *for* the department, not *with* the department. That's the difference."

Pat: "I'm starting to think about small-town policing, but I suppose there's politicking there, too."

Anita: "I think you'll find that in any big city department."

Derek: "It's the nature of the beast."

*   *

Harry Johnson has been a cop for nearly twenty years, and their comments don't surprise him.

"Most officers believe that they're on the streets for truth and justice," he says. "They want to go out and arrest the criminals, put them in jail and think, 'That's one criminal we'll never see again.'"

Two or three years later, they swing to the other extreme, Johnson believes. They've had unrealistic expectations and now they're afraid that nothing they do is going to matter anyhow.

"You take someone to jail and he's back on the street before you're even finished writing your report. You ask yourself, 'Why am I doing this?' Then you go through an even-keel period where you just go out and do the best you can, but accept that what you do isn't going to make much difference."

Johnson says he went through an extremely stressful period in 1984, and looking back, says he was "a very burned out and bitter officer."

Although the Tucson Police Department was the first agency in Arizona to provide officers with peer counseling and professional psychological services, Johnson feels that there was very little understanding of stress reduction before the mid-1980s.

The cops who counsel other cops now are highly trained, he says, "no longer taken from the street and put into the assignment for on-the-job training."

Despite the changes, Johnson feels that there's still too much negative motivation and that the department dispenses far more bad strokes than good ones.

"We have a volume of rules and procedures that tell us what we have to do, how we have to do it and what's going to happen if we don't do it that way," he says, agreeing that this may be one of the realities of working within a quasi-military operation.

Nonetheless, he says that "If a few people had come up to me, patted me on the back and told me I was doing a good job, I'd do twice as good, but usually when I thought I did a good job someone told me how I really fucked up.

"An officer who survives as long as I have without swallowing his pistol or becoming an alcoholic must understand that no matter how unappreciated you feel, you are only a part of the overall picture, and that the type of motivation that makes a good cop comes from within.

"I know when I've done a good job, I know when I've made a difference, and I no longer need to have someone tell me. Sure, it makes me feel good, but that's not what it's all about."

*   *

Those who cope best seem to do it by putting the job behind them when they go home.

"When I walk out of the (station) door, I'm Johnny Citizen and I don't need to know what's happening until I go back the next day," Les emphasizes. "This job can be rewarding and even fun, but if you don't spend your off-hours away from it, it will eat you up."

Anita nods. "I enjoy the job most of the time. I like working with people and I like helping them, but eight hours is enough. We'll never make much of a difference in society. All we can do is make small dents here and there by helping some of the people who can't help themselves."

"It's a never-ending circle," Derek agrees. "You may make the circle smaller, but it's still there."

"If I hear sirens when I'm home, I'm concerned as a neighbor, but not as an officer," Robert adds.

For Rene, though, out of sight is not out of mind. "I'll go home and watch cop shows on TV. They intrigue me, and when I hear sirens, the adrenaline begins to flow even when I'm off-duty."

*   *

As they begin their sixth year with the department, they are more aware that the job carries both a price received and a price paid. Some of what is gained is easily reduced to numbers — the annual salary of $28,260, a good benefits package, an opportunity for overtime pay and the possibility of career advancement.

That which is lost is more difficult to define.

"I've benefited, but I think my family has suffered," Robert says." They feel the stress that I feel and it just trickles down. They

286

see the world through my eyes in a lot of ways, and the shift work makes it harder for us to do things as a family. When I was a kid, my mom did shift work in a hotel and I thought she was the meanest, grouchiest bitch in the world. The other day when she was visiting, I said, 'Mom, I know now exactly what you were going through.' She got teary-eyed and hugged me."

Anita remembers when her father worked nights. "We tiptoed around the house and my mom had fits trying to keep us all quiet."

"My personal life has changed for the better," Derek observes. "I'm happily married and because of the money, I've gotten things that I've wanted. But I'm more cynical, not only about the administration, but about people in general."

Rene is still the contrarian: "People said that my attitude would change. They gave me six months, but now it's been five years. I was excited about the job when I first came on and I still am, like a kid with a new toy. It was affecting my family life for a while, but I think I caught it before it got out of hand.

"My tolerance level, though, has gone down, even when I'm off duty," he concedes. "It doesn't take as much to piss me off."

Les, who has perhaps had the most difficult time adjusting, attempts to put five years in perspective.

"When I started I thought that because of my age I wasn't going to have any problem dealing with people, but I've probably had more mood swings than any of you. I've gone from being very happy with the job to being very unhappy with it.

"I've gotten more than my share of complaints. Someone would take a swing at me and I wouldn't be satisfied until they were on the ground in a heap when I probably could have done something less physical.

"I'm not always satisfied with the department and how things are done, but I'm not in a position to change the system. Right now I'm just happy doing my job, and people can say whatever they want to me.

"We became cops to do certain things, and I think the realization has come to all of us that there are some things we just can't do."

Jeff Moore agrees. "When someone calls 911, it's our job to sort out what happened. I believe that we try our best, but we just can't please everybody and still do the job we're paid to do. Ninety percent of the people we see are basically good, but good people sometimes make mistakes, and in the end, most people are going to like us or dislike us based on what happened the last time we came into their lives.

"When you get right down to it, we need their help, and they need ours."

*   *

Back at ALETA, it's nearly midnight, and the dorms are quiet now. A young cadet strolls to the eastern fringe of the Academy, wearing only a gray T-shirt and denim cutoffs against the growing chill of the evening. Like Rene Gomez five years before him, and like the hundreds who came in between, he stands there, alone with his dreams and fears, unaware of an observer sitting in the shadows scarcely fifty yards away.

Hands grasped behind his back and fingers intertwined, the cadet looks toward the thousands of specks of shimmering light that are Tucson in the valley below. A jackrabbit ambles within a dozen feet of him, stands frozen momentarily, then turns and darts into a patch of palo verde bushes. The yelp of a lone coyote pierces the silence. It could be calling for its mate, or perhaps it's frightened, too.

The cadet lowers his head for a few seconds, then quickly pulls himself erect, pivots and walks to his dorm.

Morning wakeup is less than five hours away.